Conversations with John Cheever

Literary Conversations Series

Peggy Whitman Prenshaw
General Editor

Conversations with John Cheever

Edited by
Scott Donaldson

University Press of Mississippi
Jackson and London

Books by John Cheever

The Way Some People Live. New York: Random House, 1943.
The Enormous Radio and Other Stories. New York: Funk & Wagnalls, 1953.
Stories (with Jean Stafford, Daniel Fuchs, and William Maxwell). New York: Farrar, Straus and Cudahy, 1956.
The Wapshot Chronicle. New York: Harper & Brothers, 1957.
The Housebreaker of Shady Hill and Other Stories. New York: Harper & Brothers, 1958.
Some People, Places and Things That Will Not Appear in My Next Novel. New York: Harper & Brothers, 1961.
The Wapshot Scandal. New York: Harper & Row, 1964.
The Brigadier and the Golf Widow. New York: Harper & Row, 1964.
Bullet Park. New York: Alfred A. Knopf, 1969.
The World of Apples. New York: Alfred A. Knopf, 1973.
Falconer. New York: Alfred A. Knopf, 1977.
The Stories of John Cheever. New York: Alfred A. Knopf, 1978.
Oh What a Paradise It Seems. New York: Alfred A. Knopf, 1982.

Copyright © 1987 by the University Press of Mississippi
All rights reserved
Manufactured in the United States of America

92 91 90 89   4 3 2 1

The paper in this book meets the guidelines for permanence and durability
of the Committee on Production Guidelines for Book Longevity of the Council
on Library Resources.

Library of Congress Cataloging-in-Publication Data

Cheever. John.
   Conversations with John Cheever / edited by Scott Donaldson.
      p.   cm.—(Literary conversations series)
   Includes index.
   ISBN 0–87805–331–X (alk. paper).   ISBN 0–87805–332–8 (pbk. : alk. paper)
   1. Cheever. John—Interviews.   2. Authors, American—20th century-
-Interviews.   I. Donaldson. Scott.   II. Title.   III. Series.
PS3505.H6428Z463   1987   87-17932
813'.52—dc19   CIP

British Library Cataloguing-in-Publication data is available.

Contents

Introduction

For most of his 50-year career, John Cheever was unusually reticent about himself. As a Yankee—born in Quincy, Mass., just outside Boston—he was brought up to maintain a due reserve. If he wanted to be a writer, his parents told him, that was all right, but he mustn't pursue either fame or money. It was undignified to seek advertisements for oneself. So, Cheever used to say, he had no public image and no wish to cultivate one. When curious reporters invaded his suburban bailiwick in Westchester, he evaded their questions by taking them on hikes through the woods or by trying to get them drunk. He was, for a long time, far more honored by his fellow writers and the critical establishment (he won the National Book Award for *The Wapshot Chronicle,* 1957, and the Howells Award for the best novel of 1960–65 for *The Wapshot Scandal,* 1964) than by the general reading public, which thought of him as a short story writer for *The New Yorker.* In fact he was, next to John O'Hara, the magazine's most frequent contributor of short fiction during those years. The short story, concentrating on the interrupted event and not on continuous experience, was particularly well suited to the rapid changes of contemporary life, he contended. Besides, it was a congenial form for him. "Perhaps the first thing in the world that I can remember is being told a story," he recalled. "I suppose [that] with my last breath, I will be telling myself a story." Yet he turned to the novel as a more reliable and lucrative source of income, and the appearance of each novel was accompanied by a flurry of publicity.

Depression haunted him much of his life, and assumed a particularly virulent form immediately upon completion of a novel. After he finished *The Wapshot Scandal,* Cheever said, he "was really in trouble, I mean suicidal trouble." His solution was to spend two weeks scything the meadow. He was also sinking deeper into the abyss of alcoholism, as the interviews of the late 1960s and early 1970s testify. The book he was currently working on (a preliminary version of *Falconer*) was very likely his last one, he told Bruce McCabe in the fall of 1974.

This dismal view changed dramatically in the spring of 1975, when Cheever stopped drinking once and for all. With his release from liquor came renewed energy and a revivified sense of importance of his work and of the audience he was addressing. Now he talked willingly with reporters and interviewers for magazines and news-papers and radio and television shows—with just about anyone who asked for an hour of his time. The turning point was signalled by the publication of *Falconer*, a novel about imprisonment many took as emblematic of the author's own escape from addiction to alcohol, and by a *Newsweek* cover story and a revealing conversation with his daughter Susan that ran along with it in March 1977. From this point on, he revealed himself openly in interviews, speaking with enthusi-asm about the process and purpose of his writing, and with disarming candor about the details of his private life.

He could switch work places at will, he told reporters, moving from one room to the next in his old house in Ossining for each book. He wrote in the morning, waking early and staying at his desk until lunchtime. Looking out the window, he liked to think that his readers were out there, living in the woods behind his house. He warmed up with the journal entries he kept daily. The journal, he found, became increasingly important as he grew older and "the vividness of things passes and doesn't return to me as quickly as it used to." The principal requirements for his art, he declared, were "an extraordi-nary memory, a marvelous ear, and a passion for bringing disparities together." With these tools, he devoted himself to the basic sub-jects—love and death. Sexually explicit scenes did not interest him. Nor did psychoanalytical approaches, with their concentration on the symptomatic. "Fiction is not about what is symptomatic, it's about what's astonishing in life." He tried above all to capture *light* in his writing. "Man's inclination toward light, toward brightness, is very nearly botanical," he observed, adding that he meant spiritual light. "One not only needs it, one struggles for it."

Asked which contemporary writers he most admired, he usually mentioned Saul Bellow and John Updike, often named Robert Penn Warren and Eudora Welty and Bernard Malamud and Philip Roth, and invariably ended by insisting that "writing is not a competitive sport." They were all fellow artists engaged in a calling so important as to make such comparisons foolish, if not invidious. "Fiction," he believed, "is our most intimate and acute means of communication, at a profound level, about our deepest apprehensions and intuitions on the meaning of life and death." He wrote to make sense of his life and to help others make sense of theirs. At the same time, he was passionate about the distinction between art and life. "Fiction is not crypto-autobiography," he said again and again.

Having shucked off his New England reserve, Cheever was entirely forthright about his alcoholism and his marriage and very nearly so about his sexual orientation. He knew he would miss drinking for the rest of his life, he said, but not enough to forget "the loss of dignity, the loss of self-possession" that this "contemptible addiction" had caused. Married to the same woman for more than forty years, Cheever nonetheless characterized the wedding vows as "the most inspired and the most preposterous of all propositions." *Falconer* was a novel about confinement, he said, and he had himself been stuck in elevators and airports, emotional and erotic contracts. He could conceive of falling in love with another man, he told his daughter, but would want to "think twice about giving up the robustness and merriment . . . [of] the heterosexual world."

Interviewers drew him out on such issues as religion—"I go to church because prayer seems to contain certain levels of gratitude and aspiration that I know no other way of expressing"—and politics—*The New Masses* cited him in the 1930s as "the final example of bourgeois deterioration" and that "more or less closed" his relationship with the Communist Party. He defended suburban Westchester against the customary charges of conformity and boredom. "Ossining is wilder than the East Village," he asserted. Antonioni could not do it justice. Nowhere on earth had he encounterd "a more diverse and nonstereotyped group of people in a greater variety of circumstances." Yet he traveled a great deal in the 1960s and 1970s: to Italy, a country he loved, and Russia, a country where he was honored, and as cultural ambassador to Romania and Bulgaria, Korea and Venezuela. He told anecdotes of these trips in interviews, and also about his adventures in the remoteness of Sing Sing prison, where he taught inmates creative writing in the early 1970s. He heard things there that he couldn't have heard in any other classroom, and the classes could be very exciting. "Hey, Mr. Cheever, you'd make a great hostage," his incarcerated students told him during the Attica riots.

With the appearance of *The Stories of John Cheever* late in 1978, his critical stock took a sharp turn upward. The sixty-nine stories reprinted there, about one-third of his total production, testified to a lifetime of accomplishment, and confirmed Cheever's status as one of the country's masters of fiction. The book won the Pulitzer Prize and the National Book Critics Circle Award and (in paperback) the American Book Award. More than ever, he was in demand for interviews, and he used these occasions to broaden the range of his remarks. He inveighed, for example, against the widespread belief that an artist was a tormented person who produced some great works out of his torment and then committed suicide. Just because Jackson Pollock or Hart Crane destroyed themselves did not mean that all artists should be expected to follow suit. In fact, he pointed out, most writers could not afford to lead "messy lives," because they had to be their own disciplinarians. There was no one else to tell them to show up at their desks.

He was never happier himself than when working well and steadily. Writing satisfied that drive to be *useful* that undoubtedly came down to him, along with reticence, as a legacy of his New England ancestry. He also came to regard his vocation as therapeutic not merely for himself and his readers but for the widest possible constituency. Accepting the National Medal for Literature in April 1982, two months before he died, Cheever ventured the opinion that "a page of good prose" might constitute "the most serious dialogue" intelligent people could carry on "in their endeavor to make sure that the fires of this planet burn peaceably."

In a sense these conversations with Cheever span the universe. By the standards of sheer variety and scope of subject matter, it is hard to conceive of more interesting interviews than those he gave in the last half dozen years of his life. He held few secrets back, he had some things to say, and he said them, always, with the grace and wit of the born storyteller.

The published interviews in *Conversations with John Cheever* are reprinted without cuts or additions. Transcriptions from radio and television interviews, and from tape recordings, have been edited slightly for intelligibility. Often Cheever was asked much the same question in different interviews; often, though not always, he gave much the same answer. But the occasional repetitions that result reveal a great deal about the way Cheever and his work were perceived by various interviewers, and so have their own significance. Moreover, each interview achieves a distinctive identity as one common question leads on to other very different ones depending on the situation, the time and place, the people in conversation together. Cheever is only beginning to receive his due attention as one of the leading American writers of fiction in the twentieth century. I hope that this collection will help solidify his reputation.

SD
March 1987

Chronology

1935   Publishes "Brooklyn Rooming House" in *The New Yorker*, the first of his 121 stories for that magazine.

1937–38   Works for the Federal Writers' Project (WPA) in Washington, D.C., and in New York City, where he helps complete the New York City Guide.

1939   Meets Mary Winternitz.

1941   Marries Mary Winternitz on 22 March.

1942   Enlists in the Army on 7 May, and takes infantry training at Camp Croft, South Carolina, and Camp Gordon, Georgia.

1943   Publishes first volume of stories, *The Way Some People Live*, in March. Daughter Susan is born on 31 July. Reassigned to Signal Corps propaganda unit in Astoria, Queens.

1944–45   Lives with two other young couples in town house on 92nd Street while writing copy for films made by the Signal Corps. Goes overseas to Bataan and the Phillipines in the spring of 1945. Discharged from Army on 27 November 1945.

1946–50   Lives at 400 E. 59th Street as he continues to write increasingly complex stories and makes a number of false starts toward a first novel.

1948   Son Benjamin is born on 4 May, his mother's 30th birthday. A production of *Town House*, based on Cheever's stories, opens and closes on Broadway in September.

1949   Participates in campaign to save Elizabeth Ames, hostess of Yaddo, from a political attack instigated by Robert Lowell.

1951   Gets Guggenheim grant to write several long stories.
            Moves to Scarborough, where the Cheevers live in an
            outbuilding on the Frank Vanderlip estate.

1952   Works on pilot scripts for television adaptation of *Life with
            Father.*

1954–56   Teaches creative writing at Barnard College.

1955   Wins Benjamin Franklin award for "The Five-Forty-
            Eight."

1956   Wins O. Henry award for "The Country Husband."
            Receives a $1,000 grant in literature from the National
            Institute of Arts and Letters. M-G-M buys film rights to
            "The Housebreaker of Shady Hill." Finishes *The Wapshot
            Chronicle.* In October sails with his family for a year in
            Italy.

1957   *The Wapshot Chronicle* is published in March. Son
            Federico is born in Rome on 9 March. Elected to National
            Institute of Arts and Letters.

1958   Wins National Book Award for *The Wapshot Chronicle.*
            Joins Century Club. Publishes *The Housebreaker of
            Shady Hill* in September.

1960   Awarded second Guggenheim grant to work on a novel.

1961   Purchases house and moves to Cedar Lane, Ossining.
            Publishes *Some People, Places and Things That Will Not
            Appear in My Next Novel* in April.

1964   Publishes *The Wapshot Scandal* in January. Appears on
            the cover of *Time* magazine in March. Makes the first of
            three trips to Russia in the fall. Publishes *The Brigadier
            and the Golf Widow* in October.

1965   Awarded the Howells medal for the best novel of 1960–
            65 for *The Wapshot Scandal.*

1968   Film version of "The Swimmer" emerges.

1969   Publishes *Bullet Park* in April.

1971–72   Teaches creative writing to inmates of Sing Sing prison.

1973   Publishes *The World of Apples* in May. Falls seriously ill in
            the spring. Teaches at the University of Iowa Writers
            Workshop in the fall. Elevated to the American Academy
            of Arts and Letters.

1974–75   Teaches creative writing at Boston University. Collapses
            and successfully undergoes treatment at the Smithers
            Alcoholism Rehabilitation Center in New York.

1977   Publishes *Falconer* and appears on cover of *Newsweek* in
            March.

1978   Awarded honorary doctorate of letters from Harvard in
            June. Publishes *The Stories of John Cheever* in Novem-
            ber.

1979   Wins the Pulitzer prize and the National Book Critics
            Circle award for *The Stories of John Cheever.* Receives
            MacDowell award in mid-summer.

1980   Given Lincoln Literary Award of the Union League Club.
            Suffers two neurological seizures in the fall.

1981   Wins American Book Award for paperback edition of *The
            Stories of John Cheever.* Receives honorary degree from
            Skidmore College in May. Undergoes kidney operation in
            which cancer is diagnosed.

1982   *The Shady Hill Kidnapping* is shown as opening program
        of American Playhouse on PBS in January. Publishes *O
        What a Paradise It Seems* and awarded National Medal
        for Literature in April. Dies at home in Ossining on 18
        June.

Conversations with John Cheever

Quincy Youth Is Achieving New York Literary Career

Mabelle Fullerton/1940

Reprinted from the *Quincy (MA) Patriot-Ledger*, 6 August 1940, pp. 1, 7, by permission of the *Patriot-Ledger.*

Quincy folk will do well to watch John Cheever, son of Mr. and Mrs. Frederick J. Cheever of 67 Spear Street, Quincy, who, without fanfare, is quietly but persistently achieving a literary career in New York.

An author of exceptional modesty, he says, "I really haven't written anything worth reading, yet." All this is in the face of publications in the New Yorker, the Atlantic Monthly, Harper's Bazaar and Collier's. Several of his short stories have also appeared in annual prize collections.

Now visiting at his home in Quincy, he will return to New York this week where he is currently at work on a contemporary novel with a New England background about Boston. "Possibly it will be finished in the spring," he thinks.

After leaving Quincy, Mr. Cheever spent some time at Yaddo, an artists' colony outside of Saratoga Springs, N.Y., where he did much writing.

He says he writes "pure fiction," though when pressed, admits that some of the articles in the New Yorker were based on experiences at the dancing classes he attended in Wollaston.

As for the mechanics of the art, he considers, "you have to write in a natural style, though some magazines permit more license than others. The magazines with the huge circulations are run as big businesses and have definite editorial policies and one of them is not to offend their best advertisers. It is also important to consider both the mental and income level which the magazine reaches and govern yourself accordingly."

3

He thinks, "it takes years to get anywhere, but you can keep on polishing away until you have something. The last decade has been pretty bad, as no great writers have appeared. The war, with its constant change, is undoubtedly going to have a great effect on writers. Now they seem to be getting away from the proletarian novel and there's an indication they may even go in for fantasy."

He opines that young writers or any wishing to achieve professional status do well to seek the services of an agent.

His idea of excellent modern writing is Carson Smith McCuller's "The Heart is a Lonely Hunter."

His own literary style is ample proof that he writes naturally. It is simple, direct, forceful and has a quiet but deep humor. Because he believes he hasn't written anything "yet" and because you realize that he won't be satisfied until he has, he may be regarded as one of the white hopes of American literature.

Former Quincy Boy Courting Miracles

Mabelle Fullerton/1948

Reprinted from the *Quincy* (MA) *Patriot-Ledger*, 2 September 1948, by permission of the *Patriot-Ledger*.

So you think the day of miracles is gone?

Curtain's going up on one tonight at the Colonial theater in Boston where there will be a premiere of Max Gordon's production of the comedy "Town House" based on the now celebrated New Yorker stories, written by a former Quincy boy, John Cheever.

Mr. Cheever, who shares with Peter Pan, a look of guileless youth, contrasted by a wit that could have bandied ripostes with Voltaire, is a very shy young man and about as easy to interview as "Bambi." Son of one of Quincy's most popular and best known citizens, Mrs. Frederick L. Cheever, of 29 Spear Street, Quincy, with whom he is visiting, Mr. Cheever, after attending Thayer academy, shook off the dust of historic Quincy at the ripe old age of 16.

He explains, "I began to write then, and wrote constantly and sold quite a bit. It seemed an easy way of making a living." He spent some time "writing, writing, writing," at an artist's colony at Yaddo, near Saratoga Springs, N.Y. and during the war did some exceptionally fine work for the Army in various theatres of the war.

But returning to "Town House" "the idea for the play was mine, taken from stories I did for the New Yorker, but the play was written by Gertrude Tonkonogy, who wrote "Three Cornered Moon" several years ago. I have no special urge as a playwright, for this seems to me the perfect solution, to present the ideas and material and let someone else do the play.

"I am not a collaborator. Mr. Gordon has been considering the play for the past two years, and there were several other attempts along similar lines which didn't quite take in the theatre. Miss Tonkonogy's draft was the best. I can't imagine a finer combination than having Mr. Gordon for a producer and George S. Kaufman as a

5

director—he is a wonder. During the war, cooperative living resulted from experiences in the Army and because of the housing shortage and these along with our own experiences living in New York, form the episodes in the play."

Mr. Cheever, who assisted with the casting, thinks, "Mary Wickes is wonderful, June Duprez, just right, while Hiram Sherman and James Monks, just to mention a few are just as I realized them in the stories."

Mr. Cheever is also vastly interested in the set, which Donald Oenslager has devised and which Mr. Gordon has characterized as costing him as much, "as a 20 room house, with lights and running water." Mr. Cheever counters with a certain amount of cheer, "why some of the actors have to work practically on a vertical line" as a cross section of two floors of the town house compromise the set.

Mr. Cheever, himself, is one of those mild looking men, whose mental patterns are capable of all things, especially in the way of surprises. Tuesday afternoon, it seems, a gentle voice inquired if its owner might attend a rehearsal at the Colonial theater and when asked why, it replied, "I'm John Cheever." Broadway is unaccustomed to such a delicate approach.

Mr. Cheever, his attractive wife, Mary, (around whom one of the characters in "Town House" is built,) their five year old daughter, Susan and their four months old son, Benjamin Hale Cheever, came to Quincy after "spending the summer in New Hampshire woods," Mr. Cheever admitted with an apparent, but reluctant, kind of fondness.

After "Town House" has been checked off a hit, he will renew his intentions to a novel dealing with contemporary Eastern (N.Y. that, is) life. But he is really sold on the miraculous aura surrounding "Town House"—affirming, "the best producer and director, and a wonderful cast, everyone likes everyone." He has only one plea, that the audience laugh, because it is a comedy, and anyone who today can make the world laugh is indeed a kind of miracle maker himself: vis: John Cheever.

A Visit with John Cheever

Lewis Nichols/1964

Reprinted from the *New York Times Book Review*, 5 January 1964, p. 28, by permission of the publisher. Copyright © 1964 by The New York Times Company.

As his favorite outlet for short stories might begin it, we were met by appointment at the Ossining station by a hatless man wearing wool shirt, arctics, coat, stooped over by the weight of two huge, oyster-white bags, and followed by a radiant blonde.

"Cheever," he said. "I'll be right back."

He carried the bags into the railroad car, came down the steps as the train moved off.

"One of my wife's students at Briarcliff," he said. "Remarkably pretty girl. Drama major, naturally."

He started the car up a series of snow-covered, slippery hills.

"Errand boy, taxi—that's the trouble with working at home. It's worse when they wait for a real emergency—when the pipes are frozen and they yell for help. You have to get out and take your typewriter with you."

He lives in a house built in 1798, part of the Van Cortlandt estate. Six acres go with it, a hill suitable for a toboggan, lawns, a view of the Hudson, 25 apple trees with products available for jelly and sauce but not turned into cider, and wood that he and his son chop to size for two fireplaces.

"I've worked a good many places," he said sitting before one of these. "For three years I was in the Veterans of Foreign Wars meeting hall, under a sign saying 'One God, One Country, One Language.' I got there through having been a member of the volunteer fire department, and they were nice to me. Now for the moment I'm home. Taxi.

"Working hours depend. Usually three or four hours in the morning, quit at 12:30 and work on the place. Our elms have died and we saw them up. Sometimes we go skeet shooting. Beer can

7

launcher. Ever seen one of those? Great thing. When I'm really working, though, I work right through. Since finishing 'The Scandal' I've written five stories. One I like very much. Though I claim no favorites among stories, that's it for now. The New Yorker's bought it."

Actually, The New Yorker has published well over 100 Cheever stories, six parts of "The Wapshot Scandal" having appeared there. In the "Scandal," however, as in its companion, "The Wapshot Chronicle," he was not just writing stories, to be pulled together later with chapter headings.

"The original plan for each of the books was firmly set. If it's really set, you can write so that it can be read piece-meal—no more than a little cutting here and there. One of these days I'll probably write a footnote to the family—just for my own peace of mind."

Mr. Cheever, now 51, was born in Quincy, Mass. There is a bit of Quincy in the Wapshots' St. Botolphs, plus bits of Newburyport, Mass., remembered by his father, and bits of the farmland around Hanover (near Plymouth), Mass. He chose the name because it sounded right. So, too, the Wapshot family, which "sounded like a good New England name without too many people having it."

While getting himself started, Mr. Cheever did a number of odd jobs around New York and other places, and about one job he has definite ideas.

"I don't like to teach, although I've done it. It takes such a lot out of you, takes the skin off your back. Then, there's the politics that go on in schools—tough.

"The stories I write—I guess I take two positions. Either I'm living in a very small town or living in Paris—which I've never seen. The time it takes for a story? The one I mentioned, two months. There were 150 pages of notes for 15 pages of story. It's about a man who's at a poolside party and decides to swim the county. He's eight miles from home and swims there, pool to pool."

Acting out the saga of the swim with all the gusto of Gielgud approaching "Hamlet," Mr. Cheever donned his coat, led the way to his car, carefully searching for children's abandoned sleds before starting up. Near the house is some road construction for Route 9.

"See that? You wake up in the morning and a whole hill's gone. The railroads could handle the freight, and the only trucks on the highway seem to be construction work trucks, but still they keep on knocking down hills for more highways. I write about that, too."

Is the Short Story Necessary?

The Writer's World/1969

John Cheever, Shirley Hazzard, Harry Mark Petrakis, and
Elizabeth Janeway

Reprinted from *The Writer's World* (New York: McGraw Hill
Book Company, 1969), pp. 251–73. Copyright © 1969 by The
Authors Guild, Inc. Reprinted by permission of the Guild and
the authors.

Elizabeth Janeway: Welcome to *The Writer's World.* We're going to
talk about short stories. We are lucky to have three panelists with us
who write short stories extremely well, but who also write novels.

Many novelists begin when young by writing short stories, but they
are apt to be seduced away by that larger form, the novel, and to
relinquish the art and perhaps lose the skill. Let me introduce our
three panelists who have maintained their ability to write the short
story while also writing excellent novels.

Shirley Hazzard was born in Sydney, Australia, and educated at the
Queenwood Ladies' College in Sydney. Rarely are women writers
also officially stamped as ladies.

Shirley has lived in the Far East and in New Zealand, and now lives
in New York with her husband, Francis Steegmuller. For ten years
she worked with the United Nations. She is a contributor to *The New
Yorker,* and her first short-story collection, called *Cliffs of Fall and
Other Stories,* appeared in 1963. In January of 1966, she published
that lovely book, *The Evening of the Holiday.*

John Cheever was born in Quincy, Massachusetts. He too has
written considerably for *The New Yorker,* and for other magazines as
different as *The Saturday Evening Post.* His novels, *The Wapshot
Chronicle* and *The Wapshot Scandal* are, I'm sure, well known to
you, and he has published a number of short-story collections: *The
Housebreaker of Shady Hill; Some People, Places, and Things That
Will Not Appear in My Next Novel*—a lovely title; *The Brigadier and
the Golf Widow.*

9

Harry Mark Petrakis was born in St. Louis, and now lives in Chicago with his wife and three children, and he is the author of three novels: *Lion at My Heart, The Odyssey of Kostas Volakis,* and most recently, *A Dream of Kings.* His collection of short stories, *Pericles on 31st Street,* was one of the final contenders for the National Book Award in 1965.

Some writers confine themselves to short stories or almost do so. Kipling was one. Chekhov did it in the field of narrative fiction. His longer works were dramas. Perhaps we can best come down to talking about short stories by quoting from a most distinguished writer of short stories, and only short stories, our near contemporary, Frank O'Connor, who died only recently.

Let me offer for our panel some of Mr. O'Connor's thoughts on the short story. I'm not sure that I agree with all of them. I doubt that the panelists do.

"From the very beginning," wrote Frank O'Connor in his book *The Lonely Voice,* "the short story has functioned in a quite different way from the novel." As an example, he takes Gogol's famous story, "The Overcoat," and points out that in this story there occurs the first appearance in fiction of the little man. From this, he goes on to suggest that, while the novel must offer the reader a character with whom to identify himself, this is not true of the short story.

"The novel," Frank O'Connor says, "presupposes a normal society, while the short story does not. The modern novel has been called the novel without a hero, but the short story has never had one.

"In the short story at its most characteristic," he says, "there is something that we do not often find in the novel, an intense awareness of human loneliness. Instead of a hero, a short story offers a submerged population—Gogol's officials, Turgenev's serfs, Maupassant's prostitutes, Chekhov's doctors and teachers, Sherwood Anderson's provincials—always dreaming of escape."

John, do you agree?

John Cheever: No, not at all, no. We always say that the short story was born, of course, with Gogol, and then came out from under "The Overcoat." The short story was extremely efficient in dealing with the bureaucracies of Petrograd, Paris, and still is with Moravia's Rome. This is the obsessive thing. A man desires a pair of yellow boots, and he will make love to a number of women, and murder a number of men in order to get his pair of yellow boots.

This I think was great in the 1860s. It was perhaps the birth *not* of the short story, because we have, of course, *The Decameron* which is a collection of short stories, but rather of the *modern* short story. I think that what O'Connor was speaking of has vanished into thin air—the problem of the single man in a bureaucratic society who desires a single object, usually not a woman—has totally gone from our comprehension. The responsibilities of the short story, of course, at this point are much broader than that.

Mrs. Janeway: O'Connor seems to believe or to suggest that the short story differs from the novel because in the novel the reader finds someone with whom to identify. In the short story, he feels, characters are seen from outside. Does this seem to you true, Shirley?

Shirley Hazzard: Well, I don't know offhand. I can't think of all of the examples I'm sure exist that would refute Mr. O'Connor immediately. I agree rather with John, that it was something which perhaps seemed enormously true to him when he was saying these things, but some of them seem to me very questionable. The idea that a certain form of art *began with somebody* seems to me very strange, because, after all, a story, whether written or spoken, has always existed.

Stories have always been told; probably it was the first kind of literary self-expression, if you can call it that, that existed on the earth. It's what you tell to a child to make it go to sleep; and to adults to make them wake up, a little later.

Mr. Cheever: It's what you tell yourself in a dentist's office while you're waiting for an appointment. The short story has a great function, it seems to me, in life. Also, it's the appeasement of pain, in a very special sense—in a stuck ski lift, a sinking boat, a dentist's office, or a doctor's office—where we're waiting for a death warrant. Where you don't really have long enough for a novel, you do the short story. I'm very sure that, at the very point of death, one tells oneself a short story—not a novel.

Mrs. Janeway: Do you think then there is always someone speaking in a short story? Does it come out of the tale? Mr. Petrakis? How do you feel? Your characters are perhaps closer to the old world and the world of the bardic tale than are those of our other participants.

Harry Mark Petrakis: Perhaps closer to what Frank O'Connor himself called the storytelling as a public art.

Mrs. Janeway: Yes.

Mr. Petrakis: Since I lecture and read my stories before colleges and clubs, I feel strongly the relationship of the short story to the art of drama. But, I would like to take just a moment if I can to make a momentary digression, because there may be those in the audience who are perhaps wondering what I am doing here with Mr. Cheever and Miss Hazzard. I am here this evening because I have not published in *The New Yorker.*

I am also from Chicago, and I am very grateful that my microphone is connected. Now what was the question?

Mrs. Janeway: Where do you feel the short story came from, Mr. Petrakis, before it got to *The New Yorker?* Is there still a person speaking through it?

Mr. Petrakis: Oh, I think very definitely that there's a person speaking through it. It can be a reflective or a strident voice.

One need identify not only with characters in a novel; one can identify also with the characters in a short story. Both these forms can help us understand something of the life that goes on beneath the masks people wear with one another.

Mrs. Janeway: Perhaps I haven't explicated O'Connor well enough. Actually, I'm simply trying to provoke you. Let me read a little bit more. "If the novelist takes a character of any interest and sets him up in opposition to society, and then, as a result of the conflict between them, allows his character either to master society, or be mastered by it, he has done all that can be reasonably expected of him."

Now, perhaps, we are still back in the nineteenth century, John.

Mr. Cheever: I should say yes.

Mrs. Janeway: Back with the old-fashioned novel.

Mr. Cheever: Yes, Frank O'Connor was back with Stendhal. Yes, of course he's with Stendhal.

Mrs. Janeway: I think that one of O'Connor's points is still a valid distinction between the novel and the short story: "The element of time is the novelist's greatest asset, the chronological development of character or incident is an essential form, as we see it in life, and the novelist flouts it at his peril. For the short story writer, there is no such thing as essential form. His frame of reference can never be the totality of a human life, and he must be forever selecting the point at which he can approach it, and each selection he makes contains the possibility of a new form, as well as the possibility of a complete fiasco."

Time is certainly present in the traditional novel. In the short story is it less so?

Mr. Cheever: No, I don't think time is actually important and I can't think of an important novel or series of novels in which time, chronological time, is not totally violated. This includes *War and Peace,* as well as *À la recherche du temps perdu.* It seems to me . . . I'm here to defend the short story, right?

Mrs. Janeway: Yes.

Mr. Cheever: A rather difficult task, but it seems to me that one of the things that the short story has done is to keep the novel on its mettle. The novel is essentially massive, and is always reviewed as though it were something immense, although it might be eight hundred pages of trifling humbug. Also, it seems to me that the short story has done a good deal to invigorate poetry, because there have been decades in my lifetime when the short stories written in this country have been much more precise, much more penetrating, and much briefer than the poetry one reads.

The short story, among its other virtues, has more or less kept the novel and poetry working. Both forms are generally acceptable.

In some ways the short story is still something of a bum; but it has to be very lively or it doesn't pass.

Mrs. Janeway: How do you know when you're writing a short story and not a novel?

Miss Hazzard: I was going to ask that question, because I wonder really whether one does think to oneself, "I'm now sitting down to write a short story." If I can go back a little bit, the subject is, "Is the Short Story Necessary?" I was thinking about that, because, after all, the interesting thing about any work of art is that nobody can *prove* that it's necessary. It's more, one might say, essential. It's of our essence, it's what makes our experience coherent to us. We can't say that we will be any different if art didn't exist, and yet we know that we would be. And I think what's rather endearing about the short story is that nobody *can* show that it's necessary, but that it must be necessary—I assume we're talking of things of quality—it must be necessary to the writer. If it is to be successful, or to have any endurance, then it must be a form that happened *because* the writer had something to say that fitted into that particular form.

After all, writers are not a bureaucracy, not yet anyway, and they don't have to fall into any classification. They don't have to write a short story because that's an accepted form, or because it keeps the novel on its mettle, or makes poetry seem too long, or something of that sort. I don't think it "serves a useful purpose." If an artist writes something with a useful purpose in mind, and it succeeds as a work of art, then it succeeds in spite of his useful purpose, I rather think. It might succeed in some other way as well, but art needs no justification other than itself. It seems to me that must be essential, but the fact that it's in short-story form must be incidental to what the writer has to say.

I don't think that one should necessarily confine what one has to say into a short story or necessarily prolong it to make a novel. One selects the form most appropriate to what one has to say.

Mr. Cheever: It's a very deep impulse actually. To write at all is a very deep impulse, and it's rather like falling in love. You don't say that I'm going to fall in love for three months, or I'm going to fall in love for two weeks.

But these are your deepest intuitions, your deepest drives, and may have a duration which is determined by an endless chain of contingencies.

Mr. Petrakis: I find myself agreeing more with Mr. Cheever and Miss Hazzard than I do with Frank O'Connor here. I think though, that he must be given his due, because before I knew that you were going to quote, Mrs. Janeway, from Mr. O'Connor, I read his book on the short story, and I too felt it a very spirited defense of the short story. Like John, I'm here to defend the short story.

I think O'Connor was comparing short stories with novels which assume the guise of chronological time merely to show this basic difference—that in the novel you have a great deal more liberty with time, and that you can chronologically begin to establish the great rhythms of time. You could start with the fact that, at a given time, a man was born, and you could follow him forward through adolescence, into maturity, into marriage, to the birth of his children, through perhaps all the various aberrations which unleash themselves upon him during his life.

Whereas, the short story, by necessity, becomes an episode of selected incident. You move into it at a given time. You move into it at a given place. You are not given the liberty which you have in the novel, and you must catch the character "at a point," I believe O'Connor says, "of crisis in his life." Once the story is finished, his life is not going to be quite the same again. The greatness of the short story lies in this marvelous zeroing in. One thinks of a television camera at a football game, and thinks of the novel in terms of a camera panning the whole field, and all the players, and all of a sudden moving in on the individual play, and on the twisted, frenzied face of one of the players, the end, or the quarterback.

This, it seems to me, in terms of the conflict involved anyway, would be the difference between the novel and the short story. Each has its function, each its place; and yet as a short-story writer myself, I have an endearment for this moment of capture, this moment of revelation.

Mrs. Janeway: According to A. E. Hotchner, in his book on Hemingway—it's really a fascinating book; the amount that Hotchner believed of what Hemingway told him is absolutely fabulous—one of the things that Hemingway told him—and this I think might possibly be true; I offer it to the panel—was that he never sat down to write a novel, but that his novels all grew out of short stories. Does this happen to you, panel? Do you know when you start something whether or not it's going to be a novel or a short story? Or, do you simply start and have it tell you on the way? Shirley?

Miss Hazzard: I think to a certain extent it tells on the way. I think very often one does have, in advance, an idea of the scope. But I agree with Mr. Petrakis to a great extent about the crisis, and the incident that evokes a larger measure of life. Whereas a novel, I think, could be said to be a large measure of life that evokes a still larger one.

I think, however, that there are many exceptions to this, and that perhaps it's something easier to say than to sustain. I was thinking just now of the great short story of Joyce's, "The Dead," which does turn on a moment of crisis, which does deal with an incident you might say, and which leaves a person's life changed. The central figure's life is changed, and yet in a way the story does evoke the whole of experience. It does deal as completely with life, and with as large a scope, as any novel. One does have the whole football field wrangling and writhing as you were saying.

It's not at all that he has bitten off less than he could chew. It isn't that at all. He has sought to compress it in some tremendously artisitc and ingenious way. Of course it's quite a long story, but it's by no means a novel. Nobody could call it a short novel. It's a long short story.

Mrs. Janeway: That's a fascinating difference. O'Connor points out—and he's, I'm afraid, a bit of a straw man, but at least let me quote him once more because this is really almost a matter of fact— "Chekov's long short story, 'The Duel,' is longer than some novels that we accept as novels." In other words, length has really little to do with—or not all to do with it. Something else gets into this. There is something different about the short story. I'm particularly fascinated by it, because I've lost the ability to write short stories myself. I did write them for a while, and I've tried since then, but I find that I've gotten used to novel size. I'm a little like that Victorian husband who spoke of the deep peace of the double bed in marriage, after the hurly-burly of the chaise longue; the novel is like that wonderful double bed, and I can't seem to get back on the chaise longue.

I think this is a matter of clumsiness. Writers of short stories have a special and delicate skill, the ability to pick up just the right nexus, the right situation which will illuminate the patch of the universe that they want to explore.

John, when you begin a short story, do you foresee its end? That is, do you see it complete and as a whole when you begin?

Mr. Cheever: No more, Elizabeth, than I foresee the end of a love affair.

When Shirley mentioned "The Dead," of course, it was like striking it great. This is one of the great things. It's not a great short story. It's one of the great works that we have, great works of man, and some of the Chekhov stories are equally beautiful. As a matter of fact, the whole history of the short story, even though it's rather threadbare at this point, is great as far as understanding what other—

No, when I start a short story—but really I'm rather a retired short-story writer—I think I've written only three in the last two years; I used to write something like twelve a year. No, I do think that if it is good, it is perhaps the most intense form of writing that I've ever had any experience with. And the last story I wrote that I liked—I felt as though it had been written out of my left ventricle—I thought, "I don't want to write any more short stories, because you *don't* fool around."

The novelist, especially the German novelists in the late twenties and some American novelists now, approach the reader as though he were a ground feeder. If you've ever fished—when you fish a ground feeder, you hook him in the mouth. You start by saying, "She was raped on Thursday," and then there's a fairly interesting chapter, and then all sorts of horseradish and things come in; but the reader of the novel will go on and on and on, for something like three or four hundred pages, sometimes eight hundred pages.

With a short story, you have to be in there on every word; every verb has to be lambent and strong. It's a fairly exhausting task, I think.

Miss Hazzard: Still I don't think it ought to look as though it's "all done by hand" though, if you know what I mean.

Mr. Cheever: But it *is* done by impulse.

Miss Hazzard: By impulse, yet with care—

Mr. Cheever: No, I'm speaking of it impulsively; but when you are working on it, you can't—I'm sure you can't—walk past the room in which the manuscript lies without having a coronary thrombosis.

Mrs. Janeway: Whereas, with novels there's the feeling that, isn't it nice, there's a large thing where I can put everything in.

Mr. Cheever: Everything?

Mrs. Janeway: Yes, everything?

Mr. Cheever: Sometimes, too much?

Mrs. Janeway: Sometimes indeed, John. But specifically, sections of *The Wapshot Scandal* appeared in *The New Yorker* as separate stories. I read them there with delight, but when the book appeared, and I read them as part of the book, I found almost all of them strengthened by being read in context. Did you write them as stories first?

Mr. Cheever: No, this was entirely a commercial expedient. I've, as you know, a family, and a very demanding family, and it's virtually impossible for me to support myself writing novels. And it's virtually impossible for me to support myself writing short stories, also.

Mrs. Janeway: It's actually almost impossible for anyone to support himself by writing.

Mr. Cheever: So I've hit on the expedient of publishing novels piecemeal. At the moment, I don't have to do it anymore, but that's the way it worked out. *The New Yorker* was very gallant with *The Chronicle,* in printing "Leander's Journal" and so forth. I would much sooner not do it that way; but that's the only way I've been able to do it.

Mrs. Janeway: Well, I thought they stood up very well as stories. But as I say, I liked them better in their setting.

Mr. Cheever: It was nice of you to mention it.

Mrs. Janeway: There was a little explosion about finding out whose briefcase it was that had got lost on that terrible plane flight.

Mr. Cheever: My sense is to always put the chapter in a novel precisely where it belongs, and then take it out.

Mrs. Janeway: Yes.

Mr. Cheever: And sell it. But I know exactly where it belongs before I sell it to someone else.

Mr. Petrakis: This evening will have been my first opportunity to talk to Mr. Cheever and Miss Hazzard, who I think are marvelous short-story writers. And I think it very interesting, for instance, that Miss Hazzard mentions "The Dead," which is one of Joyce's later stories, and I think, very effective inasmuch as it foreshadows Joyce the novelist. He does a short story, and yet he does in the short story, in "The Dead," that which suggests the great scope and the great panorama of *Ulysses,* which is to come, and *A Portrait of the Artist as a Young Man.*

I, too, have had difficulty in the last few years with the writing of the short story. I do them now with considerably more burden than before. I'm grateful to the short story, because I came to the novel through the short story. I think there are many contemporary novelists who would have gained a great deal by working at the short story first. I am thinking among others of Ruark and Wallace and Robbins, who write great, bulky, exhaustive novels, from which you could cut pages and pages.

Perhaps for this reason I will not be able to write a long, eight-hundred-page novel, because having come to the novel through the short story, I try to write that which is essential. And yet, after three novels, I too feel the difficulty now of going back to the short story. I think this is significant, and probably true of a good many novelists.

The early Irwin Shaw stories, for instance, are tremendously more effective as short stories than some of the short stories that Shaw has done recently; and I don't know just why this should be. It's an area of great interest to me because, as John suggested as well, it affects my family's ability to eat, and my capacity to pay the rent; so I'd be interested in some further development along this area.

Mr. Cheever: Wallace couldn't have written a short story on pain of death.

Miss Hazzard: You said before that it was just on the pain of death that one *would* write a short story.

Mr. Cheever: Oh, Shirley! Shaw has written some marvelous short stories. He belonged to a particular era—it was up to and through the war. The fact that his novels aren't as appealing, I think, doesn't reflect either on the short story or the novel.

Mrs. Janeway: No, it reflects on his talent.

Mr. Cheever: It seems to me, as a matter of fact, that I've rather gotten us off the track. The short story is a particularly acute form with a very intense emotional spectrum. This is its only life. It doesn't go on making raspberry jam, or reporting the yacht races and so forth.

Mrs. Janeway: Some of them do though.

Mr. Cheever: Ah, but they shouldn't.

Miss Hazzard: Those *aren't* necessary!

Mr. Cheever: It's really a very rare form, and as I've said earlier, not only is it an exceptionally penetrating form of communication, it also keeps the rest of literature at heel.

Miss Hazzard: Yes. I don't know if I understand properly, but I don't regard the short story as necessarily a training for the novel. I don't think of it as a form of discipline, like being trained in sail in the days of steamships.

Mr. Cheever: No, no.

Mr. Petrakis: Perhaps I should have clarified this. I think the short story exists in and for itself. I have great affection for it. I would have preferred to have written poetry, but I could not, and since I have not felt myself qualified to write poetry, I wrote the short story, which I believe comes as close to poetry as anything can. I think, in addition to this, it can be a training ground for a novelist in that it forces him to eliminate that which is unnecessary and ponderous. There are novels in which you can spend three pages on a man's moving up in an elevator, discussing trivialities with the elevator operator. I don't think the short-story writer, trained in the discipline of the short story, trained in the discipline of the incident and the revelation, will permit himself to fall into this trap.

Mrs. Janeway: Is it a matter of compression then? Novels come in different sizes. I'd rather use that word, I think, than length. Do stories come in different sizes, too? Are some of them tighter, but bigger?

Mr. Cheever: When you define a short story, I think it's as if you were defining any piece of fiction at all. One should say that it's not a short story; it's a short narrative. Then there's the modern short story, which begins with Gogol—and I do think we do have the modern short story—and is inclined to be rather short. It deals, as in Gogol's "Overcoat," with a whole new spectrum of self-understanding, and also with bureaucracy which is actually what the story coped with, and the phobias of that particular society.

No, there's no length. Katherine Anne Porter has written short stories that run—what? Twenty-five pages?

Mrs. Janeway: At least.

Mr. Cheever: And Salinger—some of his best stories are rather long. But the impulse—There is a spontaneity, an impetuosity involved, I think, that one doesn't have in the novel.

Mr. Petrakis: Isn't this what O'Connor was talking about in a way, when he said that he was a lyrical writer? John. Your reference to the intense emotional spectrum of the short story must have been O'Connor's feeling—that he worked this way, lyrically and ex- plosively, and that he could never envisage himself maintaining this kind of emotional intensity over the span of a novel, so that he had to work in the realm of the short story.

Mr. Cheever: Yes, exactly.

Portrait of a Man Reading

Marcia Seligson/1969

Reprinted from *Book World,* 9 March 1969, p. 2, by permission of *The Washington Post.* Copyright © 1969 by *The Washington Post.*

My earliest and clearest memories are of being read to at a very young age and constantly, by my mother and grandmother. In those days, and in my particular background—my mother was English and we lived right outside Boston in what I always think of as its "Athenian twilight years"—people read all the time, even people who were not terribly literate or erudite. They read alone, to each other, in groups, to their children. Reading was the commonest form of entertainment and family activity for us New England puritans.

What did your family read to you?

All of Dickens from beginning to end, read and re-read. As soon as I could, I tackled every one of these books myself. They also read me *Treasure Island* and *The Call of the Wild,* and some of the *Tom Swift* stories, which I finished for myself when I was able.

What else did you yourself read as a child?

I loved Poe but he was forbidden. I remember my friend's father had a set of Poe which he kept under lock and key. When he went out we'd force open the cabinet and read the stories to each other. When I was about ten I was taken to a performance of *The Merchant of Venice* in Boston. I went home and grabbed the complete Shakespeare off the shelf. But my family opposed my reading such heady stuff at my age and lured me back to Jack London. There was a lot of reading but a lot of restrictions, too.

What did you read in your teenage years?

It must sound awfully precocious but I started reading Proust at fourteen. I remember being absolutely enchanted with *Swann's Way,* appalled and shocked at *The Cities of the Plain.* I have re-read

21

Swann's Way, but haven't picked up any other Proust since those years. I also read Joyce's *Ulysses* and all the Sherlock Holmes books when I was fifteen. About that time I discovered John Donne and fell in love with poetry. I devoured Yeats, Eliot, the nineteenth-century Romantics, most of the Elizabethans.

Who were your favorites?
Yeats and Donne, I suppose. Donne's lines are so firm and solid, absolutely indestructible. Reading him involves a good bit of hard work, which I appreciate—being a New Englander.

Do you still read poetry?
A tremendous amount. I probably read as much poetry as fiction. Until recently, we had a very pleasant ritual in my family where everyone—my wife, our three children and I—gathered every Sunday afternoon at five o'clock in the living room, and each of us had to recite a poem he had learned and memorized during the week. When my youngest was seven, he was reciting Robert Frost. I had great fun learning Dylan Thomas's poetry, and many of the Psalms. One of the last things I memorized, before we discontinued the event, was Donne's "The Funeral."

Why are you so attracted to poetry?
It's one of the most acute means of communication we have for the things we feel deeply. It's odd—often at moments of stress, or during small, daily crises, I'll find the lines of a poem inadvertently running through my mind. I remember once missing a plane by minutes, standing at the gate watching it take off and feeling terribly frustrated and furious. Suddenly I realized the only thing circulating through my head was the line, "The force that through the green fuse drives the flower drives my green age," from Thomas's great poem.

What poetry have you read lately?
Donne and Yeats, of course. And I really like several of the younger poets writing now, like Alan Dugan, George Starbuck, John Ashbery and Ted Berrigan, for example.

What were you reading during the Thirties?
Hemingway, naturally, with great pleasure. Thomas Wolfe with less pleasure. I liked Faulkner. *The Sound and the Fury* and *As I Lay*

Dying were favorites of mine. I was not politically obsessed, as so
many of my writer friends were in those years. But I did get caught
up in the spirit of the times to the extent that I devoted myself to
reading all of the Russians from Gogol on.

Do you read in any other languages?
Yes, French and Italian—both learned in prep school. I used to try
to read one book a year in each, but now I've gotten horribly lazy. I
must admit I haven't gotten through a novel in Italian in four or five
years, although I did prefer reading in Italian to French.

What books have you read recently in French?
Madame Bovary, several times, and *The Fall* by Camus. I chose
that particular one because it's his shortest novel.

How about reading short stores?
I've been especially interested in a few writers today who use the
short story as a form of moral parable. Dino Buzzati, an excellent
Italian writer and a devout Catholic, is one I admire a great deal. Also
Marcel Aymé, who is an anticleric, and Flannery O'Connor—another
Catholic. Their stories are based on strong moral positions, and
tremendous discipline is needed to develop these premises well in the
period of time a short story has allowed to it. John O'Hara, too,
writes highly moral tales. Look how his wicked people are always
burning in hell.

Do you read history, biography, science fiction, mysteries?
Sometimes I become very immersed in a specific period of history
and will read everything I can find. Recently I read four books on the
period from 1780 to 1812 in France. I've also done some reading on
the Risorgimento and the two Garibaldi campaigns. I've read a pile of
books on the Russian Revolution over the years, most of them quite
bad. Occasionally I read biographies; this past year I found Michael
Holroyd's biography of Lytton Strachey fascinating. I'm not at all
interested in science fiction. And I haven't looked at a mystery novel
since my entire family put down everything we were reading and for
a solid week read nothing but James Bond books.

Do you go to the theater?
Almost never. I lead a very secluded, boozy life in the woods in

upstate New York. If I'm not writing or reading, I skate, swim, visit, walk with my dogs, eat, drink. Occasionally we get to a film at the local movie theater, but mostly we all read. My wife is much more erudite than I, and our children love to read aloud. We have quite a large, serviceable library in our home, and all tend to have very catholic tastes. I often don't finish a book, may put it down after three sentences, but I'm always involved in reading *something*.

What have you read in the last year?
Let's see, I can hardly remember everything I've read—I have re-read Gibbon as well as several Dickens novels of which I'm still extremely fond. Many of my reading decisions are made for me by my family, since this is an activity we frequently do together. For instance, my son read Stephen Crane for the first time this year, so I re-read him. Also *My Antonia* by Willa Cather, a marvelous book. We all read George Eliot's *Middlemarch*. And the Nile books, by Alan Moorehead.

Do you keep up with current American fiction?
Certainly. I just finished *Portnoy's Complaint*—an absolutely glorious, important work.

Why do you feel Portnoy's Complaint *is such an important book?*
It's a most exceptional novel. The tone is always perfect, the control flawless. The book is wonderfully pure, considering his subject matter. The descriptions of fairly unsavory sexual encounters are beautifully, wittily done. And nobody has handled the subject of masturbation with any real candor until this book. Roth is masterful at pitching one mood against another—humor, pathos, self-satire. He always knows exactly what he's doing. I certainly think he's one of the best writers we have in America.

What other American writers are you interested in today?
I've always found Updike's career very exciting. He's an adventurer, a traveler. He never repeats himself and he takes all sorts of chances in the directions he's willing to go off into. For example, you know his early reputation was made as a humorous poet and his last novel swung out into a venereal obsession. We have no idea where he'll go next.

Anybody else?

I admire Mailer tremendously, especially *The Armies of the Night.* And Bill Styron, Robert Penn Warren, Saul Bellow is excellent—I think *Henderson the Rain King* is a brilliant book.

Could you choose a favorite of this group?

No, I really don't think of contemporary literature as a competitive sport. There is such a tremendous conflagration of work being done by so many writers, each attempting something different. In the same way, I'm not fond of categorization. I really don't care if a book is "journalistic fiction" or "fictional journalism" or "non-fiction fiction." Literature is a means of communication and that's all that is crucial. Also, I must admit that my own literary taste is quite impetuous and I find it difficult to diagnose such impulsive responses. I think very few writers, myself included, have trustworthy or responsible reading tastes.

Do you have a very favorite book?

Yes, definitely. *Madame Bovary.* I've probably read it twenty-five times, many of those in French.

Why is it such a great novel?

Because the writing is absolutely precise and simply perfect. This book was a considerable turning point in fiction, an innovation. Of course, all great novels are innovations but *Madame Bovary* was, for one thing, the first account we have of controlled schizophrenia. And it is a highly adventurous moral tale. You know the book was censored when it was first published and Flaubert was taken to court. Undoubtedly the most offensive point in the book is when Emma sits on a table and smokes a cigarette.

Novelist of Suburbia: Mr. Saturday, Mr. Monday and Mr. Cheever
By Wilfrid Sheed/1969

Reprinted from *Life,* 19 April 1969, pp. 39–40, 44, 46, by permission of the publisher.

For that last word in self-crucifixion, so the legend goes, catch a sensitive suburbanite by the toe on a Monday morning. "I had to settle for *this?*" he might well be ranting. "I with my dreams, I with my tastes?" Try him again on a fine Saturday and he may have trouble remembering what's supposed to be wrong with the suburbs. It is on the tip of his head, but he feels to sleepy to track it down right now.

John Cheever must be easily our subtlest and most sympathetic interpreter of this latest split in the Western mind. In his new book, *Bullet Park,* he has turned Monday and Saturday into separate people, named, a little archly, Hammer and Nailles, and sicked them on to each other. Mr. Hammer is a reformed drunk (as who is not on Monday?) and a seeker of impossible beauty; Eliot Nailles is serenely square, a dozy churchgoer and doting husband, who never ceases to thrill to the status quo. The prize they fight for is the next genera-tion—Nailles's son Tony, whom Saturday loves and Monday wants to kill.

But if you wish to ferret out these and other symbols, the essential person *not* to ask is John Cheever. For Cheever is one of those writers who instinctively deny everything, almost before you've asked it. The town is not his town, the house is not his house, the symbols are your problem. Seated in his Ossining, N.Y. living room, looking like a football-playing pixie and sipping bourbon from a silver goblet, he seems a bit like Hammer and a touch like Nailles and quite a lot like a cardsharp who won't give away his tricks. John Updike has said that he has "never met anyone quicker on his feet, both fictional and

26

real, than Cheever" and he obviously keeps in shape warding off snoopers. But in this year of blather, a reticent writer, successful or otherwise, is as fascinating as Garbo.

Cheever is unusual in other ways. To begin with, he has reversed the accepted practice in American letters of starting at the top with his best book and working his way slowly down, using his personality as a parachute. Cheever started as an avowedly minor writer, turning out small gems for *The New Yorker,* indistinguishable from all the other small gems in that magazine except for their exceptionally high polish and a certain wild gleam. Gradually his stories got better, shinier, wilder, and he managed to run some of them together into a couple of novels (*The Wapshot Chronicle* and *The Wapshot Scandal*), which any author is advised to do who wants to be taken seriously. But now, almost 57, he retains the manner of a minor writer who won't be the least annoyed if you haven't heard of him.

His moralistic New England parents had something to do with this. They took a squinty view of his writing as such. "You had to declare that you had never thought of being rich or famous," he explains. "After that they said, 'You may proceed.'"

With trifling exceptions Cheever has never been anything but a writer. "Writing well is like having a baritone voice" is all he has to say about that—reminding one once again that a WASP gentleman doesn't open his insides to casual inspection. He won't open yours either. In both his writing and his conversation Cheever leaves people's secret selves sealed up at certain points, preferring to gossip about their surface eccentricities the way the Victorians did. He understands their secret selves just as well that way and leaves them some dignity to go home in. He treats his characters, as he treats his guests, with irony and outstanding courtesy.

As Cheever's dog Flora comes up to you and his younger son Fred goes gallumphing up the stairs (his other children are Ben, studying at Antioch College, and Mrs. Susan Cowley, who teaches at Scarborough and is married to Rob Cowley, the son of the editor and critic Malcolm Cowley), one deduces another reason for his reticence—namely the protection of innocents. His characters may be imaginary, but he borrows real noses and voices and barks. And without his metronomic denials, one would soon feel oneself to be deep in Cheever country, suspecting the worst. He allows that his father, now safely dead, was the base for the frisky patriarch Leander Wapshot, and that his brother Fred turns up a time or two in his stories. "You have a father, I have a brother," he said, referring to some fiction of mine. One sitting duck is enough in any family. (As a matter of fact, I have several fathers, like everyone else.)

But Cheever goes beyond this routine defense ("Actually, I have lost my fear of libel or reaction") to a complete removal of the traces. Bullet Park sounds like a real town, but the reader should not be quite able to place it ("verisimilitude but not reality"); there are no news events to tell us what year it is; no cigarettes are lit, no brands are named. The aim is a kind of spaceless, timeless fiction in which emotions can have it out unencumbered by circumstance. If the result is a brutal vivisection of American life this particular year (and it is), so be it. He swears that is not what he had in mind.

Thus his reticence is also part of his fictional strategy: along with the calendar and the maps, the author has to go. Cheever is so intent on keeping out of the way of his creations that he almost denies his own existence. For instance, when he left New York City in the fifties, some people read this as some kind of symbolic gesture typical of his generation. "Not at all," he says; "we left for the sake of the children's education." No gesture at city? "No, I love the city. Of course, I also love the country." Thank you, Mr. Coolidge.

After a few more questions have been detonated like this, you have just the impression you are supposed to have: that the work is everything, the writer is nothing. All the answers mean the same thing: read my books. A writer's opinions will only distract you from that. This doesn't mean, as some critics have supposed, that Cheever has no social and political interests. On the contrary, once his point has been made, he is happy to talk politics—so long as it is not Cheever the Writer who is supposed to be talking. On the same principle, he won't sign petitions or angry letters, although recently he made an exception in relation to the Russian suppression of Czechoslovakia. He is exercised about the encroachment of monster highways on good countryside and may write something about it someday soon.

But even a faceless chronicler has to live somewhere. Has Cheever chosen his own locations because he thought they would be good to write in or about?

No, he said, he didn't think so, he just took what came. It was almost as if he felt that going and looking for material would be cheating. Cheever takes the accidents of life like a magician who works with whatever the audience hands him, and he constructs his world out of that, as a microscope finds it all in a snowflake.

The reader may be skeptical. After all, the accidents of his life have worked out pretty well for his purposes—colorful ancestors, fascinating parents, quaint settings. But there is something about Cheever which reminds one of the old story about the patient with the bed next to the window who invented a gaudy world outside to please the other patients, although his window overlooked a blank wall. Considering the quiet life he leads and the simple props he uses, one wonders whether Cheever's wall isn't really as blank as the next patient's, whether his ancestors weren't just as boring as the ones in your own dining room and his settings as flat as last year's summer resort.

Cheever has been called admiringly a machine for writing stories, and he has long since cut and reshaped his past into lengths of fiction. His father may not have started out as Leander Wapshot, but that's what he is now. Likewise St. Botolphs, the home of the Wapshots, may not be much like Quincy, Mass., the home of the Cheevers, but it probably contains all that Cheever cares to remember about Quincy, plus some things that *should* have happened there. When Balzac was dying, they say that he called for one of his own characters to come and cure him; Cheever might send, without expecting much, for his own Father Ransome. For such writers, memory and imagination are not two faculties but one mega-faculty. Cheever invents as he goes, and even the things that happened last week have already been improved, are halfway to being publishable.

The Blank Wall theory is borne out somewhat by *Bullet Park*. This novel looks at first glance like a close eyewitness investigation of exurban or suburban (Bullet Park seems someplace between) customs and attitudes. But Cheever says he doesn't get out that much; and on closer scrutiny, one sees how much he has milked from a few basic scenes—the train ride, the very occasional dinner party, the bathroom confrontation.

"Fiction is not crypto-autobiography," he tells his interviewers before they get their galoshes off. But he has fed enough data for several crypto-autobiographies into the distorting mechanism of fiction. No sooner had he been expelled from school, age 17, than he wrote a story about, well, somebody's explusion and sold it to *The New Republic*. (It tells a lot about his raffish conservativeness that (a) he was expelled—for laziness and smoking, he says—and that (b) he'd as soon not have the school's name published.)

After that, his brother helped him out for a while, deepening a relationship that was to form the heart of the Wapshot books, and maybe the legend of Hammer and Nailles as well—the relationship that constitutes his strongest claim on literary importance. His mother is harder to find, for reasons of camouflage, but you might not be far wrong if you looked for her in the eccentric Aunt Honora. If his wife Mary has sat for any stories, she is very cheerful and forgiving about it.

Most of his subsequent stopping places have turned up here and there in garbled form, including a short spell he spent in Washington in the '30s and annual trips to Italy, which provide the oddest item in his canon—an interview with Sophia Loren which appeared in the *Saturday Evening Post*. He is a tidy man and there is not much waste in his life. But his strongest work takes place somewhere toward the end of a branch line, probably within reach of water, where a married couple fumble between joy and despair, love and the death of love. When literal magic strikes, as it is likely to, it is in the Waspy Gothic tradition—a code for things one doesn't confront directly. Cheever is damned if he will write the least pornography "except in a triumphant sense," but his books crackle with sexual friction.

Cheever has been typed as a spiritual conservative, a celebrator of things as they are. But this is misleading. He is, to be sure, a regular churchgoer, and calls religion "a metaphor for ecstasy." The first chapter of *The Wapshot Scandal* is even read in Unitarian churches, though Cheever is Episcopalian himself. But the serenity is wrested from panic. In his most famous story, *The Swimmer* (made into a movie over which he just shakes his head sadly), a man sets out with a high heart to swim across the country, via his neighbors' swimming pools. As the day wears on, the things that gave hope to his venture—conviviality, old friends, liquor, the simple joy of swimming—become thinner and weaker. And by evening he is limping and cold and alone and his house is boarded up. So much for man's journey through life.

To ward off the spooks, no talisman is to be despised, whether it be a dream of Plaid Stamps or of bomb shelters or bacon-lettuce-and-tomato sandwiches. These perform the dignified office of fending off death and despair. Cheever's own preference would seem to be for lighting fires and walking through the woods and being baptized by thunderstorms: an immersion in nature such as Leander Wapshot undertook when, on a clear spring day, he walked into the sea and never returned. But Cheever understands about the Plaid Stamps too—which has given him a bad name in some quarters.

Cheever gives the impression of not understanding his own work too well, and discussing it only out of politeness. Otherwise he swims, skis, plays touch football, goes to the movies (saw *Rachel, Rachel* four times—but a novel is to a movie "what a bell is to a whistle. No resonance"). He reads just about all the fiction that's published and makes sly, generous judgments.

As publication approaches, he will blow the scene to escape the fuss. The residents of Bullet Park and St. Botolphs will travel along and mysteriously fetch up in the next villa, and we should have another collection of superb stories in a year or two.

Having a Drink with Cheever

Leslie Aldridge/1969

Reprinted from *New York*, 28 April 1969, pp. 48–50.

I was advised before my interview with John Cheever that I would have to have read *Bullet Park,* his new book, at least twice, that I would have to dig hard to get him to talk, and that he would be clamish, difficult, though charming. In addition, he hated interviews (perhaps even interviewers?) and hated even more having to come to New York for them.

Nevertheless, he agreed to have a drink with me one bitter cold day. I dialed him on the house phone in the St. Regis lobby and Cheever answered with a deep voice on the first ring, "Yes, come up. I'm the guy without the tie." Click. Confused—an inauspicious beginning for any interview—I rode the elevator to the fourth floor. There he was. He had come out to meet me. The guy without the tie. The only guy there, for that matter. Short, lean, compact in dark brown slacks, a blue button-down Oxford open at the neck, a neat face with blue eyes to match the shirt, short-clipped hair which subtracted a decade from his fifty-six years. He was strikingly like the image of the expensive exurbanites who people his books and stories.

He led me into a small shoebox of a room, everything in it creamy satin-bland except for a bronze clock high on the wall over the bathroom door. The place appeared totally unlived in until I saw the ashtrays overloaded with cigarette butts and ashes, and liquor bottles clustered on the chest and a jumble of ties lying in a heap on the dresser.

We camped on the beds (hotel rooms aren't for sitting). Cheever lit the first of a continuous succession of cigarettes and ordered what I expected would be a couple of drinks. The waiter arrived with a *bottle* of gin and one of Scotch and Cheever gloated, "Guess what the bill is? Twenty-nine dollars! Wait till Alfred Knopf sees that!" He chuckled boyishly. He was having a couple of days in New York, at the expense of Knopf, for the publication of his new book on April 28. And he was about to get all he could out of it, perhaps as part-payment for putting up with interviews to please everyone except himself. If there was anything liquid left, he planned to load the bottles into his suitcase and take them home with him. Meantime he poured a glass of gin, anointed it with a few drops of vermouth, and gave me a glass of Scotch. Mr. Cheever turned out to be a very agreeable and amusing man, even at moments talkative, though how much he really told me is questionable.

"I never wanted to be rich or famous, just a good writer. I like writing very much, but I'm not excited about having a book coming out. When a book is done, it's done. It has its own life. It's *not* like having a baby. When you embark on a novel, it's like a voyage, like building a house, or a bridge—I guess bridge is best—you never know if you can bring it off.

"I'm pooped out after a book." (He makes one of his many mouth noises, a pooped-out sound. WHOOOMPHFF!) "*Bullet Park* took four years to write." (It's only 250 pages, short as novels go.)

"I do read reviews of my books but they don't affect me. I've almost never had a bad review, but I would rather have an informative one than a silly rave review. When my books come out I'm always out of the country. I'm going to Curaçao and then to Rome. When my last book was published I was in Leningrad, and so busy trying to get shirts washed or take a bath that when someone came in with copies of reviews that were two weeks old, they didn't seem important."

I point out that readers are going to be guessing at his meanings. *Bullet Park,* his third novel, is a book which practically begs to be prodded for hidden symbols and mythic parallels. The protagonists are named Mr. Hammer and Mr. Nailles. There is a son, Tony Nailles, who goes to bed one day and won't get up again. There is an ending in a church where Mr. Hammer is about to murder (sacrifice?) Tony on the altar. Mr. Nailles finally breaks the church door down with a chain saw to save his son.

After reading the novel, an editor at Random House exclaimed, "Why, Mr. Hammer and Mr. Nailles are two sides of the same person." An editor at Knopf said, "The mystery that links them is the schizophrenic human psyche . . . especially the almost split-in-half American middle-class psyche of today."

I ask, what is the key to *Bullet Park,* Mr. Cheever? What is the riddle? Cheever looks at me with kind of soft blue eyes and his voice purrs. The words stream out in an accent which is a tumultuous combination of English (his mother was) and South Shore Massachusetts (his father was, and the family lived in Quincy, where Cheever was born) and it all sounds like jet-set Boston, words flowing quickly into each other like one long word embellished with sonorous sound effects. He lights another cigarette and deftly retreats from the question.

"The diagnosis of fiction is not the role of a storyteller. To write is one thing. To describe it is another. A writer is deeply intuitive when he writes. I don't know anyone who gives a good diagnosis of his own work. Metaphysical aspects are better taken care of by critics. I'm not a sociologist, a philosopher or a moralist. I'm a novelist. There's a sameness to these pursuits, but they're not similar."

"But what is it meant to *say?*" I force the question. In his first two novels, *The Wapshot Chronicle* (National Book Award 1958) and *The Wapshot Scandal* (1963) and his five volumes of short stories, most of which appeared in the *New Yorker,* Cheever has come to be known, as one critic put it, as the "Ivy League Faulkner of the New York exurbs," a keen observer of the essentially desperate, often tragic, human condition.

He leans back on the pillow. "*Bullet Park* is about a man who loves and is able to implement this love. I tried to write about two men, and one man loved his son and he saved his life. The power of love is something that can be celebrated and repeated."

"But his breaking down the church door, isn't that a symbol?"

"Yes, he cuts down the door, but I was careful to have him make a diagonal chop in it, not a cross."

"No hidden meanings, Mr. Cheever?"

"Everything is stratified. A book has resonance. There is no good story without profundity." He motions me to drink up. Alfred Knopf's Scotch makes me feel warm inside and helps me to be insistent.

"But are Hammer and Nailles the same man? Why Hammer and Nailles?"

"A book has to be taken at first on the superficial level, then, later,

on more profound levels. Why Hammer and Nailles? It's the nomen-
clature, like the idea that people named John and Mary will never
divorce." (The Cheevers, who have been married for 30 years, are
John and Mary.) "They are bound together, while Tom, Dick and
Harry will go to Reno. But Hammer and Nailles . . . they're stuck
with each other."

"Why does Tony go to bed and refuse to get up? That must have
obvious implications."

"Tony is not bored. Tony goes to bed for the reason that I *say* he
goes to bed. He feels very sad. He is *not* an indictment against
society. The book is not current history. It's supposed to set its own
climate and time. Clichés like 'generation gap' I find repulsive. Tony
wasn't concerned with inflation or the Black Panther movement. He
was just melancholy and that is a perfectly legitimate reason for him
to go to bed and not get up.

"Do I like this book? It's like shaving in the morning. Do I like the
face in the mirror? Not particularly. It's just the face I shave. But I do
like the story because I could tell it. There's a quality of exuberance in
telling a story. It's one of the most important ways of communication.
I won't say this is my best book. It's my most recent love.

"My characters at this point are the projection of my adult
imagination. They are true inventions. I had just written a character
into a book once that comes into the room in a wheelchair. Six
weeks later I went somewhere and the hostess came into the room in
a wheelchair. 'Oh Jesus, no,' was all I could think." (But I thought of
Cheever, who is himself a "swimming pool bum"—"The Swimmer"—and who likes to use a chain saw around his property in
Ossining, who adores his sons and enjoys life but sometimes finds it
terrifying—*Bullet Park*. Is he writing about himself?)

"In your books you are critical of well-to-do exurbanites. You
damn their hypocrisy, their lechery, their mortgages, their credit cards
and mink coats. You perpetrate nightmares which they seem to create
for themselves."

"I write about children, open fires, dogs, open light; they are the
things, the people I live with, associate with. I mean no blanket
criticism of affluent society." (Perhaps it is Cheever's intuitive self
which is the critic.)

"You seem always to discern the tragedy in human life."

"The human condition is not tragic, it's constricting. The conflict between grossness and aspiration. The purpose of fiction is to give a vision of life, to clarify the mistakes we've made. I'm beginning to sound like Nixon," he laughs. "If it's a distorted view, it's not good fiction. Today the novel is always a heresy. It challenges stated canons."

"Do you ever worry about being understood by young people?"

"No, the bulk of my mail comes from people under 30."

"Are writers running out of material today?"

"How can you run out of material? There are men, women, children, dogs, fires—the substance of fiction."

"What would you do if you couldn't write?"

"I'd cut wood."

He finished his cigarette and opened another pack. "I chain smoke, I chain drink, I chain everything else. I'm not shy, I'm reclusive. *Life* came up to do a spread on me and asked me to give a cocktail party and play touch football. Clichés of suburban life! This is not the way I live. I told them they'd have to take me as a boozy recluse. I love to drink. I'm hooked on it. I drink a lot but I don't drink heavily when I've got to work the next day. I love parties excessively. That's the reason I don't go to them. I drink, I dance, I eat everything that's put in front of me. We usually go out on Fridays and Saturdays. I never get drunk. When I'm not working I cut the acres of lawn or I cut down big enormous trees with a chain saw. I love to ice-skate. I'm teaching my son. And I love to ski.

"I used to write in the afternoon, but I got too excited and couldn't sleep. Now I write from 9 to 12:30 in the morning. I sit in a chair on a horseblanket because the chair isn't high enough for the rusty tin table and the rusty typewriter." (He makes a mouth noise, BAAAAAAAAGH! At the thought of the blanket? The rusty tin table? The typewriter?) "When I was younger I could write 35 pages in a couple of days. My best stories are the ones I've written straight through. I never had to change a word. But I'm not that young any more and it's very tiring, though exhilarating. I think I wrote the second chapter of *Bullet Park* that way. When I work I always wear loafers and wash trousers and a sweater. I dislike the smell of gasoline on dry-cleaned clothes. I hate wool trousers that smell of gas stations. I work in a room over a real estate agent in Ossining because there's no telephone to disturb me. I'm not distracted by people in the streets. All I see out of the window is an old bathtub sitting on a lawn near a building contractor's office, and a piece of sky.

"I must say, I miss the sky in New York. Central Park is like a bay window in a dark house. But I don't hate New York. I find it exciting. I lived in New York for about 20 years, moving up as everyone does, first on West 8th Street, then the 30s, then 92nd Street, and finally East 59th. Now I live in Ossining in an 18th-century stone house on six acres, on a hill from which I can see the Hudson River. I've always lived on my writing. Sometimes well, sometimes badly. I was stone broke a year ago. I couldn't pay the mortgage. I could scarcely buy a Christmas tree, and I had tuition bills for two kids in school." (His daughter is married to critic Malcolm Cowley's son, one son is at Antioch College, and an 11-year-old boy is in prep school. His wife Mary teaches English at Briarcliff College.) "I never take an advance from a publisher. I don't like to be indebted to people and I think I have a better relationship with my editor that way. Now I'm living on what's left of the $50,000 I got for screen rights to 'The Swimmer.'" (He didn't want to talk about the movie.) "I'd rather give a book of mine to someone awfully good rather than sell it to a big movie company for more money. I'd like to do an original screenplay sometime, but next I'd like to write a play or a libretto for an opera."

An old hand at writing, Cheever has been publishing fiction since he was expelled from Thayer Academy at 16 for smoking and getting low grades, wrote it up in a story called "Expelled" and sold it to the *New Republic*. (Ironically, it was Malcolm Cowley, his future daughter's future father-in-law, who bought it.) After a "mixed" childhood ("I don't think anyone has a normal childhood"), which culminated in his father's losing the family money during the Depression and his expulsion from prep school, Cheever decided not to go to college and to be a writer.

He has a lot of writer friends, including another John and Mary (Updike), "but I won't say who the best writers working today are. It would be like making out an invitation list. I'd always forget someone. There are many good American writers going, some smashing good writers. My wife Mary doesn't especially like my work, though sometimes she's too close to it to say. But in the choice of a wife, I wouldn't want an admirer; I want a critical intelligence, another person. I have no books of mine in the house. I don't like incomplete things around."

Although Cheever does not hide from his public ("I'm a very friendly man"), has his phone number listed in the book and allows graduate students writing Ph.D.s to come up and bother him, he tries to avoid notoriety. He tried to get *Time* to kill a cover story they were doing on him several years ago, and he admits to a certain chicanery when he is obliged to entertain reporters.

"When they come up to interview me," he confided, taking another drink, "I walk them to Croton Dam eight miles away to tire them. Then we sit by a hot fire and I give them large drinks of Scotch to get them drunk and keep them from asking too many questions." He laughs.

That is the game. I think I would have preferred being pickled in front of a roaring fire in Ossining instead of in a creamy room at the St. Regis. All right, Mr. Cheever. Another time! I will bring a bicycle for the eight-mile hike and a fake rubber plant into which I can toss the large Scotches.

I plan my revenge as I thank Cheever for the drink and leave him tieless in the room with Alfred Knopf's liquor bottles now half-empty on the chest, and the ties in a mess on the dresser and all the cigarette butts piled high in the ashtrays. I weave down the hall to the elevator, glowy all over, content that at least I know—maybe because John Cheever is really friendly and I ask a lot of questions when I drink—why a Mr. Hammer and a Mr. Nailles, why Tony went to bed and wouldn't get up and that *Bullet Park* is, as he told me, at least on one of its levels of stratification, a love story. A story about a man who loves his son.

Talk with John Cheever
Christopher Lehmann-Haupt/1969

Reprinted from the *New York Times Book Review,* 27 April 1969, pp. 42–44 by permission of the publishers. Copyright © 27 April 1969 by The New York Times Company

John Cleever does not enjoy being interviewed because he is not the sort of writer who likes to theorize about writing—his own or anyone else's. Cheever is supremely a story-teller. On the few occasions when he has been persuaded to speak about writing before an audience, he has been known simply to tell one of his stories. In fact, his fictional imagination is so strong that to be in his presence is to see events as part of a Cheever story, and oneself as a character in it.

So it would not be telling the strict truth to claim that I interviewed John Cheever. During the day that I tried to talk with him about his new novel, "Bullet Park," this is what happened: My adventure began—like Cheever's two latest novels—in a railway station. As I stood on the platform of the station in Ossining, N.Y., I realized that my suitcase was on the departing train. Cheever picked me up in his red Karmann Ghia and raced me from station to station, trying to catch up with my luggage.

Finally, on the platform of North Croton station we spied my suitcase through a crack in a large metal box that was chained to the building housing the station's waiting room. Only it wasn't a waiting room any more. The interior had been converted to an appliance showroom. One peered through its windows and beheld in the shadows row upon row of pastel-colored washing machines and kitchen ranges. A vision from a Cheever story.

While we waited for someone with a key to the metal box, we stood and talked and drank coffee in front of the pot-bellied stove in the station-master's shack. Switchmen in coveralls and conductors in vests talked about trains and schedules, while I asked Cheever about writing. At last we tired of waiting. We returned to the platform and while no one was looking I climbed headfirst into the metal box and fished out the suitcase. The morning of the interview was over.

In the afternoon I succeeded in getting Cheever within hearing of a tape recorder. (He detests tape recorders, but I insisted because I knew of a previous interviewer who had drunk too much to remember what Cheever had told him, and had had to return for another try.) Cheever avenged himself for his discomfort by plying me with Scotch. I failed to notice when the tape had run out. So the best things he said were never recorded.

I believe that John Cheever has too great a command over the artifacts of suburban life—the railroad stations and trains, the liquor, the dogs and swimming pools, the tape recorders and television sets that he has been magically animating in his fiction all these years—for me to hope to get my way. I was lucky to have escaped with the bruises I got climbing in and out of that metal box, a hangover, and the following exchanges.

My questions are identified by italics.

I want to ask you a question about your new novel, "Bullet Park."
I once got a phone call from a student. He said, "I'm having an argument about your short story, 'The Swimmer,' with my instructor. I've got him right here, and you can settle it." I told the kid that it seemed to me that a writer has a story to tell and should be granted a certain amount of innocence. Any story that is told is stratified and has all kinds of profundities if it's any good at all. It's like saying "Good morning." You can imply anything: I love you. You look awful. Drop dead. I can't live without you. And so forth. It's all in a very simple salutation. And this seems to me the privilege of the novelist.

Agreed. But there was a question about "Bullet Park" I wanted to clear up because I think it relates to something that's misunderstood about your writing. You're sometimes accused of being preoccupied with objects, things, the petty luxuries of suburan life.
Yes, I recall that a noted critic was offended by the fact that the hero of "The Swimmer" has three cars.

But why? That's part of the point of the story, isn't it?
Yuh. I don't know. Maybe he can't swim.

Anyway in "Bullet Park" the hero Eliot Nailles, spends the morning of Sexagesima, which is. . . ?

Sexagesima? The sixth Sunday before Easter.

Nailles spends part of the morning cutting wood with a chain-saw. While he's at it he recalls the words of the Epistle . . .

"Of the Jews five times received I forty stripes save one. Thrice was I beaten with rods, once was I stoned . . ."

Yes. So in a certain sense the chain-saw is sanctified by association. And in the end of the book, it's the chain-saw that Eliot Nailles uses to save his son's life.

All of which I intended. What I wanted to do—since "The Wapshot Scandal" was such an extraordinarily complex book built around non sequiturs really—what I wanted to do was something very simple. I kept thinking of William Tell: that this was a man who loved his son and was able to protect him, or, as a matter of fact, save him. And I wanted to describe a love that could be implemented, that existed in other than dramatic terms.

In a sense all three of my novels are love stories, really. "The Wapshot Chronicle" is my love for Leander. "The Scandal" is, I suppose, Melissa's love for Emile. And this is simply Nailles's love for Tony. Anything else is all in the nature of a variation. "The Chronicle," of course, is a posthumous attempt to make peace with my father's ghost . . . what I remember of him.

Was the experience of writing "Bullet Park" very different from writing "The Chronicle" and "The Scandal"?

Yes. Well, the wonderful thing about the novel is of course that the experience is always different and the form is always different. Also, there's the quality of age. I'm 56 years old and have been publishing for, what, something like 40 years? It was a question of whether or not one could bring it off, which I thought I did. It seems to have been more of an ending than I would have expected. I will never work in that line again. Or that particular voice again.

How do you mean?

I mean I have to start all over again. It's a scene, a tone, that is gone, finished. "Bullet Park" absolutely finished it for me. It seems to me that I have to start all over again.

But that's a feeling you've had before.
I guess maybe so.

You mentioned that after you'd finished "The Wapshot Scan-dal" . . .
Oh, yes! After I'd finished "The Scandal" I was really in trouble. I mean suicidal trouble. And I then spent two weeks scything the meadow next to the garden. I'd get up in the morning and grab the scythe and go out and scythe and scythe and scythe until I'd really sweated it out.

Did finishing "Bullet Park" produce . . .
No. I felt much more contented. I had done in this case precisely what I'd wanted to do. I think the sense of form in the book is such a figment of the imagination. It's almost like shaping a dream . . . to give it precisely the concord you want . . . the arch, really. It's almost the form of an arch.

So when you finished "Bullet Park" you felt you'd caught the dream?
One way I can find out if I like something I've done is if I can tell it and it's all right. For instance, I can tell "The Swimmer." The New Yorker, which had the copyright, finally asked me please not to tell it any more. I had told it while participating in a P.E.N. panel discussion and they had to scratch out that part of the tape. Well, "Bullet Park" is about a man and his son. So one day I said to my son Benjamin, "Look, I've written a story about a man with his son." And some of it is traceable. For instance, "Guys and Dolls" is one of the best musical comedy scores I know. And my children know that. So one day last summer I said, "Look, Ben, I've written a novel. Do you want to hear it?" And Ben said, "Yuh." And so I went absolutely all the way through it from "Paint me a small railway station" to "wonderful, wonderful, wonderful as it had been."

The very words?
Yuh.

You know all the words?
I did then. And I said, "Is that all right with you?" And Ben said, "That isn't me!" I said, "No. That isn't you."

What will you write next?

Right now I'm working on a Reporter-at-Large piece for The New Yorker on a state highway they want to build through the valley near here. It's caused a lot of trouble. Then, if I ever return to fiction . . .

Is there any doubt about that?

I don't know. As I said, "Bullet Park" finished something for me. I made a bargain with the devil to finish it. If I do return to fiction, I'd like to put together 12 short stories that haven't been published in a book form yet. I want to write a screenplay, a play, and the libretto for an opera.

Do you enjoy writing?

Why yes. It happens to be one of the things I enjoy doing most.

Book Beat

Robert Cromie/1973

An interview between Robert Cromie, *Chicago Tribune* colum- nist and associate editor of the *Chicago Tribune Book World,* and John Cheever, on the occasion of the publication of *The World of Apples.* The interview was taped for "Book Beat" (PBS) in May 1973 and transcribed by Dennis E. Coates. It is printed here with the permission of Robert A. Cromie.

Cheever appeared in a dark blue suit, with vest, and he seemed to be recovering from a cold, shifting uncomfort- ably in his seat and drinking often from a glass of water. He seemed older and heavier than in any of the recent photographs I have seen. He spoke with the typical pure Bostonian catarrhal dialect, his words often becoming indistinct as they degenerated into grunts. The grunts just as often transformed themselves into quiet, rolling laugh- ter, interspersing the conversation with frequent surges of the author's warm humanity.

Cromie: I think we decided that this is about your sixth or seventh book of short stories—your sixth book of short stories?

Cheever: That would be, yes.

Cromie: And you've also done, of course, *The Wapshot Chroni- cle, The Wapshot Scandal,* and *Bullet Park*—three novels.

Cheever: Yes.

Cromie: And got the Book award for *The Wapshot Chronicle.*

Cheever: Yes.

Cromie: Now you've been writing since you were seventeen or eighteen, published since you were seventeen or eighteen.

Cheever: Yes. There is a bibliography, and I think there is something like two hundred stories listed.

Cromie: To whom did you send your first one?

Cheever: The *New Republic.*

Cromie: Oh, really?

Cheever: Yes. It was pulled out of a pile of manuscripts. . . .

Cromie: How does it feel to be seventeen and have sold a short story to the *New Republic?*

Cheever: It felt precisely . . . eighty-seven dollars, that's what it felt like.

Cromie: Which was a great deal of money! Well now you stick fairly much to the short story form. You prefer that to the novel?

Cheever: I like both of them very much. I'm writing a novel now.

Cromie: Are you?

Cheever: Yes, I'm writing a very long novel, a long, massive novel, and I don't think there is any problem. They are not in any way exclusive.

Cromie: But I wondered, what attracts you about the short story especially?

Cheever: The short story has a vast number of attractions; one of them is that it is extremely great in dealing with interrupted human relationships. My feeling is not too unlike other lives in the late . . . a lad in the late nineteenth century. But we seldom know the full story when we encounter people. We are much more inclined, I think, to be travelers than we are to be farmers. We have the intense encounter, but we very often don't know the beginning and we don't know the end. And the short story is very accommodating for this sort of relationship.

Cromie: I imagine this is an impossible question to answer, but how do these short stories come into being? Do you sit down and start doodling, as it were, and suddenly you're writing a short story, or do you have an idea first?

Cheever: It of course seems to me that all writing is an expression of one's deepest intuitions about life, about, you know . . . love, death, and so forth, and to parse the process of writing is something I've never been able to do. It's like a seizure of temporary lunacy. You sit down, you write—my family's always been very accommodating. I am now writing a story, no reason can be expected of me for three or four days. . . . So I write the story and I am, I think, quite reasonable afterwards.

Cromie: You write, it seems to me, a variety of short stories, so far as type goes. Some of them are, as you indicated, episodic. They have no real beginning and suddenly they are through; and others are well-rounded and obviously well-plotted, but you don't stick only to what would be a beginning, middle and end, in your short stories.

Cheever: It seems to me that in a world that is distinguished principally by its curvatures that linear narrative, a well-plotted narrative, as you say, is very often inadequate, inefficient, and sometimes obsolete. As I say, we are travelers and my sense of fiction is that it should alter the pattern of a story, or the novel should reflect, as I said, my deepest intuitions about life, about my life. There is a story in that collection called "The Jewels of the Cabots," which is the most ambitious piece I have done in trying to change key, not only with every paragraph, but almost with every sentence, because this is very much the way we live, the way we converse, the way we love, and. . . .

Cromie: That has a main story line and some subsidiary story lines in it, too.

Cheever: It is about family, that's all.

Cromie: That's the one in which the jewels are stolen and Percy, the aunt, has one very bright son who wants to be a musician and one who is considered retarded, mentally retarded.

Cheever: Yes. My idea, of course, is to confine linear narrative, because that isn't the way anybody lives.

Cromie: They live, they are from St. Botolph's, if that's how you pronounce the name of your. . . .

Cheever: St. Botolph's is fine.

Cromie: St. Botolph's. And that is where the Wapshot family chronicle was lived.

Cheever: Yes, that's right.

Cromie: How did you imagine this place? This is your own country isn't it, I mean your area, your own. . . .

Cheever: No, it's an imaginary country.

Cromie: That's what I mean.

Cheever: There never was a St. Botolph's.

Cromie: That's what I mean by your own; I meant it was exclusively yours.

Cheever: It was what I desired, and what I disliked. It was the kind of house, the kind of country, the kind of landscape that one catches in reveries shortly after dreaming: something that you both want very much and would like to escape from. There are cows and sheep and rivers, and feckless childhoods, and angry and cruel people.

Cromie: I think, well I suppose every author's works are revealing, but I think yours are particularly revealing because in the first place you like trains very much, and you like to look out of windows at three o'clock in the morning and see who's standing there and what the town looks like. You're also obviously fond of Italy.

Cheever: Oh yes, I'm very fond of Italy.

Cromie: Because you have Italian words; and one of your towns, what was the name of the town—Mon- . . . ?

Cheever: Montraldo

Cromie: Montraldo. The story about the curious relationship between the old, old lady and the servant girl, where you—not you but your protagonist—goes and rents a house. You have lived in Italy, then, quite a bit.

Cheever: Yes, which is not that surprising, since the New England I grew up in was dominated by Florence. A very curious combination that Boston should have thought itself the city of Flowers, since it has rather inclement temperatures. And the Copley Square, of course, is intensely Florentine. There were old cousins, old aunts who went to Florence, stayed in Florence, and brought back a great deal of Florentine furniture and so forth. And so Boston was much more closely oriented to Florence than it was, for example, to Chicago.

Cromie: Part of the grand tour, I suppose, was going to Florence in the old days.

Cheever: I suppose it was. And also it was one of the last manifestations of Athenian Boston. This was culture, this was beauty, and. . . .

Cromie: Well, you, as I say, lived in Italy. When did you first go there? How many years ago?

Cheever: Precisely seventeen.

Cromie: Now have you done some of your work there, written a number of your stories there?

Cheever: Yes, I've written a great deal of my stories there. Writers write all of the time.

Cromie: There's one in which a man and woman get on a plane from Rome, from someplace nine hours away—what, New York?

Cheever: It would be, yes.

Cromie: You don't quite say, you don't quite say. But they sit a seat apart and he tries to get in a conversation. That's a charming story with a surprise ending. How was that evolved? Now what gave you that idea? Did something like that happen? Did you just think on a plane it would be kind of fun if this were true?

Cheever: Well, no. Writing is not crypto-autobiography, and it's not current events. I'm not writing my autobiography, and I'm not writing things as they happen to me, with the exception of the use of details—thunderstorms and that sort of thing. No, it's nothing that happened to me. It's a possibility. It's an idea, rather a bitter one, I'm afraid, of the sensitiveness of misunderstandings between married couples.

Cromie: Well, that came across very strongly in the story. In another one of yours, and I can't remember the title, but it's in the one about the lady, who loses her husband on that treacherous road, the road that's finally widened and then the trucks start having wrecks on it.

Cheever: She loses two husbands.

Cromie: Yes.

Cheever: She loses two husbands and then of course perches herself on a hill and shoots truckdrivers. I think she shoots something like six.

Cromie: Well, she wrecks a number of very large trucks.

Cheever: Yes, that's right.

Cromie: So she finally misses and they discover the bullet holes.

Cheever: Right.

Cromie: But that's a very powerful story—with a happy ending! She gets a third husband and moves away from the road.

Cheever: That's right. She can scarcely hear the sound of traffic. There is no more than the sound of the wind in the trees . . . the description was. That of course never happened. However, there are areas of prophecy in fiction. For example, I wrote the first sky-jacking some five years before it ever happened. It's in *The Wapshot Scandal.* And I've always regretted having written that. It was a sheer invention. And when the story that you speak of was published a series of mysterious crack-ups took place outside of Boston. And one wants to avoid that sort of thing.

Cromie: Agatha Christie recently had quite a shock because somebody murdered somebody in England using a very rare poison which she had mentioned in one of her early books.

Cheever: Yes, yes.

Cromie: You remember that?

Cheever: That sort of thing does happen. Yes, I wrote in *Bullet Park,* a man named Hammer tries to kill a young man.

Cromie: Named Wayne.

Cheever: Tony Nailles.

Cromie: Nailles, pardon me. Tony Nailles, yeah.

Cheever: I think there was a publication of a man named Hammer who tried to kill a man whose name was not Nailles, in the parking lot of a supermarket.

Cromie: But at least not on the altar of a church.

Cheever: No.

Cromie: That's a parallel I hadn't thought of, but obviously a very real one. But "Chímera," or chiméra or however it is pronounced; and I can't pronounce it because I've heard so many different ways and have never looked it up.—this is a wistful, wistful story that captured me quite, about the man who can't get along with his wife, so he starts imagining a beautiful young girl who comes and visits him.

Cheever: Yes, and of course she gradually changes.

Cromie: Yes. and finally goes away.

Cheever: Yes.

Cromie: It seems like she had other things to do.

Cheever: The point of course was that reverie grows and changes. Reverie is organic, was the sense of the thing.

Cromie: And he covers himself by thinking that if he's imagined Olga, I think her name was, then he can imagine other people.

Cheever: Hundreds and hundreds of girls.

Cromie: He's quite contented.

Cheever: Really, not very. But on the matter of prophecy, in *The Wapshot Chronicle* there is a ship called the *Topaze* which Leander is the captain of, and in the original version, the ship sank. The cable to the rudder broke and the ship sank and lots of people were drowned and so forth. We went over to Nantucket, and I thought I needed a few more details. I needed faces and so forth. There was a boat that went from Nantucket to Hyannis. Well I got on it—I was supposed to be taking notes—and the rudder cable broke and the ship started to go down. I thought, if I get off this boat I'm going to change the whole scene. Nobody was going to have a wet foot. We finally got to Hyannis, and I rewrote the whole thing.

Cromie: That's very funny. Have you ever done anything besides write? I mean, have you had other jobs? Or have you always been a writer?

Cheever: Not really, no. I was in the Army for a long time.

Cromie—Four years, wasn't it?

Cheever: Four, yes.

Cromie: What did you do?

Cheever: I was in the Infantry for two years. I was a mortar gunner.

Cromie: Whereabouts?

Cheever: Mississippi, Alabama.

Cromie: That's a good place for mortars!

Cheever: And then I was in the Signal Corps. And I was in Astoria, in Manila.

Cromie: Oh, Manila?

Cheever: Yeah.

Cromie: How did you like the Philippines?

Cheever: Oh, well, a war was going on, of course. It wasn't a question of liking the place.

Cromie: I was there originally as a war correspondent just before we went into Japan, you see.

Cheever: Well, there was absolutely nothing over waist-high in Manila. It was one of the great ruins of all time.

Cromie: Yeah, I remember. What about the Army, now, as a writer? Did you appreciate being in the Army, figuring you'd have a lot of material, or was it upsetting to you to be regimented?

Cheever: I didn't find it particularly upsetting. As a matter of fact, I met all sorts of people I wouldn't ordinarily have met, particularly in the Infantry. That was a very well motivated war.

Cromie: That's World War II, the last one, I think, that was that well motivated.

Cheever: One felt one was doing something useful.

Cromie: Do you enjoy as a writer getting out and meeting people, or are you a reclusive type at all?

Cheever: Geographically I am inclined to be reclusive because I live in the country. I live in a neighborhood in which there are no other writers, except the advertising writers. I like people, I like children, and so forth. I seldom go to New York anymore. We'll go to Russia. I go to Egypt. I go to places like that.

Cromie: Instead of the next town.

Cheever: Instead of the next town, yes.

Cromie: Well you've been described as the writer of suburbia, because almost all of your short stories are laid in the country or laid in small towns.

Cheever: Yeah, I know. But of course everybody categorizes all writers. At first I used to be the writer of the Sutton Place neighborhood. Then I was the writer of small towns in New England. Now I'm the writer of Westchester County. I cannot be all three.

Cromie: I wouldn't think so, no.

Cheever: Well, one writes about women and children and dogs, its quite simple.

Cromie: How many children do you have, by the way? I know you have at least one son.

Cheever: I have two sons and a daughter. I also have a grandson.

Cromie: Oh really? Any budding writers in the family?

Cheever: Yes, well, my daughter and my oldest son are newspaper reporters.

Cromie: How nice.

Cheever: She's in San Francisco. He's on the West Bank of the Hudson.

Cromie: San Francisco is a good town. I don't know about the Hudson, that particular area, but San Francisco is a great newspaper town. Does your wife write at all?

Cheever: My wife is a poet.

Cromie: I didn't know that.

Cheever: And a very good poet. She's also taught English for twelve years.

Cromie: Does she catch you up on things—in grammar, for example, ever?

Cheever: No, not really. As a matter of fact she seldom reads what I write.

Cromie: Do you read her poems?

Cheever: Mmhm.

Cromie: Where is she published?

Cheever: Not often; and I can't remember the names of the magazines.

Cromie: Does she use Cheever?

Cheever: Yes, she uses Cheever.

Cromie: What is her first name?

Cheever: Mary.

Cromie: Mary Cheever. I have seen the by-line, but I didn't realize the connection, obviously. Well, you've been working on a novel—a big one, you say.

Cheever: Massive.

Cromie: How massive? Four times as long as *Bullet Park,* for example?

Cheever: You'll be able to lift it to the sound of outboard motors.

Cromie: Is it modern?

Cheever: Yes, yes, of course.

Cromie: And laid in this country?

Cheever: Yes.

Cromie: I won't go into the plot anymore because that's impolite to ask an author what the plot is.

Cheever: Well, you can tell there's no answer to your question, that is the problem.

Cromie: How far into it are you?

Cheever: Eighty-four pages.

Cromie: Just started, really.

Cheever: No, it's been going slowly. I make copious notes, and organize them, and wait for what I described earlier as a temporary seizure of lunacy when everything comes together. That is, of course, the most exciting thing about writing. I totally despair [and then] observations, emotions, and so forth all of a sudden calcify.

Cromie: Now this is an actual moment when you can feel—

Cheever: Catalyze is what I wanted to say.

Cromie: You can feel it. You can tell when it happens.

Cheever: Yes.

Cromie: Is there any way you can bring it about?

Cheever: Not that I know of.

Cromie: Does it always happen?

Cheever: Oh, yes, it always has.

Cromie: If it didn't happen could you finish the book or the story without it, do you suppose?

Cheever: Well, there are a great many stories on file, a great many stories that are unfinished.

Cromie: Because this never did happen.

Cheever: Because it never happened, yes. There is a short story of mine called "The Country Husband," which closes with something like seventeen images, including a dog with a hat in his mouth, I believe, and a railroad train, and a star, and a cat wearing a dress, and a man and his wife, and so forth. They are all sort of thrown together, and it's quite marvelous. It is one of the most exciting things that can happen to anybody, I think.

Cromie: Well, now, this is a short story.

Cheever: This is a short story, yes.

Cromie: But is this one where this did happen, your moment of all coming together?

Cheever: Yes.

Cromie: All seventeen of the images!

Cheever: Yes. I must admit it's very exciting. I run out of the room saying "Look! Look!"

Cromie: You say you are writing this big novel now. Do you keep notes on your characters, on their appearance, on what they do, where they are from—do you know the backgrounds of your people, the stuff you don't put in the novel? Somebody told me, or somebody I read someplace, some author said he even knew the telephone numbers of his characters.

Cheever: Yes, I think that is customary. The man, as he walks into the room, blows his nose and walks out—you know absolutely everything about him: how much he weighs, what he had for breakfast, what sort of car he drives, his sexual relationships. If you do know all of this, then it is much easier to describe him as he is walking across a room.

Cromie: But even just somebody who has a walk-on part, a cameo part—you would know this much about him.

Cheever: I think it is profitable to do it that way, yes.

Cromie: What about your main characters? You know much more about them, I assume.

Cheever: Yes, of course, one knows what they dream.

Cromie: Their ancestors—

Cheever: Their ancestors, their digestive tract. Everything that, well, one knows about someone, who knows anything.

Cromie: It is funny you should mention just the tract, because one of the stories in *The World of Apples* is written by a man's stomach.

Cheever: Yes.

Cromie: That's a curious story, and an interesting one, and an item that had never occurred to me somehow.

Cheever: It says if you buy a *cri de coeur* you'll have a *cri de ventre*. As a matter of fact the story seems to be a little more successful than a novel written by Moravia about a man's penis. But, well, I told you it's not very successful.

Cromie: What kind of reaction do you get from your readers? Do you get a lot of mail? I would assume you would.

Cheever: It varies. It varies with magazines. When I used to contribute regularly to the *New Yorker,* the mail used to come bound in twine, which is always my idea of a good bunch of mail, with string around it. In the last novel—what did I get?—maybe a hundred and fifty letters or something like that. I was talking with Yevtushenko, and he said, "How many letters do you get, how many letters do you get?" And I said, "maybe ten a week, twelve a week, something like that," and of course he said "I get two thousand a day."

Cromie: But they are all in Russian!

Cheever: Yes.

Cromie: You are interested in the supernatural, at least you have—

Cheever: I'm interested in reverie. I'm interested in dreams. I'm interested in that which one could call unreal.

Cromie: I would like, for example, to believe in ghosts. I don't think I do, but I would like to. Have you ever seen a ghost, for example?

Cheever: No. My father said there probably are ghosts but they keep bad company.

Cromie: I like that.

Cheever: Yes, it was quite good.

Cromie: Right. There are so many people who have claimed to have seen them and I'm sure are not lying; they obviously did see them. And I'm always pleased when I find somebody who has.

Cheever: No, I've not seen a ghost.

Cromie: Nor have I, but it would be fun.

Cheever: But my father says you are the wrong company.

Cromie: Do you have a working regimen at all? Some authors do and some don't.

Cheever: I do, yes.

Cromie: How does it go?

Cheever: Keep a notebook. And I've kept it up for years and years.

Cromie: But do you get up a certain time, for example, and begin typing at a certain time?

Cheever: Yes, it's roughly nine. These days I work until noon, roughly. When I was younger I used to work straight through.

Cromie: You mean until afternoon, late afternoon?

Cheever: Yeah, I can't do that anymore, alas. Or if I do I find I can't sleep. I get too excited.

Cromie: Oh, yeah.

Cheever: I used to write very long stories: thirty-six, forty-five pages in three days. That's quite a lot of work.

Cromie: That's a lot of work; I should say so.

Cheever: And not change a word. And be terribly happy for two days. And then I absolutely crashed.

Cromie: Because you didn't like them?

Cheever: Unfortunately, no.

Cromie: Oh. That's a good point. What about the ones you've gone back to now that have been in print, say, twenty years?

Cheever: I don't, and I think very few writers do anymore.

Cromie: Because there are so many other things to do.

Cheever: Yes. . . . Also [it's] an obscene narcissism—to read something that you wrote, something that you were happy about, something you hate; all that was written twelve, fourteen years ago.

Cromie: What about the characters with whom you became greatly involved? Don't you ever want to go back and see what they are doing?

Cheever: Not really, no.

Cromie: Do they live on after the book or the novel, I mean the story or the novel is done?

Cheever: No.

Cromie: Somebody told me they do. The character keeps going and does things until he finally winds down.

Cheever: Well, of course there is a theory that the author is a pawn in the hands of his characters, that if they decide to take a train, he can do absolutely nothing about it. This I don't believe because it puts the writer in such an ignoble light.

Cromie: You don't let your characters take over. You are firm about it.

Cheever: Well, we compromise.

Cromie: Oh! Is there another train they could take?

Cheever: One wouldn't want to sit in front of a typewriter with all his people running around quite independently, because of course it's creative, you're building something and you must know what you are doing.

Cromie: Now what about this moment you speak of when it all comes together, then don't the characters sort of take over and do the things automatically? Or still are you in command?

Cheever: Oh, I think one is in command. I think a writer should be in command.

Cromie: But it becomes easier at that point.

Cheever: Yes. Because it's easier, it's more exciting.

Cromie: Do you have a book you want to write that you haven't written yet, or are you writing it now? Are you always writing it?— whatever work you're working on?

Cheever: I'm pleased with the book I'm working on now. I'm not terribly pleased with everything I've done. I hope it turns out nicely, beautifully, full of light and radiance. No, I don't have any books that I regret not having written.

Cromie: Have you written for movies now? I know you did television.

Cheever: Well, I've not actually written, I will not write a screenplay.

Cromie: Why is that?

Cheever: Because I don't think I could find . . . [independence] . . . [control]. . . .

Cromie: That's a good reason!

Cheever: It's as simple as that. Also, most offers I have to write screenplays are adaptations of stories of mine, and my feeling is that a story is done and it doesn't need any further projection. And I've done so many things, like treatments and so forth. I've been approached for it a half a dozen times I guess.

Cromie: Which of your stories have you liked once they got into the movies? Oh I liked "The Swimmer"! I loved that one. Did you like "The Swimmer"?

Cheever: No, I didn't, really.

Cromie: Didn't you, really?

Cheever: Well, there was a great deal of very involved negotiating and directors taken off and put on, and so forth. It wasn't the picture it started out to be.

Cromie: I thought Lancaster did well.

Cheever: He did very well, I thought. He worked very hard, completely dedicated to it.

Cromie: I saw that about a week ago on television.

Cheever: I think he did a marvelous job.

Cromie: Have you had anything on the screen that you did like, that you were completely satisfied with?

Cheever: No, no.

Cromie: I think most authors aren't. I know Harper Lee liked "To Kill a Mockingbird" when it got on, but most obviously aren't very happy.

Cheever: I recall that, and I think they did a good job on it.

The Inner Realm of John Cheever
Bruce McCabe/1974

Reprinted from the *Boston Morning Globe*, 23 October 1974, by permission of the publisher.

John Cheever, 62, one of the country's premier short story writers and novelists ("The Wapshot Chronicle," "Bullet Park," "The World of Apples") and winner of the 1958 National Book Award, is currently teaching creative writing two days a week at Boston University.

Several days ago on a very rainy afternoon he sat in the living room of the tasteful walkup he is renting outside Kenmore Square and talked to an interviewer. Beside him on a table were a package of filter-tip cigarettes and a glass of whiskey, both of which he resorted to rather frequently as he talked about several things, among them writing, teaching and an idea of where he is at the age of 62. Here are some excerpts:

Q. I notice you're reading Joseph Heller's "Something Happened." What do you think of it?

A. I've not read enough to react to it. All I know is that everybody associated with it, including Heller, his agent and his publisher, have gotten enormously wealthy from it.

Q. What are you writing now?

A. I'm writing a novel now, my 10th book and, I presume, my last.

Q. Why your last?

A. Because I feel rather old. It seems to me 10 is enough . . . I think 10 is a round number and I will be 63 when it's finished and that's quite enough. I'm very fond of round numbers . . .

Q. Does this mean you will stop writing?

A. Writers never stop writing. I believe it's the only occupation in which the practitioner never stops . . . I don't want to be publishing drivel as some do when they get older. I'd sooner stop . . . Writers grow old as all people do. Unlike baseball players, they can't sell

58

insurance. Unlike prostitutes, they can't be hostesses . . . The deple-
tion on ballplayers, prostitutes and writers is very high . . .

Q. What is the novel about?

A. It's about . . . confinement. I taught creative writing at Sing Sing
two or three years ago . . . It seems to me that the most conspicuous
metaphor for good and evil, including the church, is prison. Most of
the people who are confined in prison are 'bad' and most of the
people outside are 'good,' very obviously . . . I worked very closely
with prisoners for two years. None of my students has returned yet—
is a recidivist, which, incidentally, is a word I don't like . . . After
they've been in for 10 years, you know, they don't want to go out.
But, if they do, writing and reading makes an immense difference.
They help them in adjusting to everything. They've been living in a
rigid world and they have to adjust to a world where everything's
confusing . . . for all of us . . .

Q. How do you work?

A. I work in a very disorderly fashion, going back and forth and
keeping notes . . . If you'd like to see it (the novel he's working on),
this is the condition it's in. (He holds up a pile of yellow paper.)

Q. Might we photograph you with it?

A. No, my publisher would be furious.

Q. Do you do much writing in your head?

A. Where else would I do it? (Laughter) . . . The development of
an idea is a rather lengthy and chancy process. When it comes out
there is a marvelous creative ecstacy. This is true not only of writers
but many others, shoe salesmen, eyeglass salesmen . . . everyone. It
simply takes a long time. The word is 'parturition,' I believe . . .

Q. How do you like teaching?

A. I don't teach as a rule, I don't like to. I've done it but I don't like
to do it. My principal responsibility is as a writer. The students here
are responsive, which is why I do it. There's a considerable over-load
but there are almost no clinkers in the group. I couldn't think of a
better group of students beyond the fact that they are too numerous
. . . I don't teach because it's my profession, I teach for the hell of it. I
like to know what a generation younger than mine is thinking,
reading, doing and so forth and this is a good way to find out. . . .

Q. Is the novel dead—or dying?

A. The novel is, like life, resurrective. It's always coming back to life and it's coming back to life now . . . I believe fiction is the most acute and intimate means of communication, without exception. My translating varies—I can translate from somewhere between 12 and 16 languages—and this means the pleasure I feel in waking and in hearing the rain fall can be understood by people in 16 other countries. It's a marvelous means of communication . . . A man writes sentences to express his deepest feelings about life, its usefulness. It's how he exploits his gifts. There may be 2 or 3 million people who are interested and who share his doubts and enthusiasms . . . It's wonderful when you consider painting and music, the variety of styles. Literature is basic. The same language that is used to describe a . . . painting can be used to buy a pork chop. . . .

Q. What was it like being on the cover of Time magazine (in March of 1964)?

A. I tried to stop the story. It was at that time in my life that I thought publicity was abominable. I've since changed my mind. I said, 'I don't want the story' and they said, 'We didn't ask.' They ask you to pose for a portrait but if you don't there are files and files of photos they can use. You do what you want and they do what they want . . . Jerry Salinger (author J. D. Salinger) refused them and had a trauma and I wanted to avoid that . . . I went skiing in Stowe and I was followed down the slopes by a Time editor, researcher and a photographer, I guess . . . the FBI is nothing compared to being on the cover of Time. Some boys I played marbles with when I was little called me from Wilmington, Del. and said: 'What have you done wrong? Two people from Time magazine are coming up to see us in 20 minutes.'

Q. What have you read lately that's interesting?

A. (He turns to Christopher Gresov, 21, one of his students who had dropped by.) Chris, have I spoken enthusiastically of anything?

Chris: Not that I can think of.

An Interview with John Cheever

Dana Gioia, Millicent Dillon, and Michael Stillman/1976

A portion of this interview appeared in *Sequoia,* the Stanford literary magazine, in Summer-Autumn 1976, pp. 29–35. The much longer account here is from a tape recording, and reprinted by permission of the principal interviewers and *Sequoia.*

John Cheever was born in Quincy, Massachusetts in 1912, the son of a Yankee shoe manufacturer and an English emigrant. His formal education ended when he was expelled from Thayer Academy in South Braintree (a situation that was probably made easier when he quickly published a story about it in *The New Republic*). Already a published writer at eighteen, Cheever declined to go to college and immediately embarked on a highly successful career as a writer. He soon began his long association with the *New Yorker.* Sharing the pages of this magazine with John O'Hara, Dorothy Parker, Edmund Wilson, John Updike, James Thurber, and many others, Cheever achieved his enduring reputation as one of America's most distinguished writers of fiction, and quite possibly, our nation's greatest living writer of short stories.

Since his first book appeared in 1943 Cheever has published three novels and six volumes of short stories. His first novel, *The Wapshot Chronicle,* won the National Book Award in 1958, and many of his short stories, especially "The Enormous Radio" and "The Swimmer," have become among the most widely anthologized stories ever written by an American.

Mr. Cheever is a small, graceful man in his early sixties, but seems much younger. He has the gentlemanly knack of putting everyone around him immediately at ease. Speaking with the accent of patrician New England, Cheever leads a conversation with such wit and sensitivity that it is difficult for his listeners not to be carried away by its surface charm and miss the striking intelligence behind it. He is as articulate and perceptive in person as he is in print.

Participating in this interview were Dana Gioia; Michael
Stillman, a poet and director of the recording program for
authors' readings at Stanford; and Millicent Dillon, a short
story writer and instructor at Foothill College. The interview took place at the home of Professor Virgil K.
Whitaker on January 23, 1976.

Cheever (testing): My voice always comes out an octave lower than
it seems to me, with a marked English accent. Somebody played
back one of these telephone recordings: I'd said, "I'm coming
swimming in about twenty minutes!" And I came in at the house, and
she played it over, and I said, "Who's the old fruit with the English
accent?" And she said, "I didn't say that!" That's all she said. I went
swimming.

Gioia: Mr. Cheever, you're working on a novel right now? Three
parts of it have appeared in *Playboy* so far?

Cheever: No, only one. Only one part appeared in *Playboy,* and
that was because I needed money to complete the novel.

Gioia: What's it called?

Cheever: It has no title yet. [*Falconer* was published in 1977.] It
has no title yet, and I'm not sure how it ends. And I think most
novelists are very suspicious, superstitious rather, about talking about,
or describing in any detail, work-in-progress. It's rather like people
going to the race track: they won't tell anyone on the way to the track
what their bets are going to be.

Gioia: I was curious about something you said last night about
publishing in *Playboy.* Do you consider that there's a really consistently good market for quality fiction in America?

Cheever: No, alas, I don't, and it's an enormous dilemma for
people of your generation. The number of magazines has, in the
space of perhaps twenty years, gone from something like fourteen to
perhaps one and a half or two. It makes publication very difficult for
your generation to find and recognition of any sort difficult to
achieve. One can only hope the situation will improve.

Dillon: I want to ask you a question, not about the work-in-
progress, but about something you've done before, so you won't
have the feeling of superstition. In the story that you read last night—

is the title "The Swimmer"?—I wondered if you could say something about the origin of that story.

Cheever: Oh, yes, I can. I'm very fond of the story. I suppose the origin is simply the pleasure I took sitting at the edge of a swimming pool on a summer's day on which everyone had drunk too much. Also, the story is more or less factual in that occasionally someone will come to the country to interview me, and say, "Well, how did you think of the story?" And I say, "All right, well, get your trunks on and I'll show you"—and I'll take him through seven pools (which usually exhausts them). And they get on the train, or drive home again. But the impulse to write the story was sitting on the edge of a pool on a summer's day after a night on which I had drunk too much.

It was to have been a short story. I think there are thirteen pools in the story now. I think in the original version there were something like forty-five. The notes for the story (which I burned) ran something like a hundred and fifty pages. I think the finished manuscript was something like fifteen. Any questions about the story seem to me to imply that the story has failed—it should be taken at its face value. The fact that the constellations change, that the foliage changes, that all time is completely dislocated or altered in the story, ought to be taken at face value. However, as a parody of what can be done academically with the story, you can begin with the level that this is simply a reference to Ovid. And this is Narcissus, of course, and it is his face that he is pursuing, and this is the pursuit of death. It can—from the communist point of view (and it's a very popular story in Russia)—be an example of the artificiality of a personality based entirely on consumer consumption. You can cut down through about seven layers of the story, if you feel like it. I think it's an idle occupation—and if it can't be taken at its surface value, that is, if it doesn't have a response in the reader, then of course it's failed.

Dillon: The question I asked you was not so much about the meaning. I was just curious about how you arrived at the tone, which seemed so precisely perfect all the way along—whether that had taken a long time or whether it had arrived fairly quickly.

Cheever: The story took rather a long time. Most of the stories I like, however long they may be, forty or fifty pages, are usually written in three days. This took, I believe, two months. I was enormously happy with it. I don't think I've ever worked so long on a short story. I knew what I wanted, and . . . it is a sleight of hand.

Stillman: How did you feel about the film?

Cheever: Well, it was produced by Sam Spiegel, and there's one incident that I think illustrates the whole situation. Frank Perry photographed it very very blue, and Burt was painted gold, daily, and we ran Miles Davis tapes against it, and it was very very good, very funky late night music. We were going to use Coltrane but he died, so we used Davis, and this was going to be the score for the film. And Sam Spiegel said, you know, "Shit, you can't use that! I'm going to commission a score!" And he did, he commissioned a score from a man with a made-up Russian name . . . for a sixty-piece orchestra consisting mostly of strings. And that is a very good example of what went wrong with the film. That's only one of a hundred details. In order to finance a film, (it was supposed to be a full-length feature), you have to have a merchandisable screenplay. Had someone who was not a merchandising producer, someone with the freedom of Bergman, for example, done it, of course, it would have been very different. It could have been a completely subjective experience, with very few lines, if any.

Stillman: Did you think Burt Lancaster captured your character well?

Cheever: He certainly tried hard. Did everything he could. Extra-ordinarily industrious about it. And Janet Landgard I thought was very good in that it was the only film she's ever shot. I thought Lancaster *could* have done a great job. The last of it was not directed by Frank Perry, it was directed by someone whose name I don't know. Lancaster ended up in a fetal position in a very inexpensive rainstorm—Teamster's Union hose-type rainstorm. It was unfortunate. I didn't see Frank's ending, but I'm sure it was much better. Towards the end of it they cut in a few scenes that Frank had shot, and they had much more quality than what Spiegel had chosen.

Stillman: I was interested in how you feel about the use of fiction in making films. It seems to me that they're two very different kinds of art.

Cheever: I think they're vastly different. There's a clash between the two techniques. It seems to me that almost any competent novelist could write a fairly brilliant screenplay, given a good director, but one is not writing a screenplay, of course, one is writing a novel. Saul Bellow's novels don't film, John Updike's novels don't film (to mention two colleagues I greatly esteem)—and I think my work doesn't film. Simply because, if I come on a theme that could be handled more competently by a camera, I avoid it.

Gioia: Do you think, then, that by and large people in the first rank of American fiction right now have not been greatly influenced by the cinematic medium or, let's say, the medium of television?

Cheever: I think they've been influenced by it to the point that they're sophisticated; they know that very complex introspective sort of perception that one hopes to capture in a novel and the equally complex and introspective cadence that one has with a camera. Scenes are played out that obviously are for the camera eye rather than for the intellectual response of the novelist. I don't know whether this is worth taping or not: I was in the hospital—as an example of something for a camera and something for prose—and I had a very bad heart attack, and had finally been unplugged, and the doctors and nurses said, "Christ, that was a close call!" (something like that), and they had taken everything out of me, and I was lying in bed in the hospital room that was extraordinarily bleak, as they are, except for the window curtains, which had been printed with poppies and fox-glove and had obviously been chosen to cheer a man who was either dying or had just escaped death—this is a camera-detail, rather than a prose detail. I don't think a respectable novelist would bother to describe the curtains, or he would see them but would cast the detail off. There was a knock on the door, and I opened it, and there was a young priest holding the paraphernalia for Holy Eucharist, and he said "I've come to give you Holy Eucharist." And it was a question of manners (this is slightly novelistic); I didn't think that I could say, "No, thank you" or "No, thanks." I didn't know what to say, so I backed into the room. He went in, and I said, "Shall I kneel?" And he said, "Yes, please." And I knelt on the cold linoleum in my pyjamas, and he gave me Holy Communion. And at the end of the Blessing, I said, "Thank you, father" and he left. And I don't know where he came from or who he was. I've never seen him again. I never bothered to question him. But this would be much better with the camera than in prose, be much stronger. If you simply begin with the knock, the open door, go through the Mass, say nothing but the Mass—and the priest goes out. You could do it, of course, in fiction, but it's simply an example of what one recognizes as being better with film.

Dillon: So then, are you implying that television, or the film, operates in a way to set up situations that the novelist will avoid, that it's narrowed the field.

Cheever: Oh, it's rather broadened it. "Sophistication" is the word I would use. It has made the novelist aware of the fact that he has, more or less, this brother in the race who can handle certain scenes better than he. I still think that the retina used in reading prose is much more tenacious, much more lasting, than that which is taken off a screen, that a good prose paragraph, page, chapter, or book, lasts much longer than a splendid film.

Stillman: We were talking about the role of the camera in film. How do you feel about the role of the speaking voice in fiction?

Cheever: Well, it seems to me that virtually a perfect ear is as rudimentary to a novelist as his kidney, for example. That you have to be able to catch accents, to overhear what is being said four tables away. This is simply literary kindergarten as far as I'm concerned. Then what you'd have to do, of course, is to exert a good deal of taste in what you use.

Stillman: How about the voice of the narrator?

Cheever: The omniscient narrator cutting in and out, of course, is something that was used widely in the eighteenth century, and we still employ it. The novelist is perfectly free to bring in any voice he wants. Actually enjoys more freedom, I suppose, than a filmmaker.

Stillman: Do your narrators change voice from story to story? Or would you say they're spoken pretty much in John Cheever's voice with John Cheever's tone?

Cheever: Well, I would hope they're not spoken in John Cheever's voice and in John Cheever's tone. Of course, they are. That's a battle I've lost.

Dillon: In the class yesterday, when you spoke to the students, you said fiction is not crypto-autobiography.

Cheever: What I usually say is, fiction is not crypto-autobiography: its *splendor* is that it is not autobiographical. Nor is it biographical. It is a very rich complex of autobiography and biography, of informa-tion—factual information, spiritual information, apprehension. It is the bringing together of disparate elements into something that corresponds to an aesthetic, a moral, a sense of fitness. And in the class yesterday, of course, I spoke about the splendors of the imagination: how they have suffered in the post-Freudian generation is an endless source of anxiety. And I feel very strongly about that.

Gioia: Just to talk about the situation you were in yesterday, do you feel that there's a lot to be offered teaching creative writing? Is it a situation that you feel comfortable in? And do you think that the students profit by it?

Cheever: Yes, I do. Nobody likes the phrase "creative writing," of course. I try to call the classes, if I'm allowed, "Advanced Composition." It is, in my case, no more than a conversation between an old writer and a young writer. And the old writer has a great deal to learn and, in many cases, so has the young writer. It seems to me mutually a very good arrangement.

Gioia: Do you structure your classes very much?

Cheever: I don't know what you mean by structure.

Gioia: Do you give assignments?

Cheever: I give what is known as drill. My favorite drills are: give me three pages on your imagined introspection of a jogger, write me a love letter in a burning building, give me eight disparate incidents that are superficially alien and profoundly allied. I can't remember the other drills (I have about twenty). Flaubert used to drill de Maupassant, used to send him down to the Rouen railroad station where there were about twenty cab drivers and tell him to describe each face in a sentence. Then Flaubert would go down and check and see how de Maupassant made out.

Gioia: Do you think that much of the best fiction being written today is in short stories?

Cheever: No, it seems to me to be spread over short stories, novels, poetry, and plays. The forms are not competitive. It isn't the Short Story and the Novel in the Superbowl. They assist one another, they throw light on one another. They should.

Stillman: When Richard Scowcroft introduced you last night, he went into that very entertaining paragraph about possible titles for your talk. And, occasionally, the concept of innovative fiction came up, as something that you might have talked about. I wonder what you would have said about innovative fiction—who you would have had in mind, and what kinds of innovation you would have valued the most.

Cheever: Well, that's a very large question. Fiction, of course, *is* innovative. My definition of fiction would be that it is heretical—fiction is one of our most valuable heresies. It is constantly questioning, and profoundly questioning, any paradigm. The fact that the novel is declared dead three times a year is its very nature, because it's a form of resurrection. It's a very powerful and chancy way of life. And we call novels (only in the English-speaking world) something meaning a "newness" (this is the new way of looking at things)—in France and Italy, of course, they're still called *romances* (something we've never stooped to, or never been stuck with)—so that it's always a newness. The excitement of writing is that you are saying, in language that has never been used before, or in arrangements of language that have never been used before, something you don't know to have been recorded before. So it is always basically innovative. It is an exploratory and a heretical pursuit. We then have experimentation, which is something of a spinoff from innovation: experimentation in what license one can take in using words in a nonverbal or an inchoate sense. This seems to me generally unsuccessful. But fiction is innovative in its constant change of cadence. It lives on discovery.

Gioia: What is your response to the school of American writers, let's say, that you associate with John Barth, Donald Barthelme, influenced by Borges, that are innovative in the sense that they use fiction as a forum to discuss almost abstract artistic questions.

Cheever: Oh, let's see if I can remember a quotation. I wrote a short story for a retiring editor of *The New Yorker,* did I mention that? There were a number of barbs in it. There was a paragraph, I'll try to remember. "They were the sort of people that went around the world once or twice a year reading Borges and Barthelme in Statlers and Hiltons while the monsoon rains lashed the nearby temples they had come to see, but if you questioned their taste in reading, if"—there are too many ifs here—"if the world around you looks like Delacroix's *Death of Sardanopolis,* the charms of an empty canvas will seem irresistible." Right? Does that answer your question? That may be a little recondite. Do you understand what I mean?

Dillon: Well, I heard you yesterday when that young student spoke about Barthelme and Barth and the resistance he was feeling to that kind of work. Among the younger people that you're dealing with, do you notice some kind of resistance to that kind of inchoate fiction?

Cheever: Yes, I think I do. Of course, I must speak within the confinements of my age. The only thing I think lamentable in these enthusiasms is the element of vogue, how people will seize on a book, not because it's particularly sympathetic, but because it is fashionable—and in the last, what, eight years, one has seen Hermann Hesse, for example, who was read by everyone not particularly because he was comprehended, but because it was rather like wearing skirts or trousers of a certain style. He was followed by Vonnegut, whom I think a very good man, but who again was a vogue writer, then Barth, Barthelme, Coover, and Gass—a marvelous law firm!—all of whom I think are extremely interesting. And John Gardner belongs in there. And, as a matter of fact, Doctorow. Very interesting, and very important people. I much prefer Coover.

Gioia: Your own writing is concerned very much with what you'd think of as almost a traditional fiction writer's viewpoint—an interest in social textures of class, of a person's position vis-a-vis society. Do you think that that's less of an interest among young short story writers?

Cheever: It seems to me that what one is dealing with is, and I still insist on this, that fiction is our most intimate and acute means of communication, at a profound level, about our deepest apprehensions and intuitions on the meaning of life and death. And that is what binds us together, young and old. Doesn't much matter whether you write backwards or sometimes matter in which language you write. Maybe the bond of agreeing that this is an intimate and acute means of communication is the one that keeps us from flying to pieces.

Gioia: I was noticing the way you made fun of a mythic reading of a story like "The Swimmer," which would be a very natural reading, I think, for a lot of contemporary writers to give their works. Is that simply your comment on the texture of your work?

Cheever: Well, actually, when I commented on "The Swimmer," I was simply hinting lightly at the fact that it's much easier to teach fiction, not at the level of its success, but at the level of veterinary medicine, symbolism, or (as I said yesterday) anti-vivisection. It's much easier for the teacher and easier for the student who has no particular interest in literature to dissect a story than to be moved by it.

Dillon: I noticed that you were very generous in the way that you

spoke about other writers (Bellow and others), and you said something about it—that you didn't consider it a matter of competition,
really. And I wanted to ask you if, during your own experience as a
writer, whether it has been in any way helpful to you to have a
community of writers who have been supportive to you in any way,
or individual writers who've been helpful to you.

Cheever: Oh, yes. Yes, immensely. When I was seventeen or
eighteen, I guess, I had the good fortune to meet Dos Passos,
Edmund Wilson, Jim Agee was a contemporary I knew very well,
Sherwood Anderson. It was Estlin Cummings who, through at least a
similarity in background, made it quite clear to me that one could be
a writer and also remain highly intelligent, totally independent, and
be married to one of the most beautiful women in the world.
Cummings was a complete revelation and an enormous help, and I
loved him dearly. I saw Marion after his death—and his dying words
(which I think are not commonly known, which Marion hastened to
bring to me) were—he was cutting kindling on a very hot day in
September, and Marion called over, "Cummings, isn't it frightfully
hot to be cutting kindling," and he said, "Yes, Marion, I'm going to
sharpen the ax before I put it up." And with that Cummings died.
Perfect style. Now, in the case of Saul, for example—athletic analogies are pretty vulgar (they aren't as vulgar as musical analogies)—
but with Saul on the scene it's very heartening: when a man so gifted
you know is pitching, it's a pleasure to play third base or whatever,
catch. What can be very discouraging, of course, is to jog out onto
the field looking for a great game and find that you're playing with a
bunch of defrocked Jesuits and clumsy and ungifted people. I'm very
indebted to Saul.

Gioia: You mentioned before that *Humboldt's Gift,* you thought,
had been received with very bewildering reviews. Are you at all
happy with the state of reviewing in American magazines and
newspapers?

Cheever: Well, I haven't known anything different, so I wouldn't
have anything to compare—you know, anything that would strike me
as being a happier time. In Europe, there are many more critics,
actually, than we have in the United States. In Russia, literature still is
of much more importance to the lives of the people than it is in the
United States. German, French, and Italian reviews are inclined to be
criticism—and, by criticism, I mean perhaps the illumination, or a

report on the pleasure that the reader has taken in the work. In America, much more than in Europe, we have literary journalism and then literary criticism. And the journalist's responsibility is to report the price of the book, the number of pages, the nature of the book, the gist of the book, the heft of the book. As a newspaper reporter in many cases he's not competent to judge the book; and in many cases he will in spite of his incompetence go ahead. But my feeling is that books have a vitality that is invincible and, quite independently of either stupid or intelligent reviews, they will go to the millions (I think no less than millions) of people in the world who enjoy this means of communication—who enjoy books, who enjoy fiction, who enjoy serious and innovative fiction.

Gioia: Do you see yourself writing to any particular audience of Americans?

Cheever: No, I don't think that anyone can see an audience anymore. I think that came rather to a marked conclusion—or at least an obvious illustration is Virginia Woolf, who in her best books was addressing a very well-defined population. And, since that time, it seems to me, no writer has really known to whom he was speaking. To the people who're literate, obviously, but it would be very hard to describe them.

Gioia: Does that affect your writing?

Cheever: I think not. If it has any effect at all, I suppose it would be an enlargement. The fact that one doesn't know to whom one is speaking, but that they are *there,* is perhaps a more satisfactory experience than knowing precisely, as Mrs. Woolf did, where they lived, what they ate, and when they went to bed.

Stillman: I was very interested by your comments on innovation. I was wondering if there are particular kinds of innovation in the works of your contemporaries that you admire and learn from.

Cheever: Saul's work is endlessly innovative—no novel is like the other, no story is like the other, no sentence is like the other in Saul's work. Saul will chop sentence, sentence, sentence for paragraph, then cut it off with two pieces of slang from the twenties. Seems to me that John Updike is also innovative. I don't know why I should pick these two men. Just to go back over the situation, Flannery O'Connor was highly innovative. Faulkner was innovative. Hemingway was enormously innovative.

Stillman: What kinds of innovation impress you the most?

Cheever: It's emotional and intellectual adventurousness. These are unknown countries into which one steps. Always, in fiction, it seems to me.

Stillman: How do you feel about innovations in language? The way the story is being told as opposed to the way a character is being defined or the way a plot is being worked out.

Cheever: I don't know what you mean by innovations in language. You mean using made-up words?

Stillman: I mean, speaking in particularly poetic or unpoetic ways, or mixing levels of vocabulary, or tying sentences together in unusual ways, or dipping in and out of standard English and moving into, say, the language of dreams or the language of symbols.

Cheever: In word experiments, I'm old enough to recall the death of the word being announced at, yes, immediately at the end of the First World War by Gide, subsequently by Huxley, by the editors of *Transition*—the word was no longer competent to deal with our passions, our exaltations, and our dismay, we must find something else. So then we had Gertrude Stein, whose contribution was enormous. Then we had automatic writing, and forty years later we again have automatic writing, which is: you write "Bang Bang Yellow Bosh Pow Yellow Yellow Fall." You can take, as far as I can see, perhaps two or three pages of this, and then you realize that you are dealing with a dead language. In short, language has lost its urgency, has lost its ability to enable you to give or to request something from another person. And the instant this is gone, you have a dead language. Dead languages have limited charms, but limited they are. Does that answer your question? Can you think of anyone, for example, who has been a successful experimenter? Stein, I think, is probably the leading light.

Stillman: Well, I see that perhaps some of the things that are revered by readers of fiction these days you might see as the source of error. I'm thinking, for the moment, of Joyce and all his experimentation with words, particularly in *Finnegan's Wake*.

Cheever: *Finnegan's Wake* I find extremely difficult. That seems to be a universal situation. The greatness of *Ulysses*, of course, is indisputable. And *Ulysses*, with the exception of some of the Night Town, is quite traditional. But my feeling is that the introspective cadence that I have is something I share with almost everyone. One

can alter the introspective cadence in prose, as Joyce does in
Ulysses—and as James did very successfully in all of his fiction. When
one reads James, one has to sacrifice the cadence of one's own
introspection. And if you're successful at doing this, one is enchanted
with James. And when you put down James and come back to your
own introspective cadence, it is with this great sense of refreshment.
Joyce does this. He does it in *Dubliners,* he does it in *The Portrait of
the Artist as a Young Man,* and he does it extravagantly and
triumphantly in *Ulysses.* But one is giving up one's particular habitual
cadence for another man's cadence. And this does not seem to me as
innovative as it is thought by some people to have been, since one
has it in James—in Sterne—and it has appeared in literature before.
But *Ulysses* is quite a traditional book.

Gioia: What do you think of an experiment like Nabokov's *Pale
Fire?*

Cheever: I think *Pale Fire* is marvelous! "Experimental" I don't
think is quite the word. It's a triumph in inventiveness to write a novel
in terms of a footnote to a poem. It's like getting out of a human
dilemma. You find yourself in an emotional, or geographical, or even
a military situation in which your chances of survival are very limited,
and you get out by something as resourceful and inventive as writing
a footnote to a poem.

Gioia: I have another question. You've always been remarkably
commercially successful in your own writing.

Cheever: Not really, no.

Gioia: In the sense that, at least, you've been self-supporting.

Cheever: Yes.

Gioia: Do you think it's a bad idea for a writer to live in a
university?

Cheever: I don't know enough about university life, really, to
answer that question with any information at all. I found in my own
teaching that I become so excited and so absorbed in the work I am
getting from the students that it draws off an excess of energy, in the
two teaching stints (Iowa and Boston) I've not been able to do as
much work as I'd like, in many cases no work at all. Because all my
excitement is placed in the class. I have no idea what any other
teacher feels. Teaching, after all, is a profession, and an exalted
profession, and one can't assume that it is simply a way of making

money to continue some other occupation. It one tries to, the students will disabuse you of that idea very quickly.

Stillman: It would be interesting to hear you talk about *The New Yorker* magazine—as a place where fiction is often published and as a magazine that has become something of an institution in itself.

Cheever: I'd be very happy to talk about *The New Yorker. The New Yorker* first published a story of mine when I was twenty-one. Which was exciting, although I had published earlier in magazines like the *Hound and Horn* and I think also in the *Yale Review* (which was very early). Ross was editor, he was a genuine eccentric, an extraordinarily brilliant man. He liked to run rather funny brief stories—they were always called "casuals"—but he was attracted (one of his marvelous eccentricities) to rather serious stories, sometimes with quite rueful, if not morbid, endings. He used to object to them. He used to say, "Goddammit,"—he was a scratcher, he scratched an awful lot, he *itched*—and he'd say, "Goddammit, Cheever, why do you write these fucking gloomy goddamm stories?" And then he'd say, "But I have to buy them. I don't know why." And he would—he not only bought them, but he paid as much or more than any other magazine was paying for anything, including *The Saturday Evening Post* for stories of life in windjammers—and published over a period of twenty years an extraordinary list of writers. *The New Yorker* first published Nabokov, published all the early short stories of Nabokov, published, of course, Jerry Salinger, Irwin Shaw, Jean Stafford, Mary McCarthy at her best, Phil Roth, some of Saul (not much). My memory fails me on this, but there are something like twenty really first-rate people who used *The New Yorker,* or who were published in *The New Yorker* (one didn't write for *The New Yorker*). And it seems to me that the only thing they had in common, really, was excellence. They didn't deal with sharecroppers or the plight of the migrant orange picker, there's that. So they might be accused of having a class bias. But Irwin Shaw would write about an appendectomy in a submarine in the Bay of Tokyo, and Nabokov in the next issue would have a long and very elegant reminiscence of going to Berlin from Moscow on some deluxe train. And this very happy relationship was enormously enriched by the fact that in those years—I mean, you wrote a story, you gave it to the *New Yorker,* and they would take almost anything as long as there wasn't any explicit sexual intercourse—you'd give it to them perhaps on a Thursday or a Friday, it would be in final copy on Tuesday, out on Wednesday or Thursday, and went directly into the hands of those people you wanted the story to reach. And then perhaps three days later, the mail would start coming in. These were not letters that begin, "I've never written a fan letter before in my life," or, you know, "I'm sorry to take up your time"—these were letters from estimable men and women who had enjoyed what these writers had produced. It was a marvelous relationship. And also, it was instantaneous. And Ross paid handsomely, and we all *were.*

Gioia: How do you think *The New Yorker* has weathered into the seventies?

Cheever: Since I have not had anything in *The New Yorker* (with the exception of this one story that I wrote for an editor), I have not been in the offices actually for, I suppose, ten years. I couldn't say.

Gioia: Do you still read the magazine?

Cheever: Yes, I do. It was a very . . . by far the richest association I've ever had with a publication. And I'm concerned with its destiny, although I've never had any editorial voice at all.

Dillon: Can you say something about whether or not you do a lot of reading still in some of the older works, whether you find that's still fruitful and helpful for you?

Cheever: I don't read as much in the Eighteenth Century as I would like. It seems to me that I took Fielding intravenously, all of Fielding, including the attacks on Walpole and so forth. My children were told that there was no dirtier word in the language than Walpole. I love Fielding. I love [Sterne's] *Tristram Shandy.* I'm not inclined to believe that modern life is incomprehensibly difficult until I pick up a page of Fielding, and it has a luminousness and a purity that is lost to us.

Stillman: Some people would say that fiction has a social impact, that it not only mirrors its society but also tends to change it and transform it. I wonder if you share that view and, if you do, in what ways you would like to see fiction exert its power over our present society.

Cheever: Oh, well, it seems to me that the impact is questionably *social.* The political burden that literature can carry is inestimably delicate. We have very little good political fiction, as I mentioned yesterday. I can't, for example, think of a good political novel—that is, a novel that has corrective social power. The spiritual impact is, of course, what one seeks for in fiction. It is for the depth of the emotion—to make memory more coherent, more creatively accessible. Does that answer your question? Can you give me an example of what you think would be a novel with social impact?

Stillman: Well, I was interested more in your view of the current state, and process, of our society. We've been through a really extraordinary decade (the decade of the sixties). Now we're well into the seventies and on our way beyond the turmoil and conflict and trouble of those times, and I think that artists are inevitably concerned with what's going on in the social world around them. I was wondering how you feel about our having come through the sixties.

Cheever:I know the sixties primarily through the eyes of my children. It seems to me to have been a tragically chaotic decade. My son, for example, was in Cincinnati Workhouse, objecting to the war in Viet Nam quite peaceably. I had to bail him out. It was $900 for Disturbing the Peace, which is an extraordinary amount of bail to ask. And when he came home, he looked at me and said, "You know, you don't know anything until you've been roughed up by the Man! You know, augh!" My daughter was twice in the South in considerable difficulty. And it's only through their eyes, and something like sixth hand, that I have any idea of what the sixties involved. The music, of course, I heard, and the superficial aspects were apparent, but I do not know of any fiction dealing with the sixties specifically as a decade that I consider successful. Do you have anything you could suggest?

Stillman: I know that among the most popular writers, Kurt Vonnegut . . .

Cheever: Vonnegut, perhaps, is a good example. Of course, the sixties was not his decade either. Vonnegut is a man in his late fifties now, I should say. No, I think you are right. Some of the dislocations of the sixties are wonderfully reflected in Vonnegut's work—bringing together science fiction and realistic fiction, writing (as he does) affecting a very limited intelligence and possessing a very capacious mind. I think these are all good contributions to understanding that decade.

Dillon: Perhaps another way of asking that question: when you write, are there certain political or social movements that impinge on you sufficiently to actually sense it as you're writing. I take, as an example, the women's movement. Do you think that, in any way, that kind of contemporary movement puts certain pressures on your writing?

Cheever: No, I think not at all. I'm old enough to remember the force of the Communist Party in the United States as a literary lever. I was, I suppose, very young, maybe twenty, and named in the *New Masses* as the last voice of the decadent bourgeoisie. Didn't bother me at all. Because I was not concerned with social reconstruction: I was concerned with literature as an intimate and acute means of communication. And the Communist Party was very powerful, or attempted to be very powerful, in literature, and we had a great many novelists that presumably were going to change our way of thinking about capitalism. The leading one was something called *Marching, Marching* by a woman named Clara Weatherwax. It won all the Communist Party prizes, and so forth. It did not change anything at all, excepting perhaps it made Clara Weatherwax more unhappy. It's very difficult to trace—except Machiavelli's *The Prince*—any piece of literature that has had marked social impact. Marked spiritual impact is something altogether different.

Stillman: How do you feel about Solzhenitsyn?

Cheever: As you perhaps know, I'm a Russian buff, and when I was first in Russia. I think ten years ago, Khrushchev was still first secretary (I was in Russia when Khrushchev was deposed). Khrushchev, of course, locked Solzhenitsyn up for [*One Day in the Life of Ivan Denisovich*], which I think a beautiful book. I didn't meet him—he was then in the provinces, and thought to have cancer. *The First Circle* I also thought a splendid book. The CIA then obviously picked on Solzhenitsyn as a man who could be exploited to expose the stupidity, or the cantankerousness, of the Russian government—and without taking into consideration his characteristics as an orthodox Christian. It was unfortunate, I think, that they should have taken a literary character and transformed him into a political one. And that was done. The thing came to a head in the Nobel Prize. They behaved with incredible stupidity, and so I think did we. With the exception of [*One Day in the Life of Ivan Denisovich*] and *The First Circle,* Solzhenitsyn is virtually unreadable. That he should have been sold as a political identity to the book-buying public in the United States seems to me inexcusable. I've talked with the Russians about it—and, if you know Russians at all, there is a point where you realize that what you thought was a Westernized personality is a complete mystery. But one of the most moving things that was said to me was by a good friend in Moscow, when I was saying, "You are treating Solzhenitsyn as though literature were a province," and she yelled at me, "You don't understand that in my country a great novel is much more important than a great treaty!"—which seemed to me the best expression of their attitude. However, Solzhenitsyn is among us, has the strength of character, of faith—and [is], in his own giftedness, evidently to live a very happy life independently both of Brezhnev and the CIA. So it's a happy ending. And what does one look forward to? A new and splendid book from Solzhenitsyn.

Stillman: I'm not sure I fully understand. I've been reading *The Gulag Archipelago.*

Cheever: Did you like it?

Stillman: Of course, it's not fiction. And so, we're in a totally different domain by talking about it.

Cheever: But it is history written by a novelist. I've not read it, I'm sorry to say.

Stillman: It is very heavy going.

Gioia: I thought it much more impressive than I did *The Cancer Ward.*

Cheever: *Cancer Ward,* I think, is very bad. *First Circle,* I think, is quite good. [*One Day in the Life of Ivan Denisovich*] I thought splendid.

Gioia: Would you like to repeat the anecdote you told me yesterday about your and Updike's letter?

Cheever: John Updike and I were in Russia together, both of us for the first time, and were enchanted with the people and the experience. We were there for six weeks (we were only together, I think, for ten days). And as we both told the State Department, to their absolute dismay—they kept saying, "Well, what kind of experience would you describe it?"—and I said, "It was an exalting experience!" ("Whaaaa?") And it was. It was for both of us. And we were aware of Solzhenitsyn then, of course, and as soon as he was turned into a political pawn, we refrained from signing any papers objecting to the treatment of Solzhenitsyn. John would call me, or write, and say, "Well, let's hold off, let's hold off, let's see what's going to happen." Finally, the stupidity and clumsiness and brutality, in fact, of the Russians was so great that we consulted and agreed to sign a letter, with Dick Wilbur, to the Commissioner of Culture. We did. And it was a very gentle letter saying how much we loved the people and the country of Russia, and so forth. And that was absolutely the end. We were wiped out. I'd received for ten years—I'd been back to Russia twice more—at least twenty-five cards in the neighborhood of the twenty-fifth of December from the Russians, and this year I did not receive a card for the first time in ten years—in a country that cannot send out Christmas cards! (Presumably they would be New Years' cards, since Christmas is illegal). It's scarcely a country that enjoys any sort of free speech. And, of course, it's a great source of sadness to both John and me. I think the situation is very very bad there for intellectuals of any sort at this point. I've not had any letters. I heard indirectly that a very good friend who is also a dissident [Tanya Litvinov]—having refused to leave when her father was ambassador here, having refused to leave Russia under all circumstances, including starvation during the Seige of Moscow—is finally leaving. And I guess the most conspicuous proof of their loss of freedom of speech is the fact that Yevtushenko, who has the biggest mouth I've ever seen in my long life on the planet, has been silenced.

Dillon: Are you familiar with that book *Hope Against Hope* by Mandelstam's wife?

Cheever: Oh, yes, of course. That's a beautiful book. She's still lives, oddly enough, in Moscow. I didn't meet her. I didn't ask to meet her. I never ask to meet anyone when I'm there. If they want to produce someone, all right.

Dillon: Well, how do they handle something like that? You're asked by the Russian government to come, and then they present you with whomever they feel like your meeting?

Cheever: You're asked by the Russian government. I was asked by the Russian government both times.

Gioia: You said that you're not very much impressed by Solzhenitsyn's fiction. . . .

Cheever: I *am* very much impressed by [*One Day in the Life of Ivan Denisovich*] and *The First Circle*.

Gioia: Are there any other Russian writers, contemporaries, that you're . . .

Cheever: Ah, Vosnezhensky I think is a very good poet. I enjoy Yevtushenko as a performer very much (Yevtushenko is a very close friend). There's a short story writer named Yuri Kazakov who has been translated into English (most of them haven't been translated). There is a young man named [Vassily] Aksyonov, who has been silenced. I simply don't ask to see people. They say, "Well, he had to leave town" or "He was just divorced," and I know perfectly well that they don't want me to see him, that's all. So I don't pursue the matter. Yevtushenko has always enjoyed perfect freedom, up until now, last year.

Gioia: And your books are no longer appearing in Russian?

Cheever: I don't know. Also, another thing about Solzhenitsyn: the Russians *read* Solzhenitsyn! They get him in samizdat. Everyone has read Solzhenitsyn. Everything! And Americans have Solzhenitsyn on coffee tables. Nobody reads it. It's a very ironical situation.

Stillman: I'm reading it. I'm heavily into it, as a matter of fact. And that's why I'm sort of curious to know where you object to him, because there seems to be some objection.

Cheever: To Solzhenitsyn? I think I only object—and I object quite deeply—to the fact that he has been used as a political figure, and that there should be no confusion between a political and a literary figure.

Stillman: Is it by the CIA? I mean, how did this happen?

Cheever: I don't like to use the CIA, because it's gotten to be such a tedious whipping boy. Somebody in our government decided that this was a man who could be exploited.

Stillman: And you think he was being exploited when he came here and gave his speech with George Meany?

Cheever: Yes, I do.

Stillman: And the thing on *Meet the Press*—all those were essentially exploitative situations?

Cheever: Partially exploitation. The Russians, of course, made every stupid move. You couldn't anticipate how stupid they were going to be. On the other hand, I dislike seeing a literary figure being used as a political force. And I think this is true in his case. Sakharov—a much clearer cut case and, as far as the press goes, a much more articulate man (he seems to be—it's always a mistake to say so—a truly western intelligence)—is not getting nearly the publicity that Solzhenitsyn got. I don't know why we steer clear of him. Marvelous man! He *truly* seems to be a noble intellect! I'm very anxious to see what's going on now. As I say, I don't get letters anymore. My son's going over this summer, and I shall write the Writer's Union and see if I can visit him. See what the situation is. As for books being out of print, I may have mentioned, they bring out an edition in one day of what is a hundred thousand copies of my last novel, and they're sold before the day is over. Books matter tremendously to the Russians. It isn't only because they don't have other distractions. It is that they have a very deep sense of communication. The word "writer [*pisatel'*] in Russian—"author" would be the word in English (it sounds a little arty)—is a word of great reverence. All you have to say [*pisatel' Amerikanskii*], and they'll knock the cushions into shape, sit you down, and pour vodka into your ears. It's like being a priest of some functioning religion.

Gioia: Do you feel that a writer in America has any social position?

Cheever: Well, does anyone in America have any special position, I think is the question. Even millionaires are declasse now. People work very hard to get very rich and find out it's the wrong thing. Went out of style about thirty years ago.

Stillman: But they still have the money to spend.

Cheever: We do not have actually successful honorary societies in the United States. And I think it's just as well. We don't have a solid system of honors.

Gioia: Do you hold any importance for something like the National Book Award (other than the thousand dollars)?

Cheever: When I got it, I said I very much enjoyed the esteem of strangers, thank you. And somebody said, "Cheever looked as though he needed that." (I'm in the position of a clown, but I don't seem to have the grace of a clown.)

Stillman: I guess we don't have a great deal more time—at least, if it's going to be measured by the tape we have on hand. I wonder if there are various subjects or concerns that you have that we have not been able to touch upon because we haven't asked the right questions.

Cheever: No, I think the matters that I would like to emphasize today, number one, that I was in a snowbound village forty miles north of New York day before yesterday, and being a carcass I'm still responding very slowly to the fact that this seems to be an unconscionably long summer's day, there's that. That I do feel (an ax I've already ground) that the post-Freudian generation greatly underestimated the creative force of the imagination. And that literature—and this is a chestnut I've used before but I think it works—that literature is our only continuous history of man's struggle to be illustrious and remains our most intimate and acute means of communication. I wish I knew more about the dilemma of the young and their publication problems—or I wish, at least, I could do something about it. I know very few writers in their twenties, and perhaps it's because so few of them are published. One of the pleasant things about being old is that you sometimes can call attention to a young man's work and plug for him or her.

Gioia: You said that there were one and one-half outstanding magazines that still published quality fiction. What would you consider the best outlets for fiction in the country, still? For a writer of any generation?

Cheever: I'm not sure that I'm well enough informed. I expect *The New Yorker* probably still reaches as open-minded and receptive an audience as any magazine ever has in the English-speaking world. The quarterlies come and go, since they depend entirely on the caprices of their patrons. *Antaeus* published a marvelous story by Italo Calvino in the last issue. One has to look and look and look to find the good work. *Esquire* is now only publishing one piece of fiction an issue (they used to publish four). It does seem to be narrowing down—unfortunately. I think Hefner has been extraordinarily helpful. He employs Robie MacCauley, who is basically interested in good fiction and in encouraging good fiction, and he publishes Saul Bellow, John Updike, Nabokov, and so forth. And who reads it, I don't know.

Dillon: In writing the novels, do you get any kind of response?

Cheever: Yes, but in writing novels, I do, if I can leave the United States, so they can't get to me until the book is pretty much exhausted. I do this because bad reviews are sometimes disconcerting—although at my time of life they aren't any more (they were when I was younger). And, also, people are inclined to confuse you with your work. This is something, I think, that's fairly recent, where novelists count as much on the fame of their person as they do on the fame of their work. Mailer is a conspicuous example of that sort—had he not run for Mayor of New York twice, had he not been in the courts for mayhem, had he not been a conspicuous figure in television (and so forth), it would be a very different image that one felt in reading Mailer. This is not in any way to criticize Mailer for this, but it is a confusion of the celebrity of the man and the celebrity of his work. Saul, of course, is ideally the opposite. His personal life is completely unknown. He exists as a novelist, and he is known through his work (except to his friends). And one would sooner have it that way. If you brought out a book, and if people are terribly excited about it, then they assume that they're also excited about you, and sometimes they're gratified and sometimes they're not—or if they don't like it, then they're angry at you. And so it's easier for me just to leave the country. It's always nice to be complimented. And sometimes, of course, to be detested does throw some very helpful light on one's own limitations—where one has limped when one should have run. But when you have finished a book, and if you've finished to your own satisfaction, you really don't give a damn whether anyone likes it or not. I mean, you do want someone to like it, because it was addressed to someone in the darkness, out there, but you're usually tired and you're gratified.

Gioia: Can I ask one more question (this is totally off the field)? You talked almost exclusively about American contemporaries. Do you feel that there are any writers who consistently admire, either in Britain or, let's say, British colonials that write in English, or even Canadians or Australians?

Cheever: Yes, I do not wish to be nationalistic, since literature, of course, is international (like science, all the exalted occupations of mankind). But I do think American literature is much more diverse, much richer than any other. This is because Italian is the only language I can read other than English, and I know of almost no one writing in Italy today of any particular interest to me. Montale, I think, is a marvelous poet, but Montale's about eighty. And Moravia has written very little recently.

Dillon: Have you read Natalia Ginzberg?

Cheever: No, I don't know her.

Gioia: Do you like Calvino's work?

Cheever: Oh, I liked the short story much better than I've liked anything else by Calvino. The only thing I know is *Baron in the Trees,* I think, which I liked. But I thought the story was a triumph over his method, over himself, over everything. It was beautiful. Calvino now lives in France and translates from Italian as if he had written in French. There's no trace of Italian in his translations, though. English: I can't offhand think of anyone. I think Graham Greene an estimated man, a highly estimable man, and a man who might possibly be neglected (which is why I mention his name). I read a novel by an Englishman a week or so ago, called [Malcolm] Bradbury which I thought quite good. I know very few of the young English novelists—well, there are very few. In France, we have Robbe-Grillet, Nathalie Sarraute (whom nobody could read), Sartre (who was a long time ago). I do think the American scene is much much more resplendent, much richer than anything else today. Not only because it's easier for me to read.

A Talk with John Cheever

Shirley Silverberg/1976

Reprinted from *Westchester*, May 1976, pp. 64–68, by permission of Shirley Silverberg.

"This is being written aboard the S.S. Augustus, three days at sea. My suitcase is full of peanut butter, and I am a fugitive from the suburbs of all large cities. What holes! The suburbs, I mean. God preserve me from the camaraderie of commuting trains, and even from the lovely ladies taking in their asters and their roses at dusk lest the frost kill them, and from ladies with their heads whirling with civic zeal . . .

"God preserve me," he continued, "from women who dress like toreros to go to the supermarket, and from cowhide dispatch cases, and from flannels and gabardines. Preserve me from word games and adulterers, from basset hounds and swimming pools and frozen canapés and Bloody Marys and smugness and syringa bushes and P.T.A. meetings." (From "The Trouble of Marcie Flint," by John Cheever.)

He was standing at the door as I drove up on a February afternoon, a furred Cossack hat on his head, a well-worn camel's-hair coat over corduroy pants tucked into leather boots. His three retrievers bounded down to the car to greet me. The wooden columned porch from which the dogs had come was comfortably cluttered with the paraphernalia of winter. Ice skates, skis, some firewood. And it all looked somewhat battered, comfortably and genteely battered. As did John Cheever himself, I thought.

"You had trouble finding the house?" He sounded apologetic.

We walked into the house, a beautiful, old, welcoming farmhouse it appeared to be.

There was no foyer so that the room we walked into was actually the dining room. On the right a large kitchen was visible, kitchen appurtenances hanging from racks built over the stove. Straight ahead was a split flight of stairs, an old chest of drawers on the landing, an interesting looking red fan in a frame over the chest. We walked up the whole flight of stairs into a large wood-paneled living room and settled ourselves around the fireplace. There was nothing new-looking in the room; the wooden floors were not highly polished, but they were beautiful. The sun shone brightly into the far corner of the room which was filled with plants.

The atmosphere was all warm, inviting, and suburban—high class, low-key, unpicture-window suburban, but definitely suburban.

What? Cheever a suburbanite?

How could the author of those words be so pleasingly entrenched in the same land he strips bare so unmercifully, not once, but over and over again in his stories?

Was I also going to find that John Cheever, notorious for the high percentage of acidity in his domestic tales, in reality thinks women are sweet tabbies, marriage a long, white thornless rose, and happiness as available as cornflakes?

He laughed. "I don't hate women, and I don't hate the suburbs. I've been known as the annalist of the small New England town; I've been called the chronicler of the expatriate in Italy, and now it's the suburban label. Critics just love to put labels on people, but fiction is never cryptoautobiography."

His voice is soft and the words come out fast, almost mumbled; one must almost strain to catch them.

"Fiction," he repeated emphatically, "is never cryptoautobiography. It is bringing together very disparate elements into a third force. The complexities transcend one's own life.

"I use the suburbs because in them you find as rich a variety of people as one can find anywhere in the country, people whom you can get to know intimately and with whom you can sustain a relationship. I use its rituals and appurtenances because they offer a splendid panorama against which to display the condition and behavior of the men, women, children, and dogs who interest me.

"There is something rather awesome, you know, in the spectacle of fifty to sixty housewives all lined up at the station, the beautiful Hudson in the background."

Although Cheever feels rituals are easier to see in a suburban society, the suburbs have never struck him as an artificial way of life.

"I resent the preconception of the suburbs as a place where people live in uniform houses, make love to each other, and then commit suicide. I have never encountered a more diverse and non-stereotyped group of people in a greater variety of circumstances anywhere on the earth. I find living in the environs of the city a comfortable and stimulating life."

The Cheevers came up to Ossining from the city in 1952. They lived for ten years in a gardener's cottage on the old Vanderlip estate, and they have been in their present home for fourteen years.

"I love the country," he says, and, indeed, Cheever chopping wood, Cheever romping through the countryside with dogs have become the clichéd phrases of the writers who write about this writer. But clichés are born out of truth, and the truth is that Cheever's deep and abiding love of nature runs through his own life and through the most despairing pages of his fiction like a lyrical thread of hope.

He admits to a special affection for the sights and smells of the western side of the county (although he has so little acquaintance with the sound side, he says, that he feels ill equipped to make comparisons).

"I like the smell and the look of the river. And there is a small bakery in the hollow near St. Augustine's Church on the Old Post Road in Ossining. I like the smell of the freshly baked bread."

He feels very much a part of the community and the county although his role has always been a quiet one: "The television people are distressed that I don't have an image. I don't make speeches, and I've never run for public office."

He has been a member of the volunteer fire department (a commitment he has considered sheer pleasure, not pathos as critics of *Bullet Park* interpreted that action of its hero). He attends Trinity Church on Sundays quite regularly; and on Fridays quite regularly he lunches at Dudley's (a neighborhood restaurant owned by the grand-son of Mr. Vanderlip) together with the other members of his "Friday Club"—Arthur Spear, publisher; Tom Glazer, folk singer; John Dirks, a cartoonist and sculptor; Barrett Clark, an actor; and Roger Willson, a professor of history.

Ossining is no longer quite the sleepy town it was when Cheever arrived, but it is still an old town and he is grateful for that.

"We're quite defenseless before change, but Ossining is one of the more fortunate old places. Urban renewal has torn down the unsightly buildings and by and large has left the beautiful old ones."

Cheever likes old houses. His own dates back to 1799, and offhandedly, but obviously caring about it, he will point out the provenance framed on his wall.

Can this rather exquisite feeling of durability and tradition ever be achieved in "the uniform houses of the newer suburbs"?

"Absolutely. It's quite interesting," he says, "to see what two dozen years have wrought. Housing developments which were ugly in the beginning have taken on, twenty-four years later, the characteristics of their owners—a triumph of human invention."

Invention—or improvisation, a word Cheever is partial to—and tradition are concepts not unfamiliar in his fictional world. For if his characters lead lives of quiet desperation, it is not so much because they are materialistic suburbanites but rather because they are spiritual nomads, traveling in an unmarked wilderness where the past has been lost and the future has not been found.

"I write about people who have lost their sense of tradition, and they must improvise. No man or woman can improvise a sound sense of environment, a whole moral society in the space of a lifetime. We need to be able to count on an inherited sense of good and evil. One needs to rely, however small, on an element of tradition."

Cheever's own roots are strong New England—he is a puritan, a strong New England moralist, critics often say of him. He was born in Quincy, Massachusetts, in 1912, one of two sons of Mary Liley Cheever, an Englishwoman, and Frederick Lincoln Cheever, a Massachusetts Yankee whose family records in Newburyport go back to the Revolution.

"I come from the seafaring branch of the family," Cheever says, "and my ancestors, I am told, sailed the seas for the China trade."

The red fan, framed over the chest on his stairwell, was brought back from such a voyage.

His great-grandfather, Benjamin Hale Cheever, was a celebrated ship's master whose "boots are in the Peabody Museum, for some strange reason, filled with tea from the Boston Tea Party." Cheever laughs.

But the heritage of the sea ended with his grandfather. Cheever's father owned a shoe factory, and by the age of 12 Cheever knew he himself was not going to be a seaman but a writer.

"It was an empirical decision. I liked doing it. My family praised me for doing it. It brought happiness to everyone. There seemed no reason not to pursue it." He feels, incidentally, that he is not unique, that most writers feel their "calling" quite early.

Cheever recollects his life as going along on a predictably even keel up until his postadolescence. "At that time, my father lost his money, I realized my mother and father detested each other—they separated around this time for a period of a year or so—and I was disenchanted with my education."

He was attending Thayer Academy at the time, an institution he felt was unduly dedicated not to giving an education but to getting its students into Harvard. His discontent plus conditions at home led him into being a "cantankerous pest" who smoked illegally, dis-regarded the syllabi, and generally asked for expulsion. He got it.

The bottom had fallen out of the tradition barrel for Cheever—a bewildering fate not uncommon to many of his heroes.

He never continued with a formal education. Instead, he wrote a short story about his experience at Thayer. "Expelled" was accepted for publication by the *New Republic* in 1930, and as the saying goes, his career was launched. In the past forty years he has written three novels, has compiled six collections of short stories, and has earned the distinction of having contributed more short stories to the *New Yorker* than any other writer—120 in all. In 1948, he received the Benjamin Franklin Short Story Award for "The Five-Forty-Eight," and in 1956 he was honored with the O. Henry Award for the "Country Husband." In the same year he won a National Institute of Arts and Letters Award. His Wapshot novels each took an award, *The Wapshot Chronicle* winning the National Book Award for fiction in 1958, and *The Wapshot Scandal* earning him the very prestigious Howells Medal for Fiction in 1965.

Although he has firm ideas about the role of fiction, he lays down few dicta about the craft itself. "Although I generally set aside the hours of 8:00 A.M. to 1:00 P.M. when I am writing, I don't set aside a special place in the house in which I write. It could be any one of a number of rooms. I can't say for sure how long a story will take to finish. It took me three days to write 'Goodbye, My Brother' (his most poignant and touching story) but on the other hand, it took me two months to write 'The Swimmer' (the story which was made into a movie starring Burt Lancaster). In general, though, a short story takes three or four days, a novel four years."

He's in the last stages of writing one now. What is it about? He shakes his head. "It's bad luck to talk about a book before it comes out." This much he would say—it's not set in the suburbs.

If critics and public are wont to render pronouncements about Cheever and the suburbs, they can be equally vociferous on the subject of Cheever and women: Cheever's women are domineering, they are omniverous, they are castrating.

It all pains him, particularly that word castrating. "All that business of unconscious penis envy—I don't buy it."

His grandmother, he said, left England because women's rights didn't exist there, and his mother was a woman's righter, too— "although I have to say I resented the fact that she always seemed to be out raising money for some progressive school that invariably failed rather than being at home when I needed her."

But a woman who did nothing except soothe and smooth her mate's path could only be a bore, he insists. His own wife, Mary, teaches English at a secondary school, and "a damn good teacher she is too.

"I don't hate women at all. On the contrary, I am quite devoted to them; I would be quite lost without them." He doesn't see his men and women as engaged in a conflict or struggle because those words imply a victory, and there is no victory for one or the other.

"Quite simply, it's that men and women continue to mystify one another. It's the richest relationship on our planet and, therefore, the most complex. To simplify it is tragic.

"I'm always amazed, for instance, at the ability of a man at one quarter of a mile away in bad light to pick out the woman he wants to live with."

Did he do this himself? Yes, the first time he saw his wife, he says, was in the elevator of a Fifth Avenue building on a rainy evening, and he knew.

Is the durability of such a relationship as equally and chemically mysterious? In a way.

If Cheever's stories leave one with the impression that marriage as a state is somewhat less than ecstatically blissful, here at least there is no dichotomy between reader and writer.

"Marriage is a splendid aspiration," he says. "One cherishes the vision of an ideal relationship, but just look at the marriage vows. . . ."

He gets up and moves over to the bookcase where the *Book of Common Prayer* is already out lying on the shelf as if much in use. He reads the vows we are all so familiar with. . . .

"They are the most inspired and the most preposterous of all propositions. In rural societies where men and women have to work together, there is a natural bond that ties them. Now and here we have more freedom, more latitude to question the relationship. There is no need economically to sustain it. It has to be rich in and of itself.

"The 'Imponderable of Love' is what binds a man and woman. Unfortunately, in my point of view, that love is neither strong enough nor even enough in most cases to last a lifetime."

His own marriage has made it for at least thirty years so far and has produced three children: Susan Cowley, the eldest and now divorced, a Pembroke graduate, is an associate editor at *Newsweek;* Ben, an Antioch graduate, is married, is a father and is in the editorial department of *Reader's Digest;* and Federico, who was born in Italy— "so how could we just call him Frederick"—is just eighteen and is awaiting word from Stanford University. (Although he himself never completed his formal education, Cheever would have been distressed had his children not. "They were not insanely dedicated to being a writer as I was; a university education was important in helping them shape their futures, I felt.")

Although it has had its threatening moments, he confidently sees his marriage as continuing another thirty(!). "Man's redeeming feature," he says, "is that he does feel some sense of his capacity to live happily with another.

"Many of my characters do, you know. I got so cross with critics always saying that all I could write about was unhappy people that I sat down and wrote 'Worm in the Apple.' "

This is a story about the well-to-do Crutchmans who lived in Shady Hill and

> . . . . were so very, very happy and so temperate in all their habits and so pleased with everything that came their way that one was bound to suspect a worm in their rosy apple and that the extraordinary rosiness of the fruit was only meant to conceal the gravity and the depth of the infection.

Among the neighbors, the speculations were rife about how soon and at what turn in their lives the worm would emerge. Mr. Crutchman's participation in the life of the community was very vigorous: what was the sorrow that drove him? Their daughter's feet were too big. Mrs. Crutchman was often heard to comment:

> "Rachel's feet are so immense, simply immense." Now perhaps we see the worm. Like most beautiful women she is jealous; she is jealous of her own daughter. She cannot brook competition. She will dress the girl in hideous clothing, have her hair curled in some unbecoming way and keep talking about the size of her feet until the poor girl will refuse to go to the dances . . . but when the girl enters the room she is pretty and prettily dressed and she smiles at her mother with perfect love. Her feet are quite large, to be sure, but so is her front. . . .

The worm does not emerge in the life of their daughter, nor of their son. Not even after their children are married do the Crutchmans suffer "the celebrated spiritual destitution of their age." They lost neither teeth nor hair nor money . . . instead, they "got richer and richer and lived happily, happily, happily, happily."

Unfortunately, their happiness is a worm in *our* apple. We can scarcely believe in it. We ask ourselves, "Has Cheever with his wonderful cynicism written this story tongue in tooth, picking out pieces of the worm, secretly enjoying a joke he's playing on us?" Because the truth is that even when one of his people does emerge triumphant, an overwhelming, compassionate sadness is usually what the reader feels. There's very little hootin', hollerin' happiness in Cheever's stories.

Maybe because he doesn't feel happiness is a hootin', hollerin' affair?

Cheever can define better what happiness is not than what it is. "Happiness is not taking it to the bank in a wheelbarrow," he says, "but I would be hard put to define what it is. Perhaps the ability to carry on the rhythm, order, and obligations of life in a relative sense of peace and serenity."

Does he consider himself happy? His answer is a very contained "Relatively so. I have no regrets professionally, and I've made no compromises professionally. Emotional compromises are something else again."

There are other whispers—the lines on his face go more than sixty years deep. Both in his fiction and in his conversation psychiatry is a subject that gets its lumps, suggesting an acquaintance of a more than passing and a less than productive nature. When talk turns to his brother, a reticence is perceptible. Sensitivity prevents further indelicate intrusion. What price prying? What matter if happiness cannot be spewed out in ecstatic pronouncements about one's past and one's present?

Here is a man who was thoughtful enough to remember to have tonic on hand the second time round for a casual visitor, and who is modest enough to refrain from name dropping. In three hours of conversation, he chose to relate only one incident which related the measure of esteem he is held in by his confreres. It concerned "Papa" Hemingway whose wife came to see Cheever after Hemingway's death because she had to tell him how deeply his story "Goodbye, My Brother" had affected her husband.

Here is a man whose writing has illuminated the world, not primarily with its cynicism but with its compassion and its innate sense of man's ultimate ability to triumph. He says of himself, "I used to be a lot meaner than I am now," a statement that is likely true. But one senses a vulnerability that must surely always have made up for the meanness.

For once, fiction may well merge with autobiography because that's the way it is with Cheever's people. Buffeted by forces they scarcely understand, they may do cruel and hateful things to each other, but they are not unforgivable or wicked people. We understand and sympathize with their frailties, and we can bear their vicissitudes because hope rarely is permitted to desert us totally. John Cheever knows, and through him you know and I know, that we can go out into the starry night and find "kings in golden suits" who "ride elephants over mountains."

John Cheever:
The Art of Fiction LXII

Annette Grant/1976

Reprinted from *Writers at Work: The Paris Review Interviews, Fifth Series*, pp. 113–35, by permission of Viking Penguin Inc. Copyright © 1981 by The Paris Review, Inc. The interview first appeared in *The Paris Review*'s Fall 1976 issue.

The first meeting with John Cheever took place in the spring of 1969, just after his novel *Bullet Park* was published. Normally, Cheever leaves the country when a new book is released, but this time he had not, and as a result many interviewers on the East Coast were making their way to Ossining, New York, where the master storyteller offered them the pleasures of a day in the country—but very little conversation about his book or the art of writing.

Cheever has a reputation for being a difficult interviewee. He does not pay attention to reviews, never rereads his books or stories once published, and is often vague about their details. He dislikes talking about his work (especially into "one of those machines") because he prefers not to look where he has been, but where's he's going. Where he has been is impressive.

His collections of short stories are *The Way Some People Live* (1943), *The Enormous Radio and Other Stories* (1953), *Stories and Others* (1956), *The Housebreaker of Shady Hill* (1958), *Some People, Places and Things That Will Not Appear in My Next Novel* (1961), *The Brigadier and the Golf Widow* (1964), and *The World of Apples* (1973). His novels are *The Wapshot Chronicle* (1957), *The Wapshot Scandal* (1964), and *Bullet Park* (1969). He has recently finished another, due out in the spring of 1977.

For the interview Cheever was wearing a faded blue shirt and khakis. Everything about him was casual and easy, as though we were already old friends. The

Cheevers live in a house built in 1799, so a tour of buildings and grounds was obligatory. Soon we were settled in a sunny second-floor study where we discussed his dislike of window curtains, a highway construction near Ossining that he was trying to stop, traveling in Italy, a story he was drafting about a man who lost his car keys at a nude theatre performance, Hollywood, gardeners, and cooks, cocktail parties, Greenwich Village in the thirties, television reception, and a number of other writers named John (especially John Updike, who is a friend).

While Cheever talked freely about himself, he changed the subject when the conversation turned to his work. Aren't you bored with all this talk? Would you like a drink? Perhaps lunch is ready, I'll just go downstairs and check. A walk in the woods, and maybe a swim afterwards? Or would you rather drive to town and see my office? Do you play backgammon? Do you watch television?

During the course of several visits we did in fact mostly eat, drink, walk, swim, play backgammon or watch television. Cheever did not invite us to cut any wood with his chain saw, an activity to which he is rumored to be addicted. On the day of the last taping, we spent an afternoon watching the New York Mets win the World Series from the Baltimore Orioles, at the end of which the fans at Shea Stadium tore up plots of turf for souvenirs. "Isn't that amazing," he said repeatedly, referring both to the Mets and their fans.

Afterwards we walked in the woods and as we circled back to the house, Cheever said, "Go ahead and pack your gear. I'll be along in a minute to drive you to the station." . . . upon which he stepped out of his clothes and jumped with a loud splash into a pond, doubtless cleansing himself with his skinny-dip from one more interview.

Interviewer: I was reading the confessions of a novelist on writing novels: "If you want to be true to reality, start lying about it." What do you think?

Cheever: Rubbish. For one thing the words "truth" and "reality" have no meaning at all unless they are fixed in a comprehensible frame of reference. There are no stubborn truths. As for lying, it seems to me that falsehood is a critical element in fiction. Part of the thrill of being told a story is the chance of being hoodwinked or taken. Nabokov is a master at this. The telling of lies is a sort of sleight-of-hand that displays our deepest feelings about life.

Interviewer: Can you give an example of a preposterous lie that tells a great deal about life?

Cheever: Indeed. The vows of Holy Matrimony.

Interviewer: What about verisimilitude and reality?

Cheever: Verisimilitude is, by my lights, a technique one exploits in order to assure the reader of the truthfulness of what he's being told. If he truly believes he is standing on a rug you can pull it out from under him. Of course verisimilitude is also a lie. What I've always wanted of verisimilitude is probability, which is very much the way I live. This table seems real, the fruit basket belonged to my grandmother, but a madwoman could come in the door any moment.

Interviewer: How do you feel about parting with books when you finish them?

Cheever: I usually have a sense of clinical fatigue after finishing a book. When my first novel, *The Wapshot Chronicle,* was finished I was very happy about it. We left for Europe and remained there so I didn't see the reviews and wouldn't know of Maxwell Geismar's disapproval for nearly ten years. *The Wapshot Scandal* was very different. I never much liked the book and when it was done I was in a bad way. I wanted to burn the book. I'd wake up in the night and I would hear Hemingway's voice—I've never actually heard Hemingway's voice, but it was conspicuously his—saying, "This is the small agony. The great agony comes later." I'd get up and sit on the edge of the bathtub and chain-smoke until three or four in the morning. I once swore to the dark powers outside the window that I would never, *never* again try to be better than Irving Wallace. It wasn't so bad after *Bullet Park* where I'd done precisely what I wanted: a cast of three characters, a simple and resonant prose style and a scene where a man saves his beloved son from death by fire. The manuscript was received enthusiastically everywhere, but then Benjamin Demott dumped on it in the *Times,* everybody picked up their marbles and ran home. I ruined my left leg in a skiing accident and ended up so broke that I took out working papers for my youngest son. It was simply a question of journalistic bad luck and an over-estimation of my powers. However, when you finish a book, what-ever its reception, there is some dislodgement of the imagination. I wouldn't say derangement. But finishing a novel, assuming it's something you want to do and that you take very seriously, is invariably something of a psychological shock.

Interviewer: How long does it take the psychological shock to wear off? Is there any treatment?

Cheever: I don't quite know what you mean by treatment. To diminish shock I throw high dice, get sauced, go to Egypt, scythe a field, screw. Dive into a cold pool.

Interviewer: Do characters take on identities of their own? Do they ever become so unmanageable that you have to drop them from the work?

Cheever: The legend that characters run away from their au-thors—taking up drugs, having sex operations and becoming Presi-dent—implies that the writer is a fool with no knowledge or mastery of his craft. This is absurd. Of course, any estimable exercise of the imagination draws upon such a complex richness of memory that it truly enjoys the expansiveness—the surprising turns, the response to light and darkness—of any living thing. But the idea of authors running around helplessly behind their cretinous inventions is con-temptible.

Interviewer: Must the novelist remain the critic as well?

Cheever: I don't have any critical vocabulary and very little critical acumen and this is, I think, one of the reasons I'm always evasive with interviewers. My critical grasp of literature is largely at a practical level. I use what I love, and this can be anything. Cavalcanti, Dante, Frost, anybody. My library is terribly disordered and disorganized; I tear out what I want. I don't think that a writer has any responsibility to view literature as a continuous process. I believe that very little of literature is immortal. I've known books in my lifetime to serve beautifully, and then to lose their usefulness, perhaps, briefly.

Interviewer: How do you "use" these books . . . and what is it that makes them lose their "usefulness?"

Cheever: My sense of "using" a book is the excitement of finding myself at the receiving end of our most intimate and acute means of communication. These infatuations are sometimes passing.

Interviewer: Assuming a lack of critical vocabulary, how, then, without a long formal education, do you explain your considerable learning?

Cheever: I am not erudite. I do not regret this lack of discipline but I do admire erudition in my colleagues. Of course, I am not uninformed. That can be accounted for by the fact that I was raised in the tag-end of cultural New England. Everybody in the family was painting and writing and singing and especially reading, which was a fairly common and accepted means of communication in New England at the turn of the decade. My mother claimed to have read *Middlemarch* thirteen times; I dare say she didn't. It would take a lifetime.

Interviewer: Isn't there someone in *The Wapshot Chronicle* who has done it?

Cheever: Yes, Honora . . . or I don't remember who it is . . . claims to have read it thirteen times. My mother used to leave *Middlemarch* out in the garden and it got rained on. Most of it is in the novel; it's true.

Interviewer: One almost has a feeling of eavesdropping on your family in that book.

Cheever: The *Chronicle* was not published (and this was a consideration) until after my mother's death. An aunt (who does not appear in the book) said, "I would never speak to him again if I didn't know him to be a split personality."

Interviewer: Do friends or family often think they appear in your books?

Cheever: Only (and I think everyone feels this way) in a dis-creditable sense. If you put anyone in with a hearing aid, then they assume that you have described them . . . although the character may be from another country and in an altogether different role. If you put people in as infirm or clumsy or in some way imperfect, then they readily associate. But if you put them in as beauties, they never associate. People are always ready to accuse rather than to celebrate themselves, especially people who read fiction. I don't know what the association is. I've had instances when a woman will cross a large social floor and say. "Why did you write that story about me?"

And I try to figure out what story I've written. Well, ten stories back apparently I mentioned someone with red eyes; she noticed that she had bloodshot eyes that day and so she assumed that I'd nailed her.

Interviewer: They feel indignant, that you have no right to their lives?

Cheever: It would be nicer if they thought of the creative aspect of writing. I don't like to see people who feel that they've been maligned when this was not anyone's intention. Of course, some young writers try to be libelous. And some old writers, too. Libel, is, of course, a vast source of energy. But these are not the pure energies of fiction, but simply the libelousness of a child. The sort of thing one gets in freshman themes. Libel is not one of my energies.

Interviewer: Do you think narcissism is a necessary quality of fiction?

Cheever: That's an interesting question. By narcissism we mean of course clinical self-love, an embittered girl, the wrath of Nemesis and the rest of eternity as a leggy plant. Who wants that? We do love ourselves from time to time; no more, I think than most men.

Interviewer: What about megalomania?

Cheever: I think writers are inclined to be intensely egocentric. Good writers are often excellent at a hundred other things but writing promises a greater latitude for the ego. My dear friend Yevtushenko has, I claim, an ego that can crack crystal at a distance of twenty feet; but I know a crooked investment banker who can do better.

Interviewer: Do you think that your inner screen of imagination, the way you project characters, is in any way influenced by film?

Cheever: Writers of my generation and those who were raised with films have become sophisticated about these vastly different mediums and know what is best for the camera and best for the writer. One learns to skip the crowd scene, the portentous door, the banal irony of zooming into the beauty's crow's feet. The difference in these crafts is, I think, clearly understood and as a result no good film comes from an adaptation of a good novel. I would love to write an original screen play if I found a sympathetic director. Years ago René Clair was going to film some of my stories but as soon as the front office heard about this they took away all the money.

Interviewer: What do you think of working in Hollywood?

Cheever: Southern California always smells very much like a summer night . . . which to me means the end of sailing, the end of games, but it isn't that at all. It simply doesn't correspond to my experience. I'm very much concerned with trees . . . with the nativity of trees, and when you find yourself in a place where all the trees are transplanted and have no history, I find it disconcerting.

I went to Hollywood to make money. It's very simple. The people are friendly and the food is good but I've never been happy there, perhaps because I only went there to pick up a check. I do have the deepest respect for a dozen or so directors whose affairs are centered there and who, in spite of the overwhelming problems of financing film, continue to turn out brilliant and original films. But my principal feeling about Hollywood is suicide. If I could get out of bed and into the shower I was all right. Since I never paid the bills, I'd reach for the phone and order the most elaborate breakfast I could think of and then I'd try to make it to the shower before I hanged myself. This is no reflection on Hollywood, but it's just that I seemed to have a suicide complex there. I don't like the freeways, for one thing. Also, the pools are too hot . . . 85°, and when I was last there, in late January, in the stores they were selling yarmulkes for dogs—My God! I went to a dinner and across the room a woman lost her balance and fell down. Her husband shouted over to her, "When I told you to bring your crutches, you wouldn't listen to me." That line couldn't be better!

Interviewer: What about another community—the academic? It provides so much of the critical work . . . with such an excessive necessity to categorize and label.

Cheever: The vast academic world exists like everything else, on what it can produce that will secure an income. So we have papers on fiction, but they come out of what is largely an industry. In no way does it help those who write fiction or those who love to read fiction. The whole business is a subsidiary undertaking, like extracting useful chemicals from smoke. Did I tell you about the review of *Bullet Park* in *Ramparts?* It said I missed greatness by having left St. Boltophs. Had I stayed, as Faulkner did in Oxford, I would have probably been as great as Faulkner. But I made the mistake of leaving this place, which, of course, never existed at all. It was so odd to be told to go back to a place that was a complete fiction.

Interviewer: I suppose they meant Quincy.

Cheever: Yes, which it wasn't. But I was very sad when I read it. I understood what they were trying to say. It's like being told to go back to a tree that one spent fourteen years living in.

Interviewer: Who are the people that you imagine or hope read your books?

Cheever: All sorts of pleasant and intelligent people read the books and write thoughtful letters about them. I don't know who they are but they are marvelous and seem to live quite independently of the prejudices of advertising, journalism, and the cranky academic world. Think of the books that have enjoyed independent lives. *Let Us Now Praise Famous Men. Under The Volcano. Henderson The Rain King.* A splendid book like *Humboldt's Gift* was received with confusion and dismay but hundreds of thousands of people went out and bought hard-cover copies. The room where I work has a window looking into a wood and I like to think that these earnest, loveable and mysterious readers are in there.

Interviewer: Do you think contemporary writing is becoming more specialized, more autobiographical?

Cheever: It may be. Autobiography and letters may be more interesting than fiction, but still, I'll stick with the novel. The novel is an acute means of communication from which all kinds of people get responses that you don't get from letters or journals.

Interviewer: Did you start writing as a child?

Cheever: I used to tell stories. I went to a permissive school called Thayerland. I loved to tell stories and if everybody did their arith-metic—it was a very small school, probably not more than eighteen or nineteen students—then the teacher would promise that I would tell a story. I told serials. This was very shrewd of me because I knew that if I didn't finish the story by the end of the period, which was an hour, then everyone would ask to hear the end during the next period.

Interviewer: How old were you?

Cheever: Well, I'm inclined to lie about my age, but I suppose it was when I was eight or nine.

Interviewer: You could think of a story to spin out for an hour at that age?

Cheever: Oh, yes. I could then. And I still do.

Interviewer: What comes first, the plot?

Cheever: I don't work with plots. I work with intuition, apprehen-sion, dreams, concepts. Characters and events come simultaneously to me. Plot implies narrative and a lot of crap. It is a calculated

attempt to hold the reader's interest at the sacrifice of moral conviction. Of course, one doesn't want to be boring . . . one needs an
element of suspense. But a good narrative is a rudimentary structure,
rather like a kidney.

Interviewer: Have you always been a writer, or have you had
other jobs?

Cheever: I drove a newspaper truck once. I liked it very much,
especially during the World Series when the Quincy paper would
carry the box scores and full accounts. No one had radios, or
television—which is not to say that the town was lit with candles, but
they used to wait for the news; it made me feel good to be the one
delivering the good news. Also I spent four years in the Army. I was
17 when I sold my first story "Expelled" to *The New Republic. The
New Yorker* started taking my stuff when I was 22. I was supported
by *The New Yorker* for years and years. It has been a very pleasant
association. I sent in twelve or fourteen stories a year. At the start I
lived in a squalid slum room on Hudson Street with a broken window
pane. I had a job at MGM with Paul Goodman doing synopses. Jim
Farrell, too. We had to boil down just about every book published
into either a three, five, or a twelve page précis for which you got
something like five dollars. You did your own typing. And, oh,
carbons.

Interviewer: What was it like writing stories for *The New Yorker* in
those days? Who was the fiction editor?

Cheever: Wolcott Gibbs was the fiction editor very briefly and
then Gus Lobrano. I knew him very well; he was a fishing companion. And of course Harold Ross, who was difficult but I loved him. He
asked preposterous queries on a manuscript—everyone's written
about that—something like thirty-six queries on a story. The author
always thought it outrageous, a violation of taste, but Ross really
didn't care. He liked to show his hand, to shake the writer up.
Occasionally he was brilliant. In "The Enormous Radio" he made
two changes; a diamond is found on the bathroom floor after a party.
The man says "Sell it, we can use a few dollars." Ross had changed
"dollars" to "bucks" which was absolutely perfect. Brilliant. Then I
had "the radio came softly" and Ross pencilled in another "softly."
"The radio came softly, softly." He was absolutely right. But then
there were twenty-nine other suggestions like, "This story has gone

on for 24 hours and no one has eaten anything. There's no mention of a meal." A typical example of this sort of thing was Shirley Jackson's "The Lottery" about the stoning ritual. He hated the story; he started turning vicious. He said there was no town in Vermont where there were rocks of that sort. He nagged and nagged and nagged. It was not surprising. Ross used to scare the hell out of me. I would go in for lunch. I never knew Ross was coming, until he'd bring in an egg cup. I'd sit with my back pressed against my chair. I was really afraid. He was a scratcher and a nosepicker, and the sort of man who could get his underwear up so there was a strip of it showing between his trousers and his shirt. He used to hop at me, sort of jump about in his chair. It was a creative, destructive relationship from which I learned a great deal, and I miss him.

Interviewer: You met a lot of writers during that time, didn't you?

Cheever: It was all terribly important to me since I had been brought up in a small town. I was in doubt that I could make something of myself as a writer until I met two people who were very important to me: One was Gaston Lachaise and the other was E. E. Cummings. Cummings I loved and I love his memory. He did a wonderful imitation of a wood-burning locomotive going from Tifflis to Minsk. He could hear a pin falling in soft dirt at the distance of three miles. Do you remember the story of Cummings' death? It was September, hot, and Cummings was cutting kindling in the back of his house in New Hampshire. He was sixty-six or seven or something like that. Marion, his wife, leaned out the window and asked, "Cummings, isn't it frightfully hot to be chopping wood? He said, "I'm going to stop now, but I'm going to sharpen the axe before I put it up, dear." Those were the last words he spoke. At his funeral Marianne Moore gave the eulogy. Marion Cummings had enormous eyes. You could make a place in a book with them. She smoked cigarettes as though they were heavy, and she wore a dark dress with a cigarette hole in it.

Interviewer: And Lachaise?

Cheever: I'm not sure what to say about him. I thought him an outstanding artist and I found him a contented man. He used to go to the Metropolitan—where he was not represented—and embrace the statues he loved.

Interviewer: Did Cummings have any advice for you as a writer?

Cheever: Cummings was never paternal. But the cant of his head, his wind-in-the-chimney voice, his courtesy to boobs and the vastness of his love for Marion were all advisory.

Interviewer: Have you ever written poetry?

Cheever: No. It seems to me that the discipline is very different . . . another language, another continent from that of fiction. In some cases short stories are more highly disciplined than a lot of poetry that we have. Yet the disciplines are as different as shooting a twelve-gauge shotgun and swimming.

Interviewer: Have magazines asked you to write journalism for them?

Cheever: I was asked to do an interview with Sophia Loren by the *Saturday Evening Post.* I did. I got to kiss her. I've had other offers but nothing as good.

Interviewer: Do you think there's a trend for novelists to write journalism, as Norman Mailer does?

Cheever: I don't like your question. Fiction must compete with first-rate reporting. If you cannot write a story that is equal to a factual account of battle in the streets or demonstrations, then you can't write a story. You might as well give up. In many cases, fiction hasn't competed successfully. These days the field of fiction is littered with tales about the sensibilities of a child coming of age on a chicken farm, or a whore who strips her profession of its glamour. The *Times* has never been so full of rubbish in its recent book ads. Still, the use of the word "death" or "invalidism" about fiction diminishes as it does with anything else.

Interviewer: Do you feel drawn to experiment with fiction, to move toward bizarre things?

Cheever: Fiction *is* experimentation; when it ceases to be that, it ceases to be fiction. One never puts down a sentence without the feeling that it has never been put down before in such a way, and that perhaps even the substance of the sentence has never been felt. Every sentence is an innovation.

Interviewer: Do you feel that you belong to any particular tradition in American letters?

Cheever: No. As a matter of fact I can't think of any American writers who could be classified as part of a tradition. You certainly can't put Updike, Mailer, Ellison or Styron in a tradition. The individuality of the writer has never been as intense as it is in the United States.

Interviewer: Well, would you think of yourself as a realistic writer?

Cheever: We have to agree on what we mean before we can talk about such definitions. Documentary novels, such as those of Dreiser, Zola, Dos Passos—even though I don't like them—can, I think, be classified as realistic. Jim Farrell was another documentary novelist; in a way, Scott Fitzgerald was, though to think of him that way diminishes what he could do best . . . which was to try to give a sense of what a very particular world was like.

Interviewer: Do you think Fitzgerald was conscious of documenting?

Cheever: I've written something on Fitzgerald, and I've read all the biographies and critical works, and wept freely at the end of each one—cried like a baby—it is such a sad story. All the estimates of him bring in his descriptions of the '29 Crash, the excessive prosperity, the clothes, the music, and by doing so, his work is described as being heavily dated . . . sort of period pieces. This all greatly diminishes Fitzgerald at his best. One always knows reading Fitzgerald what time it is, precisely where you are, the kind of country. No writer has ever been so true in placing the scene. But I feel that this isn't pseudohistory, but his sense of being alive. All great men are scrupulously true to their times.

Interviewer: Do you think your works will be similarly dated?

Cheever: Oh, I don't anticipate that my work will be read. That isn't the sort of thing that concerns me. I might be forgotten tomorrow; it wouldn't disconcert me in the least.

Interviewer: But a great number of your stories defy dating; they could take place anytime and almost any place.

Cheever: That, of course, has been my intention. The ones that you can pinpoint in an era are apt to be the worst. The bomb shelter story ("The Brigadier and the Golf Widow") is about a level of basic anxiety, and the bomb shelter, which places the story at a very particular time, is just a metaphor . . . that's what I intended anyhow.

Interviewer: It was a sad story.

Cheever: Everyone keeps saying that about my stories, "Oh, they're so sad." My agent, Candida Donadio, called me about a new story and said, "Oh, what a beautiful story, it's so sad." I said, "All

right, so I'm a sad man." The sad thing about "The Brigadier and the
Golf Widow" is the woman standing looking at the bomb shelter in
the end of the story and she is sent away by a maid. Did you know
that *The New Yorker* tried to take that out? They thought the story
was much more effective without my ending. When I went in to look
at page proofs, I thought there was a page missing. I asked where the
end of the story was. Some girl said, "Mr. Shawn thinks it's better this
way." I went into a very deep slow burn, took the train home, drank
a lot of gin and got one of the editors on the telephone. I was by then
loud, abusive and obscene. He was entertaining Elizabeth Bowen
and Eudora Welty. He kept asking if he couldn't take this call in
another place. Anyhow I returned to New York in the morning. They
had reset the whole magazine—poems, newsbreaks, cartoons—and
replaced the scene.

Interviewer: It's the classic story about what *The New Yorker* is
rumored to do—"remove the last paragraph and you've got a typical
New Yorker ending." What is your definition of a good editor?

Cheever: My definition of a good editor is a man I think charming,
who sends me large checks, praises my work, my physical beauty
and my sexual prowess, and who has a stranglehold on the publisher
and the bank.

Interviewer: What about the beginning of stories? Yours start off
very quickly. It's striking.

Cheever: Well, if you're trying as a story-teller to establish some
rapport with your reader you don't open by telling him that you have
a headache and indigestion and that you picked up a gravelly rash at
Jones Beach. One of the reasons is that advertising in magazines is
much more common today than it was twenty to thirty years ago. In
publishing in a magazine you are competing against girdle advertisements, travel advertisements, nakedness, cartoons, even poetry. The
competition almost makes it hopeless. There's a stock beginning that
I've always had in mind. Someone is coming back from a year in
Italy on a Fulbright Scholarship. His trunk is opened in Customs and
instead of his clothing and souvenirs, they find the mutilated body of
an Italian seaman, everything there but the head. Another opening
sentence I often think of is, "The first day I robbed Tiffany's it was
raining." Of course, you can open a short story that way, but that's
not how one should function with fiction. One is tempted because

there has been a genuine loss of serenity, not only in the reading public, but in all our lives. Patience, perhaps, or even the ability to concentrate. At one point when television first came in no one was publishing an article that couldn't be read during a commercial. But fiction is durable enough to survive all of this. I don't like the short story that starts out "I'm about to shoot myself," or "I'm about to shoot you." Or the Pirandello thing of "I'm going to shoot you or you are going to shoot me, or we are going to shoot someone, maybe each other." Or the erotic thing, either "He started to undo his pants, but the zipper stuck . . . he got the can of three-in-one oil . . ." and on and on we go.

Interviewer: Certainly your stories have a fast pace, they move along.

Cheever: The first principle of aesthetics is either interest or suspense. You can't expect to communicate with anyone if you're a bore.

Interviewer: William Golding wrote that there are two kinds of novelists. One lets meaning develop with the characters or situations, and the other has an idea and looks for a myth to embody it. He's an example of the second kind. He thinks of Dickens as belonging to the first. Do you think you fit into either category?

Cheever: I don't know what Golding is talking about. Cocteau said that writing is a force of memory that is not understood. I agree with this. Raymond Chandler described it as a direct line to the subconscious. The books that you really love give the sense, when you first open them, of having been there. It is a creation, almost like a chamber in the memory. Places that one has never been to, things that one has never seen or heard, but their fitness is so sound that you've been there somehow.

Interviewer: But certainly you use a lot of resonances from myths . . . for example, references to the Bible and Greek mythology.

Cheever: It's explained by the fact that I was brought up in Southern Massachusetts where it was thought that mythology was a subject that we should all grasp. It was very much a part of my education. The easiest way to parse the world is through mythology. There have been thousands of papers written along these lines— Leander is Poseidon and somebody is Ceres, and so forth. It seems to be a superficial parsing. But it makes a passable paper.

Interviewer: Still, you want the resonance.

Cheever: The resonance, of course.

Interviewer: How do you work? Do you put ideas down imme-diately, or do you walk around with them for a while, letting them incubate?

Cheever: I do both. What I love is when totally disparate facts come together. For example, I was sitting in a cafe reading a letter from home with the news that a neighboring housewife had taken the lead in a nude show. As I read I could hear an Englishwoman scolding her children. "If you don't do thus and so before Mummy counts to three," was her line. A leaf fell through the air, reminding me of winter and of the fact that my wife had left me and was in Rome. There was my story. I had an equivalently great time with the close of "Goodbye My Brother" and "The Country Husband." Hemingway and Nabokov liked these. I had everything in there: a cat wearing a hat, some naked women coming out of the sea, a dog with a shoe in his mouth and a king in golden mail riding an elephant over some mountains.

Interviewer: Or ping-pong in the rain?

Cheever: I don't remember what story that was.

Interviewer: Sometimes you played ping-pong in the rain.

Cheever: I probably did.

Interviewer: Do you save up such things?

Cheever: It isn't a question of saving up. It's a question of some sort of galvanic energy. It's also, of course, a question of making sense of one's experiences.

Interviewer: Do you think that fiction should give lessons?

Cheever: No. Fiction is meant to illuminate, to explode, to refresh. I don't think there's any consecutive moral philosophy in fiction beyond excellence. Acuteness of feeling and velocity have always seemed to me terribly important. People look for morals in fiction because there has always been a confusion between fiction and philosophy.

Interviewer: How do you know when a story is right? Does it hit you right the first time, or are you critical as you go along?

Cheever: I think there is a certain heft in fiction. For example, my latest story isn't right. I have to do the ending over again. It's a question I guess of trying to get it to correspond to a vision. There is shape, a proportion and one knows when something that happens is wrong.

Interviewer: By instinct?

Cheever: I suppose that anyone who has written for as long as I have, it's probably what you'd call instinct. When a line falls wrong, it simply isn't right.

Interviewer: You told me once you were interested in thinking up names for characters.

Cheever: That seems to me very important. I've written a story about men with a lot of names, all abstract, names with the fewest possible allusions: Pell, Weed, Hammer, and Nailles, of course, which was thought to be arch, but it wasn't meant to be at all. . . .

Interviewer: Hammer's house appears in "The Swimmer."

Cheever: That's true, it's quite a good story. It was a terribly difficult story to write.

Interviewer: Why?

Cheever: Because I couldn't ever show my hand. Night was falling, the year was dying. It wasn't a question of technical problems, but one of imponderables. When he finds it's dark and cold, it has to have happened. And, by God, it did happen. I felt dark and cold for some time after I finished that story. As a matter of fact, it's one of the last stories I wrote for a long time, because then I started on *Bullet Park*. Sometimes the easiest seeming stories to a reader are the hardest kind to write.

Interviewer: How long does it take you to write such a story?

Cheever: Three days, three weeks, three months. I seldom read my own work. It seems to be a particularly offensive form of narcissism. It's like playing back tapes of your own conversation. It's like looking over your shoulder to see where you've run. That's why I've often used the image of the swimmer, the runner, the jumper. The point is to finish and go on to the next thing. I also feel, not as strongly as I used to, that if I looked over my shoulder I would die. I think frequently of Satchel Paige and his warning that you might see something gaining on you.

Interviewer: Are there stories that you feel particularly good about when you are finished?

Cheever: Yes, there were about fifteen of them that were absolutely BANG! I loved them, I loved everybody—the buildings, the houses, wherever I was. It was a great sensation. Most of these were stories written in the space of three days and which run to about thirty-five pages. I love them, but I can't read them; in many cases, I wouldn't love them any longer if I did.

Interviewer: Recently you have talked bluntly about having a writer's block, which had never happened to you before. How do you feel about it now?

Cheever: Any memory of pain is deeply buried and there is nothing more painful for a writer than an inability to work.

Interviewer: Four years is a rather long haul on a novel, isn't it?

Cheever: It's about what it usually takes. There's a certain monotony in this way of life, which I can very easily change.

Interviewer: Why?

Cheever: Because it doesn't seem to me the proper function of writing. If possible, it is to enlarge people. To give them their risk, if possible to give them their divinity, not to cut them down.

Interviewer: Do you feel that you had diminished them too far in *Bullet Park?*

Cheever: No I didn't feel that. But I believe that it was understood in those terms. I believe that Hammer and Nailles were thought to be social casualties, which isn't what I intended at all. And I thought I made my intentions quite clear. But if you don't communicate, it's not anybody else's fault. Neither Hammer nor Nailles were meant to be either psychiatric or social metaphors; they were meant to be two men with their own risks. I think the book was misunderstood on those terms. But then I don't read reviews, so I don't really know what goes on.

Interviewer: How do you know when the literary work is finished to your satisfaction?

Cheever: I have never completed anything in my life to my absolute and lasting satisfaction.

Interviewer: Do you feel that you're putting a lot of yourself on the line when you are writing?

Cheever: Oh yes, oh yes! When I speak as a writer I speak with my own voice—quite as unique as my fingerprints—and I take the maximum risk at seeming profound or foolish.

Interviewer: Does one get the feeling while sitting at the typewriter that one is godlike, or creating the whole show at once?

Cheever: No, I've never felt godlike. No, the sense is of one's total usefulness. We all have a power of control, it's part of our lives: we have it in love, in work that we love doing. It's a sense of ecstasy, as simple as that. The sense is that "this is my usefulness, and I can do it all the way through." It always leaves you feeling great. In short, you've made sense of your life.

Interviewer: Do you feel that way during or after the event? Isn't work, well, work?

Cheever: I've had very little drudgery in my life. When I write a story that I really like, it's . . . why, wonderful. That is what I can do and I love it while I'm doing it. I can feel that it's good. I'll say to Mary and the children, "All right, I'm off, leave me alone. I'll be through in three days."

Talk with John Cheever

John Hersey/1977

Reprinted from the *New York Times Book Review,* 6 March 1977, pp. 1, 24, 26–28, by permission of the publisher. Copyright © 1977 by The New York Times Company.

One end of the living room in a house built in 1799, in Ossining, N.Y. A table has been pushed against the left-hand wall; under a large print of Hadrian's tomb spouting frenetic fireworks. Cheever, in a brown pullover, is seated beyond the table, with a window at his back. He is 64; looks like a man of 34 who has been to a hilarious but awfully late party the night before. Face flushed: recent skiing in Utah mountains. Nut brown hair. Sharp eyebeams. The brilliant glow behind him is mist-filtered sunlight. Two large glasses of dark amber liquid on the table—iced tea. Cheever is smoking.

Seated at the outer edge of the table, facing the wall, is a visitor, at whom Cheever is looking with some alarm. The bastard is fiddling with a cassette tape machine.

Center and right: the rest of a living room that doesn't seem to have jumped out of any known Cheever story. Lived-in. Two comfortable chairs. Chinaware brought from Canton by Cheever's seafaring grandfather. On far wall, a Paxton, a painting of a woman on a summer's verandah. Right, a wide reach of pine paneling (restored) over a fireplace; a Seth Thomas clock. Fire of applewood logs cut by twice-warmed Cheever. Wood smoke in the air. A golden retriever, Edgar, settles down for a nap.

John Hersey: Could we test your voice?

John Cheever: Three, five, seven.

Recorder *(playing back)*: Three, five, seven.

(Hearing this, Cheever performs one of his remarkable repertory of groans.)

113

JH: Sing Sing? If a crow flew from here. . . .

JC: About five miles. Approximately 15 minutes by car.

JH: I remember it from my boyhood, at the Ossining station, the walls and lookout towers looming near the tracks. You've been here 20 years. Has it seemed to you to loom as a presence all that time?

JC: Not particularly.

JH: Did we hear some time ago that you were working in the prison?

JC: I taught at Sing Sing for two years. Falconer is *not* Sing Sing. I used the imaginary prison of Falconer principally as a metaphor for confinement. It would be the third large metaphor I've used. The first is St. Botolph's, a New England village which has the confinement of traditional values and nostalgia; the second was the suburban towns, Bullet Park and Shady Hill, again areas of confinement; and the third is Falconer. *Not* Sing Sing. My students—some of whom are still in prison and some of whom I continue to see—are *not* characters in the novel.

JH: Of course not.

JC: I feel very strongly about this. Fiction is not crypto-autobiography. Fiction seems to me a much more important means of communication. St. Botolph's never existed. Nor did Bullet Park. Nor Falconer. The smells, sounds, noises and lights are all there, but from a variety of places.

JH: How did you happen . . .

JC: I taught in prison because at a party someone said there were two thousand inmates and six teachers. One doesn't marry in order to write about women nor have children to write about children nor teach in prison to write about prisoners.

JH: What do you mean by confinement?

JC: I think I mean the confinements of the improvised sense of right and wrong that, socially, we are in agreement on. My first-hand experience with confinement, on a surface level, has been of sorts we're all familiar with, such as being in in-transit areas—in airports—during blizzards, when you're in for 32 or 36 hours, in places where you can't speak the language and are not sure what plane you're supposed to be on. Being stuck in elevators, and particularly, again, in countries where you don't know how to yell "Help!" or "The elevator won't work!" Being stuck in sentimental or erotic contracts that are extraordinarily painful and difficult to extricate oneself from.

Cheever stubs out a butt and at once lights a new cigarette. An illusion: the coils and swirls of brilliantly backlit cigarette smoke seem not to move; they hover, as if painted on the air—seem to have been hung out on purpose to hide the restless animation of the face beyond. As the conversation goes on, this motionless blue-white curtain blurs quick facial shots of surprise, puzzlement, delight, annoyance, explosive amusement.

JH: Besides confinement, one finds in "Falconer" many vivid, small recurrences from other books of yours: An older man endangered by the sea. Yard work. Figures seen in the buff. Sailboat races. Family turmoil. Glimpses of the sky. Beaches. . . .

JC: This is obviously the mortal furniture of one's life—what one lives with and dreams of. The strong reprises, though, have been, I think, the confinements of an improvised society and the thrust of life in determining to vary them. Escape is not the word one means. There doesn't seem to be any word for eliminating confinement. It is the effort to express one's conviction of the boundlessness of possibility.

JH: Mind if I check to see if this damn thing is recording? It makes me so nervous.

JC: Not half as nervous as it makes me.

Recorder: . . . conviction of the boundlessness of possibility.

The dog, Edgar, leaps to his feet, alarmed that his beloved, voluble Cheever seems to be throttled in the box in the guest's hands. The golden-retriever temperament immediately translates concern, however, into licking and tailwagging.

JC: *(delighted):* His master's voice in the Victrola! *(Cheever's laughter comes in a rush, like the few chugs of an outboard motor not quite catching.)*

JH: *(resuming):* Where do the sounds in your written voice in *Falconer* come from? We know you read: there's that dentist in the *Chronicle*, Bulstrode, wonderful name you ripped off from *Middlemarch*.

JC: It seems to me that the people of my generation, and yours, when asked for influential books, cannot stop at a thousand. Well.

The sound of my grandmother's voice, perhaps, reading to me. She was an Englishwoman. In my day it was customary to have almost all of Dickens read to you as a child. My father was a north-shore Yankee. He did not have a marked accent. He had, I should think, a very good prose style—he wrote some of Leander's journal in the *Chronicle.* The voices of southern Massachusetts, and of course of the people one loves. Literary voices? Surely this is the most intimate of all the choices a writer makes. One hopes one has chosen those that are strongest and most radiant. I consider myself lucky, for example, to have read Donne when I was very young.

JH: What about Chekhov? You're well known as the American Chekhov.

JC: If I'm known, it's as the oldest living short story writer. *(He laughs.)* No, I love Chekhov very much. He *was* an innovator— stories that seemed to the unknowing to have no endings but had instead a whole new inner structure.

JH: Your voice has a blurted quality—shifts, ellipses, disjunctions.

JC: I have always felt there is some ungainliness in my person, some ungainliness in my spiritual person that I cannot master. Perhaps you mean that.

JH: No, It's fascinating. A matter of form-speed.

JC: I do find myself more concise than I would like to be. There are paragraphs which had been chapters. For instance, the Cuckold's jewelry business. It's simply in three sentences which could have gone on and on. There were other situations. I could not accept them. The line was there, and I had to throw everything out and keep it concise. When I was younger I could run all over the pasture and come back. Now I seem to be going much more directly to what I have to say. I was unable to be digressive in this case. I trust I'm more mature. *(He laughs again.)* My father's speech was most precise. I can recall that he'd never had a dry martini. I made him one, and he drank a good deal of it, and all he said was, "Strong enough to draw a boat." Which is a very good example of his powerful laconic speech.

JH: Your spiritual person. . . .

JC: I have been a churchgoer for most of my adult life—a liturgical churchgoer, I am very happy with Cranmer's *The Book of Common Prayer.* The current schisms of the church concern me not at all. It seems to be one of God's infinite mercies that the sexual disposition of the priest has never been my concern. The religious experience is very much my concern, as it seems to me it is the legitimate concern of any adult who has experienced love.

JH: Any desk rituals?

JC: As a matter of fact, I seldom have a desk. At the moment I am working in a third-floor room with a broken television set, a Miro print and a chair that is bound together with picture wire. That should be a source of petulance. But it really doesn't matter. When I finish a book in one room, then I don't particularly want to get back into that room. Since the house has seven rooms, I have a couple to go. I'm very fond of ceremony, but as far as writing goes—just this: I work in the morning, I work with the light. I come down to breakfast very early, in the dark, before the light. The cats want their breakfast at once. I truly never have been cruel to a cat, but when they start climbing up and down my legs, I say to them *(he speaks now in a sharp tone, leaning down to the edge of the table),* "I'm celebrated for my cruelty to cats!" The intelligent ones stop.

JH: Does confinement start with the body? Have you felt confined since your heart attack four years ago?

JC: I like to think of it as no more than a part in the stream of experience. Cardiomyopathy is, along with much medical science, still in an investigative stage. Little is known. For example, altitude. I was cross-country skiing at Alta in Utah, last week, and I didn't know how high I could go. I thought I wasn't supposed to go over six, but we started at six, so I got on the lift and went to nine, and it was perfectly all right, so I went up to twelve.

JH: Testing?

JC: I was testing! *(Here he laughs most mischievously.)* To live physically is extremely important to me. I was brought up to take some of the responsibilities in maintaining a house. Cutting firewood, for example. I bicycle, skate, ski, walk, swim. It's very, very important to me to be continuously in touch with my environment.

JH: You once said, "I chain smoke. I chain drink. I chain everything." I know you've stopped drinking.

JC: I stopped drinking two years ago. I was an alcoholic. It was something of a struggle to stop drinking. But it has been accomplished.

JH: Any connection with Farragut's getting clean in the book?

JC: There may be. But no. I've had clinical trouble with alcohol and also with drugs, but that really was not, I think, what I was concerned about. I wanted to use *that* as a metaphor, too, as the prison was to be, for confinement.

JH: Is love a confinement? Family?

JC: Mary and I have been married for 38 years, I think. That two people—both of us temperamental, quarrelsome and intensely ambitious—could have gotten along for such a vast period of time is for me a very good example of the boundlessness of human nature.

JH: Any children?

JC: *(Another small groan, hardly more than a sigh.)* I have not been very good as a sedate parent. I'm particularly aware of this for my two sons. I've offered, for example, to wear a hat and take commuting trains if they would be more comfortable about it, and they said that really wouldn't make the difference. They felt that there was a lack, and then I said to both of them, "Coming of age, when you find a lack in me, you'll be able to find plenty of other men who'll be able to play out the role of father for you." The most exciting thing in my life *(the cadence changes, the voice is suddenly brisk)* has been the birth of my children and watching them grow and take up their lives. I want them to walk away from me without rancor. One has gotten to be defensive about the enormous pleasures, and diversity, the richness of life in a family, because, God, beginning with Samuel Butler the family was thought to be the shield of hypocrisy, and it's taken us that long, nearly two centuries, to be candid about the enormous pleasure we take in one another and relationships.

JH: The book is dedicated to your son Federico?

JC: It is to my son Federico, yes. He's a freshman at Stanford. I went out last week, after Utah. I said, "Do you want this kind of book dedicated to you, Fred?" He had read it, and considering the nature of the book. . . . As I finished large sections of it, I would read them to Mary, Suzie [Cheever's daughter], Fred, by the open fire. They were all very pleased with it. It did seem rather a curious performance. What I wanted, of course, was a very dark book that possessed radiance. And they seemed to feel that's what it was.

JH: You spoke of fiction as an important means of communication.

JC: Writing is for me a means of communication. It is for me my ultimate—as far as I know—usefulness. It is talking with people whose company I think I would enjoy if I knew them. And it's speaking to them about my most intimate and acute feelings and apprehensions about my life, about our lives. *(Cheever leaves the room to refill the iced-tea glasses. Comes back talking.)* The point of this communication is that it is a *useful* performance. The force of reality in fiction and the force of reality in a dream are very much the same. You find yourself on a sailing boat that you do not know— don't know the rig—going along a coast that is totally strange to you, but you're wearing an old suit, and the person besides you is your wife. This is in the nature of a dream. The experience of fiction is similar: one builds as if at random. But whereas the usefulness of the dream, in a rudimentary sense, is only for your own analyst to interpret, fiction builds toward an illumination—toward a larger usefulness.

JH: For parties on both ends of the communication?

JC: Yes. It is a mutual enterprise. I have something to say, and I would like your response. *"Ich habe etwas gesagen."* I said that yesterday, and somebody said, "Why do you say it in German?" The imperative implication in English is not very strong. "I have something to say." But it *is* an imperative. *(Cheever is talking very loud now.)* I have something to say, and if you are interested, I would like your response. We can't quite say it in English. *"Ecoute!"*—you know. "Listen" isn't sharp enough. But it is an imperative: "I would like your response to what I have to say."

JH: Do you visualize a reader to whom you're saying this?

JH: I always think of the reader as being in the woods. *(He seems to love this idea. It sounds as if the outboard is really going to start this time.)* Now and then you see a form. Not hidden, actually—but readers don't, for an American novelist, *appear.* I think perhaps Mrs. Woolf and the English novelists knew pretty much the income group, the sartorial tastes and the education of the people they addressed. The American novelist does not. We have no idea where they come from, where they went to school, what they wear, eat, do. But they are numerous enough to support—modestly, in any case—a novelist. There are enough of them so that fiction is quite independent of

commercialism—commercial interests—commercial power or influence. The readers are interested, and they seem to be intelligent. This
is an astonishing and marvelous thing.

JH: If your pleasure in writing is the usefulness of this communication, what is the pain?

JC: Pain? I have no memory for pain.

JH: You spoke of darkness and radiance. There is a lot of darkness
in *Falconer,* all right. It makes the light in the book seem specially
intense. A patch of sky. . . .

JC: Oh, sky! How I miss it, in anyone's fiction, when there is no
sky! I look through chapter after chapter, thinking, well, there *may* be
some sky.

JH: The light in the prison courtyard. . . .

JH: Radiance and light, I suppose, originate with fire. I suppose it's
one of the oldest memories man has. In my church, the mass ends, of
course, not with a prayer, not with an amen. It ends with the acolyte
extinguishing the candles. Which goes back, probably to the close of
the most savage congregation, which was the scattering of fire. Light,
fire—these have always meant the possible greatness of man.

JH: Fire suggests fear. I see another kind of light in your writing—
more joyous.

JC: The whiteness of light. In the church, you know, that always
represents the Holy Spirit. It seems to me that man's inclination
toward light, toward brightness, is very nearly botanical—and I mean
spiritual light. One not only needs it, one struggles for it. It seems to
me almost that one's total experience is the drive toward light. Or, in
the case of the successful degenerate, the drive into an ultimate
darkness, which presumably will result in light. Yes. My fondness for
light is very very strong and, I presume, primitive. But isn't it true of
us all?

A Duet of Cheevers

Susan Cheever Cowley/1977

Reprinted from *Newsweek*, 14 March 1977, pp. 68–73, by
permission of the publisher. Copyright © 1977 by Newsweek,
Inc.

John Cheever has ended up in an eighteenth-century
house with iron balustrades, broad stone terraces and
white wooden porches. He spends these winter afternoons in the paneled downstairs living room, wearing
blue jeans and a blue Shetland pullover, slumped in the
yellow wing chair, drinking a shot glass of dark cold tea,
chain-smoking, reading, talking. Three golden retrievers
lie before the fire on an Oriental carpet. Although the
house, the hunting dogs and his tasseled loafers suggest
the easy life of a country gentleman, my father hasn't
lived that life; and the throw-away elegance of his home
in Ossining, N.Y., is a long way from the lunatic fringes of
Boston society in which he grew up. "Three times my
palm has been read," he says. "Once by Candida Donadio [his literary agent], once by a homosexual poet and
once by a dragoman in Luxor. They all said I had an
untraumatic childhood." They were wrong.

My father was brought up in Quincy, Mass., the second
son of a North Shore Yankee who lost all of his money
and some of his mind in the 1929 crash, and an Englishwoman who ran a gift shop to keep the family in baked
beans. At 16, he was expelled from Thayer Academy for
smoking. His first story, "Expelled," was published in *The
New Republic* when he was 17. Since then, except for an
Army stint and some teaching, he has never done anything but write fiction.

At first, he wrote in a rented room on Hudson Street in
New York City—a room so squalid that Walker Evans
immortalized it in a photograph. After he married my
mother, Mary, in 1941, he wrote in their one-room apartment in Chelsea. Later, when he was living on Upper
East Side, he wrote in a windowless storage space in the

basement of our apartment house. In the morning he put on his one suit, went down in the elevator with other men on their way to work, took off the suit, hung it up and wrote in his boxer shorts. At lunchtime he would put on the suit and come back upstairs.

In 1951, we moved to the suburbs—Scarborough, N.Y.—and he wrote in the guest room of the little-house-on-a-big-estate where we lived. In 1956, when we went to Rome for a year, he worked on the ormolu dining-room table of our flat. In 1961 we moved to the house in Ossining, where he wrote *Bullet Park* in the maid's room off the kitchen, *The World of Apples* in the second-floor bedroom I left when I got married and, last year, *Falconer* in my brother Ben's old bedroom at the top of the house. Ben is married and lives nearby; he is an editor at Reader's Digest. My other brother, Fred, is a freshman at Stanford. I am a writer at *Newsweek,* and interviewing my father makes us both a little nervous.

Susan Cheever Cowley: How did you start writing?

John Cheever: Uhh, telling stories and writing came very easily to me. In grade school, if the class was obedient, the teacher would say, now John will tell you a story. I don't remember what they were like except that they involved a great deal of suspense . . . the idea was to get the teacher so excited she would have to cancel the next class.

Q: Did your parents encourage you?

A: No. When I was about 11 they took me to see *The Merchant of Venice* and I got so excited that I raced downstairs early the next morning to read Shakespeare and this upset them. Soon after that my mother took me to see *Hedda Gabler*—she thought it was a musical. She tried to get me out but I wouldn't budge. When I was about 12 I announced that I wanted to be a writer and they said they would have to think it over. After a couple of days they said that I could be a writer as long as I didn't seek wealth or fame. Your family has never been conspicuous—it was thought vulgar and pushy to seek wealth or fame. So I said, that was not what I was seeking—a remark I've often regretted.

Q: What kind of writer were you? I know that a lot of people—including the ones who design your paperback-book jackets—seem to think that you are principally a chronicler of the suburban party circuit, and they'll probably be a little upset with *Falconer.*

A: I think I have sometimes been mistaken as a social observer. You can't say, "I don't deserve it," but the fact that I can count the olives in a dish just as quick as John O'Hara doesn't mean I am O'Hara.

Q: Do you feel that you've been misunderstood?

A: No, I've never felt misunderstood. Although I was told, by an editor, that I shouldn't try to be serious, that my only gift was to report cocktail conversation.

Q: Would you say that he misunderstood you?

A: No, I would say he was mistaken.

Q: Do you think you have developed as a writer?

A: *(delightedly)* Oh yes! Oh yes! I've developed tremendously. My prose is much closer to the substance. I've rid myself of persiflage. It's like having a voice and finally finding the right music.

Q: Do you think that being a so-called New Yorker writer held you back?

A: I never wrote *for The New Yorker,* and I never stopped writing for *The New Yorker*—they bought my stories.

Q: Not for much, as I remember.

A: In the golden days of *The New Yorker,* I was never paid over $1,000 for a story and sometimes under $500. I think Ross's feeling [Harold Ross, *The New Yorker's* founding editor] was that if I was paid any more, if I stopped eating in cafeterias, for instance, I would get prideful, arrogant and idle . . . and he may have been right for all I know.

Q: Well, you've often said that Ross was kind of a father figure for you. Why did you need a father figure?

A: I had a profoundly troubled adolescence. My father and mother were intensely unhappy. Their life together was miserable. My father was a self-made man who had lost everything. The whole scene struck me as being bankrupt in every way.

Q: I guess your brother was the only person you could talk to around there. I remember when Fred died last spring you talked a lot about your love for him.

A: That's right. In fact, the strongest love—not the most exciting or the richest or the most brilliant—but the strongest love of my life was for my brother. We were planning to live together; he was going to be the businessman and I was going to be the novelist. It would have been a perfectly acceptable arrangement in Boston, but it finally seemed unacceptable to me. When it was apparent to me that it seemed an ungainly closeness, I packed and shook his hand and left. I went to New York.

Q: I think your relationship with him was often very difficult: you were always ambivalent about him. The figure of the recalcitrant brother appears in a lot of your work, and in *Falconer* the brother is murdered. Did you ever want to kill Fred?

A: Well, once I was planning to take him trout fishing up at Cranberry Lake, which is just miles away from everything in the wilderness, and I realized if I got him up there he would fall overboard. I would beat him with an oar until he stayed. Of course, I was appalled at this.

Q: So you didn't go to Cranberry?

A: No, I went to a psychiatrist.

Q: Did you ever fall in love with another man? I mean, because of the homosexuality in *Falconer,* people are certainly going to ask you that.

A: The possibility of my falling in love with a man seems to me to exist. Such a thing could happen. That it has not happened is just chance. But I would think twice about giving up the robustness and merriment I have known in the heterosexual world.

Q: Well, have you ever had a homosexual experience?

A: My answer to that is, well, I have had many, Susie, all tremendously gratifying, and all between the ages of 9 and 11.

Q: What about the heterosexual world? You know, women who don't know what a kind and generous and loving man you are might be upset by your portrait of the bitch-wife Marcia in *Falconer.* A lot of your women characters are pretty cold—beautiful but narcissistic, women to be worshiped instead of loved. Is that the way you feel?

A: You're putting a narrowness on it I hoped I didn't have. I don't really have any message on women. I've known a lot of women and it seems to me they are distinguished by their variety. I don't think of them as creative or destructive, serious or empty-headed.

Q: What about your marriage?

A: Well, it's been extraordinary. That two people of our violent temperament have been able to live together for nearly 40 years as we have seems to me a splendid example of the richness and diversity of human nature . . . and in this 40 years there's scarcely been a week in which we haven't planned to get a divorce.

Q: But in *Falconer* you seem to be saying that the salvation of men is in their relationship with other men.

A: No, I don't feel that at all. I think the salvation of men and women is in men and women. I think the salvation of men and women is in men, women and children. The one stubborn, obdurate fact that I've been able to discern in life is that a man and a woman, ardently loving, will produce a third life.

Q: Lately you've been saying that everything you've written has been about confinement. The confinement of a small town like St. Botolphs, the suburban confinement of Shady Hill, the confinement of the Falconer State Correctional Institution. Has your marriage been a kind of confinement?

A: No, not really. The confinements I have felt have been when I've been stuck in elevators or airports, especially where I couldn't speak the language. I've been stuck in Leningrad and in Cairo, both for a long time, once by a blizzard and once by a BOAC slowdown. I have also been stuck in sentimental and erotic contracts that excited in me the desire for escape.

Q: One of your experiences with confinement was when you were teaching at Sing Sing. What was that like?

A: It was very exciting. When you went in you weren't always sure you were going to get out. It was exciting during the Attica riots when they kept saying, "Hey, Mr. Cheever, you'd make a great hostage." There was the student response; some of them had never read at all before. I heard things I couldn't have heard in any other classroom.

Q: But you got really depressed about the whole experience.

A: Yea. First I went there as a do-gooder, but then the horror of prison—an imponderable I've tried to put in the book, the blasphemy of men building, stone by stone, hells for other men—got to me. After that I went there very unwillingly. It seemed to me to be participating in an obscenity.

Q: But you didn't stop.

A: I didn't stop until I had the heart attack.

Q: That was four years ago. After that you had all kinds of confinement. Confinement in the intensive-care unit of Phelps [Memorial Hospital in Tarrytown, N.Y.], confinement at Boston University. Confinement finally in Smithers [an alcoholics rehabilitation center in New York City].

A: After the heart attack I didn't drink for a while; I went and taught a semester at the University of Iowa and was reasonably sober. But then I came back and I was intensely unhappy with my work and everything. I started drinking heavily and took a job at B.U. [Boston University], which was very unfortunate.

Q: A sort of return to childhood confinements?

A: Yes, I was in Boston when I was 17 and I thought I had gotten away completely. When I returned I found I had made no progress at all. All the images, the ghosts and anxieties I thought I had escaped were still there. I couldn't, for example, go to Symphony Hall because my mother was there. There were whole areas of the city I couldn't go into. I was not mature enough to return to the scene of the crime.

Q: I remember that things got so bad you were almost arrested for drunkenness. Do you want to tell about it?

A: Well, sure. I was walking down Commonwealth Avenue in freezing weather, not wearing an overcoat. There was this bum drinking out of a brown paper bag, so I sat down with him. This was precisely what my parents would have not wanted me to do. We both drank out of the brown paper bag—it was some kind of fortified wine—and a policeman came along and threatened to arrest us.

Q: And?

A: I told him that my name was John Cheever and that he was out of his mind.

Q: And?

A: Well, he said he would arrest me if he ever saw me again.

Q: When you came back from Boston you were a wreck. I ran into John Updike at a Playboy Awards lunch and he had seen you in Boston and said you were in a daze most of the time. "I keep thinking the John Cheever I know is in there somewhere," he said.

A: Everyone who liked me thought I was dying. My reaction was "so what."

Q: Well, you came home and went into Smithers for a month. Grim.

A: The dreadfulness of the place was therapeutic. The fact that men had presumably jumped out of the window in the ward where I slept—it made me realize this was a critical matter.

Q: What made you change? What made you stop drinking, when you had drunk all your life?

A: The turning point, I think, was when I appeared to be dying. It made me realize that my ardor for life was quite genuine, and anything I could do to continue alive and useful I was quite willing to do. The important thing about Smithers is that I have not had a drink since I left.

Q: I think we all felt, feel, that you had come back from the dead—to be part of the family again, and to write *Falconer.* Don't you think that all your own imprisonments, at Sing Sing, at Smithers, at Phelps, helped you write the book?

A: What I want to make absolutely clear is that this novel was not written out of a singular experience of alcohol or drugs. I like to think it is the sum of my living. I like to think my teaching at Sing Sing is a small part of it. I did no *research* there. I did not, for example, ask to see the showers or the cells. I like to think my confinement at Smithers is a small part of it. I like to think of *Falconer* as the sum of everything I've ever known and smelled and tasted.

What your question brings up is the difference between reporting—journalism—and fiction. Journalism is conscientious to the available facts. In fiction one uses the available facts merely to create a mood, an illusion. I didn't go to Sing Sing to gather material any more than I got married and had children to gather material.

Q: But you noticed all the cats at Sing Sing and I know that you've had mixed feelings about our cats. Is that why you wrote the cat-massacre scene in *Falconer?*

A: I have never been unkind to a cat excepting Delmore [a former Cheever cat]. I do tell the cats when they climb up and down my legs at 6 in the morning that I have an international reputation for cruelty.

Q: What do they do then?

A: Climb up and down my legs.

Q: When you left Smithers, you seemed to be on a kind of high— it seemed that you had been miraculously saved from death. You sat down and wrote *Falconer* at top speed and you were so excited about it that you read it to us chapter by chapter.

A: Yes. I guess it took about a year to write the book. I started somewhere around the middle of May and I finished, I remember distinctly, on Maundy Thursday.

Q: I remember about halfway through the book when you realized what the end was going to be. We were standing on the porch in the sun. "He gets out," you said. "Farragut gets out." How did you feel?

A: As happy as I've ever been, and for longer. I was very happy with *The Wapshot Chronicle*. While I was working on *Scandal* I was suicidal. I got sick in the middle of *Bullet Park*. *Falconer* was a high that lasted ten months. It seems to me that at the end of the book, when Farragut gets off the bus, his degree of self-possession equals freedom. He's all right. He's free of the fear of falling. And he's going to be all right.

Q: After Smithers, you started going to church every Sunday again. Why?

A: I go to church to make my thanksgivings. Period. The level of introspection I enjoy on my knees is something I enjoy nowhere else.

Q: What would you like to give thanks for in your children *(smile)*?

A: I hope that we should all succeed in love and usefulness. I know it sounds like a chestnut but it's what I believe.

Q: Well, how do you rate yourself compared with other writers?

A: Writing is not at all a competitive sport. I don't think of myself as being less than Saul Bellow or better than Herbert Gold. The essence of literature is always the singularity of the writer.

Q: Do you think that, as you've changed, your attitude toward your readers has changed? You seem a lot more willing to talk about your life and your work than before?

A: I used to detest being interviewed. I used to detest giving readings. I used to dislike meeting people, especially people who'd say, "How can I thank you for all the hours of reading pleasure you've given me!" My stores of contempt were much higher then. Now, it's clear to me that I count on this audience of strangers to whom I speak my most intimate thoughts. I'm dependent emotionally upon their response—never more so than with *Falconer* because it deals with controversial matters. If there were no response, I would have to think my emotions were so eccentric as to have no universality at all.

Q: So you think you've mellowed?

A: Well, I think maybe I've matured. Why don't you ask me how I feel about getting older?

Q: *(obediently)* How do you feel about getting older?

A: *(reading from notes made in anticipation of the interview)* Since I have no clear and responsible sense of the seasons of life, and since I would not want to be one of those old men who claim to be burgeoning and burdened when there's not a leaf in sight, I count on you and your brothers to keep me posted.

"Not Only I the Narrator, but I John Cheever"

Eleanor Munro/1977

Reprinted from *Ms.*, April 1977, pp. 74–77, 105, by permission of Georges Borchardt, Inc., and the author.

John Cheever is that rare and disputable thing among American fiction writers today—a devotee, in an old-fashioned mode, of women. His hundreds of stories and first three novels are not only beautiful, comical, and true-to-life (as he himself said of one of his character's works) but are also often parables on Love between the sexes consummated in that "preposterous lie . . . the Vows of Holy Matrimony." A lie it may be, Cheever has been saying for more than 30 years, and still we humans are not to be despised for our longing for permanence. Rather, fallible humankind is to be pitied and loved. For have many of us not the same innocent wish? And are not the shaky forms of permanence we have invented—like marriage and the domestic clusters in which many live—evidences not of hypocrisy but rather a "guise or mode of hope"?

Then pity poor Pilgrim, I was thinking as I drove out to Cheever's home in the lovely, light-splashed Hudson Valley of New York the other day. For as in the old morality tales, Pilgrim must ever and ever fall away from brightness and find himself on the downward path to the cold. Bitter, haunted figures stalk many of Cheever's works, looking for vengeance or a way back to lost innocence. *Falconer,* his powerful new novel, is set in a prison. Once upon a time, Cheever implies, there was an Eden, but far behind. Now time must be served in that penultimate place-of-no-progress, the jail cell. The root feeling is claustrophobia. Escape must be found, call it birth, rebirth, epiphany, ecstasy, orgasm, love, or Holy (in this case) Communion.

Leander Wapshot, clan father in Cheever's best-known saga, *The Wapshot Chronicle,* had in his blustery middle age the face of "a boy [but] a boy who had seen the Gorgon." Photographed after the writing of *Falconer,* Cheever had that very look—melancholy and

130

shocked. In person, however, he's neither of these, but a tight-knit, darting figure, more crinkled than gouged by time, with scrutinizing blue, blue eyes, rugged useful country hands, and the witty, harassed manner of a man torn between endearing hospitality and a preference not to be trapped, now, by interviewers.

His book is finished, and there's more on his mind than books. Ice skates, for instance. He'd lost his own, the pond was frozen, and he'd just been to buy new ones. "All they had was plastic for God's sake! Plastic! With some kind of gold scribbling all over them! Worse than cellophane and how I hated that." Then two golden Labradors came to nuzzle him. One is a favorite, but the other, Edgar, Cheever can't stand, for two cardinal dog sins. "He's dumb and he has no memory." Still on one of the half dozen breaks Cheever would make over the next couple of hours (for tea, more wood, matches, kindling, more tea) he would also jump up and run outside to throw Edgar a ball.

We sat in his 18th-century stone-ended house in a haze of applewood smoke. Mary, his wife of 37 years, a teacher of English, was off gathering pine boughs. The light was cold and dim on polished floors and old Turkish carpets, but it was natural light. We sat by windows, looking into shadows of rooms beyond. Deliberately the Cheevers picked this style of house, instead of "a box with great sheets of glass," for its generous providing of dusky corners. In and out of the light and dark Cheever goes. He finishes a book in one room, he explained, then leaves that workplace behind and has to find another spot. Still, unlike hapless Farragut, victim of the fall in *Falconer,* Cheever's found home.

Eleanor Munro: Begin at the beginning. What was the first one like—that "home" you keep coming back to in your stories, as a source of "lightness and strength"?

John Cheever: When I was a boy we lived in Quincy, Massachusetts, in a big Victorian house on a hill, and the Cheevers really did once own sailing ships that went back and forth to Canton, as the Wapshots did. But I've never tried to exploit myself as a remnant of a famous China Trade family because when strangers at bars and parties think they recognize me, they usually imagine it's because they've seen me at the racetrack in Saratoga or Belmont and I enjoy this more than an ersatz historical prominence. However, both my father and grandfather were born to fathers over fifty, so just three generations of Cheevers do go back into the eighteenth century. When I was a boy, it was the twilight of Athenian New England, but even so late in time, New England families shared a strong sense of what was practical in the establishment. In marriage, or personal display. When the evening meal should be eaten. The role, so far as appearances go, of the sons, the daughter, the husband. Naturally there were deviations—cruel and tragic ones—but in my estimation these didn't render the community overwhelmingly hypocritical. We went unwillingly to dancing classes and assemblies, but it seems there are some advantages to learning the forks early in life. And of course, we were very industrious. Everyone in New England chopped wood. It was a useful occupation and a mark of probity, character, and thrift. If you were rich, you chopped wood in the front yard.

Then there was always an excitement in our lives. At lunch on Sundays everyone would be arguing. An uncle would be singing in the *St. Matthew Passion* in a Boston church, a cousin was a concert pianist, his mother painted portraits. An aunt founded the Shakespeare Society, my mother founded the Current Events Club, and my father could be called on to recite "Casey at the Bat." These families had the zeal of a people who felt life in this country to be adventurous and new. An attitude I see reasserting itself today.

Munro: Many of your stories refer to a golden age that's gone. The men fall from grace while the women, once they lose the Way, so to speak, spin off into lives of waste or bitterness. Are you literally thinking of the falling-away of Americans from that shared culture and morality? Do you ever wish things were as they were, mothers in their places, sons in theirs?

Cheever: Definitely not! It's tremendously important to make this clear. For instance, I use the word "nostalgia" I hope as the Europeans do. The Italians say "la nos-tal-*gee*-a"—one of the greatest human emotions. Not regret for the past, but a keen sense of the present, saying, How splendid it was! But spoken without regret.

In fact I have a kind of running feud with some critics in the New York *Review of Books* and other places whose sense of life seems confined to the past, the past imperfect, and the remote past. For example, you and I have never met in this room before. I have just learned your married name. You may just have observed that my socks don't match. These are the excitements of the present. How absurd—and how customary—it would be to cast all this in the past—to say this *was* that late winter twilight when Ellie Munro drove out from New York and wouldn't take anything but tea and a weak scotch.

On the other hand, there's the other kind of insidious mannerism where the writer says something like, "The phone rings and it's Mrs. Woolf calling to say Lytton's hemorrhoids are better . . ." Now I say that's a misuse of the *present* tense!

This kind of confusion is related to the prolonged psychoanalytical conversations many of my generation experienced, where too great an emphasis was put on our motives and too little on the thrust of life. To "mine" was the term the doctors used, and when you fell in love, you "mined" your motives to see if your love was escapist. Diving into a cold pool—which I love—was thought to be narcissistic. We became accustomed to seeking motives for our present acts and then coming up triumphantly with something sordid from the past. As I see it, the continents of motive are far away and unknown, and their coastlines are out of sight.

Munro: Then what does persist and have meaning for you as a writer now?

Cheever: To write is to make sense of one's life, to aim to succeed in one's usefulness and one's loves, and to share this excitement with strangers. Much of this is mysterious, just as one doesn't understand why certain effects of illumination and smell and touch move us. For example, I'm fascinated by the sight of leaves falling across the headlights of a car. Now it's hard to decipher the moral meaning of this sight. Yet yesterday I had a letter from Rumania, saying "I read your book, and *I too* thrill at leaves crossing the light." So these letters come in, dozens of them, from Russia, from Japan, from all over, and almost always about the mysteriousness and universality of our responses.

Munro: It's men you write about in most depth. Your women are essentially love objects—or even more unfashionably today—religious Presences, Holders of the Grail. I think of those unforgettable images of naked women coming out of the green sea, or Clarissa nursing her baby under a pear arbor in the rain, or any number of women in lamplight placing a china serving dish on the table. But I don't recall your dealing with a "liberated" woman, whose frustrations are unconnected to her domestic situation, except Honora and Justina, and of course they're aged, asexual, and magnificently eccentric. Possibly it's worth adding that both these controlled the family trust funds!

Cheever: Well, I'm not sure about that. I have written about a variety of women, but I've seldom known a passive and an unliberated one. This is not to overlook the cruel loneliness and bewilderment enforced on many women. My maternal grandmother, for example, was an English emigrant who complained bitterly of her past. "I am a very well-educated English woman," she would say. "I can take tea in French and hem a pocket handkerchief." Yet she and all her friends considered themselves free spirits. One of her friends was the novelist Margaret W. Deland. These women had the urge to save the world. One day Grandmother was walking with the Delands in the slums of Boston and saw women rapping their rings against their windows. "Why are they doing that?" she asked. "Because they are *whores*," explained Mr. Deland, who was a successful publisher.

It turned out that many of the girls would come down pregnant from the mills in Lowell and Lawrence, have their babies at the Diocesan Home, and then find the only livelihood open to them was hustling. So Grandmother and Mrs. Deland began to take these girls and their babies into their homes and teach them housekeeping. Then they'd put ads in the Boston *Transcript* and find them jobs. I have to admit that along the way they also provided themselves with good maids.

My own parents had no money at all to begin with. My father left Newburyport on the last of the sailing ships, graduated from the Phillips School with honors and went to work the next day. The top of his career was when he owned a shoe factory in Lynn. I used to be taken there once a year and allowed to blow the whistle. But later on, he lost everything, and Mother went out and opened a gift shop, just like Sarah Wapshot. I was fifteen or sixteen. My brother and I blew the last of the money we had on a summer in Germany and then I began a new life in a Hudson Street furnished room. It was squalid, cold, lonely, and I remained deeply disconcerted by the harm my mother's working did to my father's self-esteem. Whenever I cleared ten dollars, I would send it to him and he, of course, would spend it on a lunch at Locke-Ober's. He was a self-made man from a ruined, seafaring family, and suddenly he found himself helpless, unable to support his family. He tried to kill himself. She, on the other hand, was ecstatic to be independent. I didn't understand it at all. But today for me to grant what I think of as sovereignty to other men and women is one of the most thrilling experiences I know, and when I finally realized that my mother, managing her gift shop, felt herself to be sovereign, I was happy to get the news.

Munro: How do you like the new genre of women's fictionalized confessions?

Cheever: A distinction has to be made, I think, between fiction and crypto-autobiography. Any confusion between the two debases fiction, one of the most exalted and acute means of communication we have. Reality has something like the same place in fiction that it has in dreams. In a dream you are on an unknown ship on an unknown river, but you're wearing an old suit and the man beside you is your brother. In a dream these fragments—this collage of the real and the unreal—remains meaningless until it is analyzed. In fiction, the collage is mastered and coherent. The writer's vocation is to make sense of this larger reality.

Munro: I expect the women would say that's their aim too.

Cheever: Well, whose books do you like? X's? Y's? I won't mention their names because I love them dearly as people. But the books! Z's novel, for instance, is sloppily felt. There's no velocity in her perceptions, no keenness in her chain of her impressions. On the other hand, Flannery O'Connor was one of the glories of our time. Jean Stafford is splendid. Joan Didion is brilliant. I love Elizabeth Bishop, Mary McCarthy's best stories. Katherine Anne Porter's contribution. Adrienne Rich. Levertov. Erica Jong's first book . . . but the list would be too long.

Essentially, the fact that the war between men and women has been lifted out of its comic-strip status into a legislative and spiritual realm seems to me a great advantage to us all. That, and the fact that women are today allowed to describe their erotic expectations and responses. However, sexual explicitness does, I think, bring up the difference in values between a truth and a fact. Capote writes in *Esquire* that you can get blown in the balcony of a movie theater for fifty cents. This may be a fact, but it does not correspond in any way to my sense of truth. Incidentally, *Esquire* failed to publish that bit of information in its Dubious Achievements issue.

Munro: Can a male writer succeed in telling the truth about a female character?

Cheever: Whether or not a man can write with, forgive me, penetration and depth about a woman brings us back to the first canon of aesthetics, which is "interest." If a man or a woman or a homosexual can bring off their opposites with interest, I think they've been successful. In the long history of the English novel no triumph is comparable to the brilliant and profound description of both men and women that we find in George Eliot. Actually, male or female, what a writer has to have are an extraordinary memory, a marvelous ear, and a passion for bringing disparities together. I love giving exercises like these to my students: write a love letter from a burning building. Or, three pages on your idea of the introspections of a jogger. Exercises that force you to rush on to the consummation, not pausing but in the end conveying to the reader what you feel.

Sometimes you even have to just let the story go. Writing "The Swimmer," for instance [one of Cheever's most famous short stories, made into film starring Burt Lancaster]. When I began, the story was to have been a simple one about Narcissus. I started with that image of the boy looking into water. Then swimming everyday as I do, I thought, it's absurd to limit him to the tight mythological plot—being trapped in his own image, in a single pool. This man loves swimming! So in my first version, I just let him out and he swam in an immense number of pools—thirty of them! But then I began to narrow it down, and narrow it down, and something began happening. It was growing cold and quiet. It was turning into winter. Involuntarily. It was a terrible experience, writing that story. I was very unhappy. Not only I the narrator, but I John Cheever, was crushed.

I've said before, and I say still, if a writer hasn't mastery over his characters he shouldn't be in the business. But there are forces larger than character. Destiny. Nemesis. Sometimes a character's fall or ascension seems irresistible. There's nothing you can do. *Falconer,* for instance, is set in jail and all I knew was, Farragut had to get out. Out of drugs. Out of the delusions of drugs. Out of . . . Hell. I know from my years of teaching at Sing Sing what the inside of a prison looks like, but my only firsthand experience with confinement had been in stuck elevators, fogged-in airports, and mistaken erotic contacts. But we all know the taste of confinement—the prison is a metaphor of course—and as soon as I had described his predicament I knew he had to get the hell out.

Munro: Is Farragut's break for freedom—or liberation—something most of us aspire to?

Cheever: Look what happened the other day. I had been lecturing at Cornell on Chekhov and afterward we went out for a walk in the snow. We were all standing on a high ridge overlooking the valley and we saw a snow-bow—that spectrum that forms in very cold weather just to the right of the sun. And then we all exclaimed, "We've never seen this before!" And it occurred to me, aside from polite conversation, how often we break out and say to one another or to ourselves, "I've never seen this before!" You dive into a pool and you say, "I've never felt such cold water before!" Or, "The waves were never so high!" Or, "I've never seen Cassiopeia so bright!" It occurred to me what a sense of marvel we still have. What a freshness there is to our experiences, and then an innocence to our expressions. Standing there on that ridge in Ithaca, with people I had never met before and might never meet again, it seemed to me, for a minute or two anyhow, that our exclamations made some progress toward improving our responsiveness to our strangeness, still, to this planet.

Munro: Is it to tap repeatedly this sense of liberation, or of marvel and strangeness, that you have held on to certain, as you say, "lies" and rituals, like going to church every Sunday and taking Holy Communion?

Cheever: I said it in *Falconer:* ". . . to profess exalted religious experience outside the ecclesiastical paradigm is to make of oneself an outcast . . ." and that's a condition we live with. Still there are other ways! We had this neighbor, an amazing, wonderful man now dead, an Italian with an enormous ego, who came to me one day with arms outstretched and said, "Cheeeeever! How do you account for my incrrredible ebooolience?" And then he answered himself, "It is because I have the philosoff!"

As for ceremony, I have a taste for it because it's a way of making sense of one's life and one's chances. In Tbilisi, I went to the poet Noneshvili's house for dinner. His wife covered the table with a vast,

snowy damask and then, after setting the table, spilled a glass of red
wine at every place. "It's an old Georgian ceremony," she explained.
"It promises you can't mess things up any more than I've already
done, for the next couple of hours."

And then of all the unscientific and marvelous forces we cope with
or come in contact with from time to time, the one of greatest
astonishment, what moves us most, is love. The other day at a lunch
party, there was a woman who turned suddenly to her husband
sitting across the table and said, "Sweetheart . . . listen." I hadn't
heard anyone say, "Sweetheart" for, oh, years and years. I've been
waiting ever since, to hear it again.

But it's getting dark and I'm thinking about your long drive home.
Take these apple logs for your fireplace. Those plastic city logs aren't
any good. They don't have any smell at all!

John Cheever: The Author Faces the Demands of Fame

Robert Baum/1977

Reprinted from the *Quincy (MA) Patriot-Ledger,* 19 April 1977, by permission of the *Patriot-Ledger.*

John Cheever had just returned to his hotel room after being one of seven writers at a luncheon/book fair in Boston. He had taken off his tie and now sat back in an armchair and smiled wryly.

"They wanted me to make a speech to sell my book. Goddamned if I can sell a book. So when it was my turn. I just stood up and said, 'My name is John Cheever. I was born in Wollaston.' Then I sat down."

The book in question, the novel *Falconer,* has sold over 105,000 copies, anyway. It has also brought Cheever new acclaim—perhaps even a new critical reputation. It has been called a great American novel. And while the 64-year-old writer has surely earned a niche as a satirist and reporter of the suburban scene, that's quite a way from "great novelist."

Now, many critics are reevaluating his place in American letters after *Falconer.*

The man, too, has apparently changed quite a bit recently. For one thing, this is his first promotion tour ever; in the past, even interviews were rarely granted. He has recovered from a heart attack suffered four years ago, and has successfully emerged from a bout with alcoholism two years ago.

It was a warm spring day in Cheever's "author" suite at the Ritz; we poured 7-Ups from squat-necked little bottles, and sat near the windows to catch the breeze.

Cheever's wife, Mary, said goodbye, and he, still thinking about the book fair, asked, "Did the ambassador (Henry Cabot Lodge) sell out his book?"

"Noooooo!" she answered. They exchanged a grin.

She left, we sat back and I had an opportunity to study him.

John Cheever, then, at 64. Sandy-haired with a face both craggier and more interesting than most photographs make him look. Small and thin. (Those who knew him from Wollaston described him as heavy, and some early photos show him that way.) Wears shirts with soft collars that look more comfortable than fashionable. Smokes filter-tip cigarettes. Speaks softly, sometimes mumbles.

And, on occasion, smiles the damnedest smile. It seems to come on a random thought and say, "Hello! What absurdity have we here!" Far from mocking; rather gentle, bemused and tentative. The image that presents itself—albeit, a grotesque one—is of an owl blinking in unaccustomed sunshine. The smile seems to seek perspective, possibly on a stranger—not me so much as the public John Cheever.

Or maybe, like his novel *Falconer,* the smile is meant to tell of a newfound lack of confinement. Who knows? But Cheever warned several times during the interview, "Fiction is not autobiography."

Falconer takes a Cheever suburbanite and puts him into prison, convicted of killing his brother. An unlikely locate, even more unlikely when one finds it the setting for Cheever's most hopeful work. For, in the end, the hero escapes, not only from prison, but from drug addiction and many fears. In between, though, he experiences riots, a homosexual love affair, and a stomach turning massacre of cats. Why a prison locale?"

"I taught for two years in Sing-Sing (which is near Cheever's home in Ossining, N.Y.), so it's not accidental. But the Falconer Prison in the book is not Sing-Sing. I took all I could of the smells and sounds of Sing-Sing, but none of the characters."

His voice slowed down considerably, as he added:

"I used prison as a metaphor for confinement, something I have experienced personally only when I've been stuck in elevators or airports, especially where I couldn't speak the language. I have also been stuck in emotional and erotic contracts."

His voice slowed, and he even interrupted to ask if he was going too fast for me. Before he finished I realized that this was almost word-for-word what he had told his daughter, Susan Cheever Cowley (a Newsweek editor) in a recent Newsweek interview.

Apparently, it was of special importance to him to say that just right, and to be quoted just right. Throughout the interview I waited for other slow downs, but they didn't happen.

Falconer then was not a prison novel, but a novel of confinement.

"Drug addiction is another metaphor for confinement—loss of freedom. In *Falconer,* I responded to a man's being able to regain self-possession and leave confinement."

Farragut's (the hero's) escape from prison in a canvas sack meant to carry a corpse—was this intended to symbolise a spiritual rebirth?

Cheever looked doubtful. "Well, he recaptured his self-possession. I look on it as an achievement. His escape was not so much running away from something, but spiritually positive. I know Farragut isn't going to return."

Has the critical reaction to *Falconer* surprised him?

"It's exciting to see a serious novel well-received. For a serious work of fiction there's an audience of maybe 50,000 who will buy the book. At times, it can be stretched to 100,000, and that's encouraging. And it's very heartening that one cannot sell pornography."

How would he rate *Falconer* compared to his other work?

The smile. "It's obviously my most mature work . . . since I was oldest when I wrote it."

Falconer is a work laden with symbolism. How aware of symbols is Cheever when he writes?

"The writer should be aware of . . . richness . . . symbolically in the material in which he works, but, on the other hand, well, one reviewer said the relationship between the brothers in *Falconer* was that of the Egyptian bird gods Seth and Horus and that even the name of the prison, Falconer, stood for a bird of prey." He laughed. "That is not necessarily the ideal reader."

"Meaning is one of the secondary uses of fiction. You like fiction in an emotional way."

What is the first thing that comes to him when planning a story . . . the plot, an image, an abstract thought?

"Something I urgently want to say—an idea and an emotion. It must have urgency."

The theme? An idea, then, is first? ("And an emotion," he adds. "Ideas and emotion.")

But your fiction is so filled with concrete details.

"One uses details to hold attention and to convince that your story is significant."

You mean like the white enamel bars at Falconer worn black in spots by the hands of prisoners?

"Yeah." Cheever stood and twisted the neck of a 7-Up bottle. "Yeah," he said, pouring, "So they'll say, 'That guy really knows what he's talking about!' "

"But the basic test of fiction is 'Is it interesting?' That's the principal canon in writing—interest."

How does "interest" differ from "entertainment"?

"The difference is seriousness. I'm not a money player, nor are any of my colleagues that I esteem."

Do you like going on these promotion tours for your books?

"This is my first ever. The only reason I'm here is that I come from Quincy."

Will he visit Quincy?

"No. There's no time, and what I remember of Quincy has vanished. I'm not complaining, mind you, when a man reaches his sixties . . ." he finished with a shrug.

He said he recalled elms growing in Quincy Center, the smallness of the center he knew, and the beauty of the Thomas Crane Library.

"I remember I used to deliver the Quincy News in a truck in Houghs Neck. I used to pick up the box-scores of games for the paper. It's one of my best Quincy memories."

He was born on Wollaston Hill on May 27, 1912. He developed his narrative skill young, and his teachers often let John tell the class a story.

He wasn't a delight for the establishment, however; he attended Thayer Academy in Braintree and got kicked out for smoking. This gave him the material for his first published story. Appearing in *The New Republic,* the story "Expelled" was a satire.

—"Satire? It was meant to be an attack," Cheever said, "You know there was a delegation of students from Thayer at the book fair today and they were saying things hadn't gotten any better, either."

(A Ledger editor recalls picking up a copy of the *New Republic* to read Cheever's story, and being thought a Communist by the Quincy of that day when he was seen with the magazine.)

So Cheever at 17 was a published writer and went to New York and found himself a hovel so wonderfully squalid that his friend, photographer Walker Evans, recorded it for posterity. He wrote more stories and the *New Yorker* bought several.

In 1957, some twenty-eight years after his first short-story, he published his first novel, *The Wapshot Chronicle* on the doings of South Shore suburbanites. It won for him the National Book Award in 1958, and wider attention. Some critics, however, suggested that his was another case of an excellent short story writer forced by economics or neglect to produce a novel.

Why did he wait so long?

"Most of one's experience is unfinished (like a short story). It was only after 18 years of marriage and three children that I felt I had had a sustained experience and I wrote a novel. The difference is like that between a sprint and a marathon."

Who influenced his writing?

"I couldn't list fewer than a thousand. Writing is not a competitive sport. It can be best compared to a relay . . . and what I'm about to say is too damn pious, and please quote me as saying so . . . but one does not so much succeed as make a contribution."

Success for Cheever (in others' estimation at least) has increased with *Falconer*. Still, he has doubts that he may be writing too long.

"I've asked my children to tell when the time comes—to say 'Go on writing, but don't publish!' "

It would be hard to stop writing.

"Writing is the only serious (he underlined serious with his voice) means of communication we possess that is quite free of commercialism."

A good exit line for Cheever, so I said goodbye.

As we were walking to the door, however, Cheever hit me with a stunning irrelevancy:

"You know there's a museum in South Dakota just for used eyeglasses worn by famous people. Got a letter from them some years back," he chuckled. "They've got a director and an assistant director and everything!"

"Did you give them a pair of your old eyeglasses?"

"No. I didn't wear them then!"

I was almost out the door when his meaning became clear. Famous People Used Eyeglass Museum, indeed! Cheever had come through illness and written a most serene and hopeful book. A man who seldom granted an interview in a 57-year career went on his first promotion tour. New knowledge, perhaps? A most private man was doing his best to respond to the public. Used eyeglasses and fame!

As the door closed, John Cheever was laughing.

John Cheever Comes Home

June Beisch/1977

Reprinted from the *Boston Herald,* 28 August 1977, by permission of the *Herald.*

Coming back to Boston had not been an easy thing for John Cheever, even though this time he was returning in the glow of acclaim for *Falconer,* his new novel about prisons, addiction and love; even though this time around a chauffeured limousine whisked him from his rooms at the Ritz to his various appointments in the city; even though his name was everywhere and his face loomed soberly from the cover of news magazines. There was still an ambivalent feeling about Boston. It had always been there, though. Childhood memories—unhappy memories—crowded in upon Cheever whenever he came back home. There was a vagrant fiber in him that was always exacerbated whenever he was in Boston—alcohol had become such a problem that years ago he had almost been arrested for drunkenness on Commonwealth Avenue. During his stint as visiting professor in creative writing at Boston University, his life was in disarray and his drinking problem increased. Cheever refers to the time as his "cranky years."

After a few days in Boston, he seems ready to try a *rapprochement* with the city. He is feeling buoyant. His mood is expansive. "I've never seen Boston looking more beautiful," he admits, lighting a cigarette and settling back. "The skyline is varied now, and I'd forgotten how marvelous Copley Square is . . . Trinity Church and the new library. Truly beautiful and rich."

Ten years ago, John Cheever had addressed a crowd assembled at the New School for Social Research in New York. There was always a feverish sense of anticipation at such lectures. The audience was keenly aware of the immense strides being made in fiction. At that time, Cheever was recognized as one of the country's finest short story writers.

145

But the truth was, no one expected a great novel out of Cheever. A decade later, *Falconer* came as a great surprise.

John Cheever is a small man who wears a look of weary disdain, who has a raffish wit, and whose edgy intelligence makes others feel somewhat sluggish by comparison. He looks older now . . . his face is more lined, but it laughs easily. He now lives in Ossining, N.Y. Does he still consider himself a New Englander? He shouts back. "I like to think of myself as John Cheever."

But, there is still a good bit of Boston in John Cheever. "I was born in Quincy," he says. "But in Boston there was a high degree of accepted eccentricity. People were often characterized by the rather odd things they did, such as wearing raincoats to church or wearing a dinner jacket to dinner with no socks. I don't know if this still goes on in Boston, but it certainly did then.

"I like to think I know nothing about madness," Cheever says drily. "As for marriage, I do think that the vows of holy matrimony are surely the most preposterous and surely the most hopeful that one could ever make. The fact that I've been married for almost forty years to a woman as temperamental as myself—each week we declare an impending divorce—I owe to the vows of holy matrimony.

"I think freedom is splendid. Freedom abused, of course, is not freedom at all." He pauses deliberately for a moment and continues: "You are not free unless you are sufficiently well-informed and sufficiently intelligent to exploit it."

John Cheever's previous books and short stories, have described the world of the anguished suburbanite. His women are the kind who wear polo coats and carry six-packs. His men are their mates. They lead "normal" lives. Rarely do issues complicate the plot. Politics are never present. Never are there any *pronunciamentos* on the drug culture, the counter culture, the sexual revolution. "The political burden," he explains, "that literature can bear, it seems to me, is an extremely delicate question. No . . . I don't think that novelists are usually political. It seems to me that the canvas of the novelist is the emotional and spiritual landscape of people and if he offers a political idea, he almost always offers a solution. I cannot think of a writer who offers a solution behind perhaps the refreshment of one's courage."

Do writers lead messy lives? John Updike insists they do. "But

John doesn't lead a messy life at all," argues Cheever. "He's one of the most organized people you'll ever meet. Basically, writers cannot lead messy lives because they are their own disciplinarians. There is no one there to tell them when to show up at their desks. They are the ones to set their own challenges. They have to be highly disciplined and cannot afford to be messy." Cheever looks exasperated.

Many writers, Cheever explains, are self-destructive because they deal with imponderable, intangible, perilous matters. His own life had been somewhat hell-bent on destruction, but he seems to have recovered his equilibrium. Still, he doesn't like to discuss his past drug addiction: "I wouldn't dream of writing under the influence of drugs or alcohol. I wouldn't dream of going into the room where I work unless I was very level headed. Faulkner drank near the end and it seems to me that you can tell. You can practically smell the whiskey and bourbon on Faulkner's worst work."

Another New Englander, Henry David Thoreau, once asked, "How can I sit down to write when I've not yet stood up to live?" John Cheever doesn't feel that he's missed out. "I feel I've given up nothing," he says forcefully. "Writing has heightened my life, has brought me reason and the fragrance of common sense. I don't see myself as a shut-in or a sedentary person."

Interview with John Cheever
Compiled by James Valhouli/1977

Reprinted by permission of James Valhouli.

On December 2, 1977, John Cheever gave a reading at
Bradford College. Beaming with good health and humor,
he read two of his favorite stories, "The Swimmer" and
"The Death of Justina." Following his reading, he talked
casually about his writing, his career, his recent novel,
Falconer, and art in general. In the brief dialogue that
ensued, Mr. Cheever answered various questions posed
by students, faculty, and friends from the reading community at large. The following is a transcription of some of
those questions and answers.

Q. Hearing you read has been a delight, and it has added an
additional dimension to your writing. Do you enjoy reading your
stories?

A. I regarded reading with utter contempt until last year. When I
agreed to read in the past, and I did it once a year, I used to get part
drunk and gesticulate wildly. I always knocked the water pitcher or
the glass on the floor half way through the first page. I regarded
anyone who bothered to dress to come out in the evening to hear
anyone read as an absolute cretin. Within the last year, it suddenly
occurred to me that I was dependent on my readers as much as they
were and are dependent on me. Writing is very much like a kiss. It's
something you can't do alone. I've come to enjoy reading immensely.

Q. How have critics interpreted either or both the stories you read
today?

A. The interpretations of "The Swimmer" have always fascinated
me. There is the Freudian interpretation that the swimming pool is
Jocasta and this is his mother that Neddie Merrill is completely

148

raping. The mythological interpretation makes Neddie Narcissus pursuing his image from pool to pool. There are countless interpretations, and they go on and on. Actually, it's quite simple: "I like to swim."

Q. You've been writing for nearly half a century and you have published a great deal. Can you say something about how you see yourself as a writer in relationship to other people?

A. I'm deep into writing now. I've been fortunate enough to make it my profession. People who cannot make it their profession also make a tremendous contribution. Writing is not a competitive sport, and the successful novel is never really successful or triumphant. In my particular generation, and I include writers like John Updike and Saul Bellow who are dearest of friends, we don't cut one another's throats, as Faulkner and Hemingway used to. It is very much the sense that whatever John Updike does marvelously helps *me* along towards understanding my own life, and whatever I do, John is grateful to me. The same thing is true of Saul. People who write in their spare time and who keep journals all share in their universality and their consciousness some concern for the welfare of the commonwealth and the welfare of men and women in general. Sometimes failures are, in a sense, more successful than best sellers.

Q. Could you describe your average writing day?

A. I don't have an "average" day anymore than anyone else does. When I'm working intensely, I can work from eight 'til around two, then I do something physical—ski, swim. I worked that way on *Falconer* for about eight months. I go out of town once a month for about three days to visit another part of the States or the world. That was pretty regular. I always work in the morning. Saturday morning, I look at my mail and Sunday morning, I go to Holy Eucharist. The rest of the week, I work. As a writer, you have to discipline yourself.

Q. Do you have a ritual that you follow in your writing?

A. I keep a journal—this is something I insist on from my own students. I keep a journal every day of the year. This is partly, I think, because I come from a seafaring family. My grandfather went around the Horn. He kept a ship's log. My father was a catboat sailor, but he also kept a log. The logs are fairly open. They always begin, as most journals do, with the weather, prevailing winds, ruffles of the sails. They also include affairs, temptations, condemnations, libel, and occasionally, obscenities. Keeping a journal is particularly important now that I have gotten older and the vividness of things passes and doesn't return to me as quickly as it used to. There are three things that I insist on from my students: (1) that they have one language other than English; (2) that they can read music; and (3) that they keep a journal through the entire year, with the exception of Christmas and New Year. A journal is a valuable measure of yourself.

Q. How do you use your journals?

A. I might go back two-three weeks to examine a line I have heard spoken, to see my response to a distant light, a keen fragrance. I didn't use my journals as much when I was younger as I do now. I'd recommend keeping a journal to anyone who's interested in writing.

Q. Have you written any poetry?

A. No. The disciplines for poetry and the novel, the short story, seem to be vastly different. The impact of the word in prose is so unlike that in poetry.

Q. Can you say something about the composition of *Falconer* and how you went about imagining yourself a prisoner?

A. I'm glad you asked that. Confinement is something that has always concerned me—it still concerns me. I taught at Sing Sing for a couple of years, so I am familiar with the environment, the smell, the touch of prison. I'm also very familiar as a man, I think most of us are, with being confined in stuck elevators, particularly in countries where you can't speak the language. If you yell "help!" they don't know what you're talking about. Being confined in transit areas and airports; being confined in love affairs that are mistaken—that you can't see any way out of them; being confined in indebtedness; being confined in bank statements—there're all sorts of confinements. I'm also familiar with the vision of leading another kind of life. Confinement and freedom is very much like Good and Evil and, to use a marvelous new metaphor we have now, it's like gravity and weightlessness. I have written about confinement in the past. In the *Wapshot* novels, it is confinement of the provincial village. In the suburban stories, it is the confinement of an improvised society. I expect I will write about freedom and confinement 'til the day I die.

Q. Can you elaborate on what you mean by freedom?

A. We all must know what it means to love and to be loved, to live in peace—that's what I mean.

Q. What has been your most satisfying achievement in your writing career?

A. There are about twenty stories that I was terribly happy about. I was very happy when I finished *Falconer*. I was very happy when I finished *Bullet Park*. I was suicidal when I finished the *Scandal*. It's always quite a strain.

Q. How do you see the state of fiction at the moment? Is the novel really dead?

A. One leaves "the death of the novel" to bores! Everyone who is familiar with the medium knows how it counts on iridescence for its vitality. It's one of those forms of communication that is constantly dependent on the power to relive its courage. American literature is in marvelous condition. It's robust. It's healthy. It's also enviably read all over the world.

Q. Why did you choose writing as your vocation?

A. It's the thing that I could do best. It's the thing that 'made the most sense out of my life. And now that I've gotten quite old, it seems to me a marvelous occupation. It's really the most acute and intimate means of communication we have. It's a way in which we expess to one another loneliness, the need for love, courage, all sorts of imponderables that we have no other way to communicate to one another. It's also the only means of communication that we have that is judged entirely on merit—absolutely the only one.

Q. You have published nearly two hundred short stories. Have you followed any particular principle of aesthetics or composition?

A. The short story is as fluid as your life. The only canon of aesthetics that I regard seriously is interest. If a story is interesting, then it is worth reading—and of course—writing.

John Hersey Talks with John Cheever
John Hersey/1977

John Cheever is the author of the recent bestseller *Falconer.* He has written several volumes of short stories and three other novels, including *The Wapshot Chronicle,* for which he won the 1958 National Book Award. As a teacher, he has worked at the Iowa Writers' Workshop and at Sing Sing Prison in New York. John Hersey, Pulitzer Prize-winning novelist, has just published his twentieth book, *The Walnut Door.* He served as Master of Pierson College from 1965 to 1970 and is Adjunct Professor of Writing at Yale. He interviewed John Cheever in July under the sponsorship of the Yale Summer Term.

I'd like to talk first to you, John, about some of the things behind the work—matters of education, family, experience, and so on—that have given you the resources you've dealt with so well. You're one of the best educated men, to say nothing of writers, that I know. But you are a paradigm of the man of letters who is unspoiled by higher education. You raise the question in our minds whether writers should go to school at all. Your formal, or institutional, education was broken off when you were bounced from Thayer Academy at the age of seventeen. I wonder if you'd like to begin by telling us about that experience?

I was delighted to be expelled from Thayer. It was not unreasonable on their part. They would have liked very much for me to go to Harvard, and I sensed intuitively that that would have been disastrous. So I was very happy when the headmaster threatened me with expulsion, and I immediately went home and wrote an article for *The*

New Republic, called "Expelled," which *The New Republic* published. I was seventeen when it was published, and I was very happy about it.

What was the immediate cause of your expulsion?
Smoking, an expulsion offense.

Who caught you? Were you caught with the crime blazing?
I was caught by a teacher.

Was it exciting?
It was intentional, John.

Your own written voice is so strong that it's hard to find allusion or influences in it, but one can't read many pages in your work without running across a mythological figure—Actaeon, Daphnis, Cassiopeia, Artemis. What gave you the love of the classics?
I expect a good deal of it was that I was brought up in Quincy, Massachusetts, in the twilight of Athenian Boston. There was a great deal of cultural activity, all of it quite genuine, none of it pretentious—at least in recollection. Any preciseness in my prose style I like to attribute to my father, or to the fact that I come from a seafaring family. They all kept journals or ships' logs, and it seems to me that the laconism of New England is quite useful.

Can you tell us more about your father?
My father came from Newburyport. Whether or not he was an adequate father is something that has been thrashed over on psychiatrical couches for years. No conclusions have been reached. His concern for sartorial preciseness was exhaustive. He took a cold bath every morning at six, howling like a walrus, and dressed and went to business. He had a small shoe factory in Lynn. Psychiatrically, our relationship was never in any way consummated, but he did leave me his journal, which I used in a novel of mine called *Wapshot Chronicle.* So we achieved the kind of thing that I think writing can attain, which is a profound and a posthumous peace.

What about your grandparents? As I remember, your grandmother was one who read to you when you were small.
Yes, I had an English grandmother who read, I think, the complete works of Dickens to me and used to correct my pronunciation, which

was Massachusetts. She said, "Did you have a good time?" I said, "An awful good time." And then she would say, "A *very* good time," and I would say, "No, it was really an awful good time." She was quite rigid.

Let me read about a family from a Cheever story. "The branch of the Pommeroys to which we belong was founded by a minister who was eulogized by Cotton Mather for his untiring abjuration of the Devil. The Pommeroys were ministers until the middle of the nineteenth century, and the harshness of their thought—man is full of misery, and all earthly beauty is lustful and corrupt—has been preserved in books and sermons. The temper of our family changed somewhat and became more light-hearted, but when I was of school age, I can remember a cousinage of old men and women who seemed to hark back to the dark days of the ministry and to be animated by perpetual guilt and the deification of the scourge. If you are raised in this atmosphere—and in a sense we were—I think it's a trial of the spirit to reject its habits of guile, self-denial, taciturnity and penitence." Does this describe at all the family in which you grew up?

Yes, it does. Of course I am describing a character in fiction, and any confusion between autobiography and fiction is lamentable. The darkness—the capacity for darkness that was cherished by New England—certainly colored our lives. My father used to point to his veins and say, "There is nothing in these veins but the blood of shipsmasters and schoolteachers." As a matter of fact, he had a couple of old cousins who were obviously native Indians. I don't know how he included them. The Cheevers, I believe, did marry Indians.

Could you talk about your childhood?

How truthfully or how persuasively, I don't know. I recall it as having been extremely sunny. This may be a reaction to the tradition of the novelist as being a man who had a wretched childhood, an even worse adolescence, and spent the rest of his life trying in some way to rectify these injuries—something one would not want to encourage. My recollections of childhood are of the Cape and of southern Massachusetts. All seemed quite pleasant. The traumatic years that I went into in psychoanalytical conversations dealt with my adolescence, and with the fact that my parents separated. My brother and I became extremely close—morbidly close, it seemed to me. It was a very intense relationship in traditional Boston which was, at that point, so anxious to fortify its own eccentricities that anything so peculiar as two brothers who were inseparable was greeted enthusiastically. It seemed to me that two men living with such intense intimacy was an ungainly arrangement, that there was some immutable shabbiness about any such life. He was a cotton textile manufacturer, and I was to be the novelist. At the age of nineteen we traveled in Europe together, and then I walked, so far as possible, out of his life.

The brother figure in your work, certainly in Falconer, *is one who suffers at the hand of the narrator. And yet you were very close to this brother.*

I don't suppose that I have ever known a love so broad as my love for my brother. I've known loves that are much more enduring, much richer, much more brilliant, much more rewarding. But this seems to have been a very basic love. The brother theme appears in a great many stories. I strike him in some, I hit him with sticks, rocks; he in turn also damages me with profligacy, drunkenness, indebtedness, and emotional damage. And in *Falconer,* the brother is killed. There are, of course, historical precedents: Osiris and Set in Egypt; Cain and Abel; the Dioscuri in Rome. So that the brother theme, though it is not one of the dominating themes in literature, has some universality.

A minute ago, you said, "I strike my brother." How close are you to your narrator?

It seems to me that any confusion between autobiography and fiction debases fiction. The role autobiography plays in fiction is precisely the role that reality plays in a dream. As you dream your ship, you perhaps know the boat, but you're going towards a coast that is quite strange; you're wearing strange clothes, the language that is being spoken around you is a language you don't understand, but the woman on your left is your wife. It seems to me that this not capricious but quite mysterious union of fact and imagination one also finds in fiction. My favorite definition of fiction is Cocteau's: "Literature is a force of memory that we have not yet understood." It seems to me that in a book that one finds gratifying, the writer is able to present the reader with a memory he has already possessed, but has not comprehended. Does that make sense?

It does in terms of the relationships we've been talking about—father/son, brother/brother, and so on. The father/son theme occurs again and again very strongly in your work, and occasionally the mother appears in a vivid way. What about your own mother?

Here again, John, it was a relationship that I was able superficially to requite. I was correct. I visited both my parents four times a year until they died. My father asked that I read Prospero's speech over his grave, which I did. It was not requited in any way in the sense that my relationship, and my wife's relationship, is to our children. It was never intimate, but it seems not to have been destructive. The psychiatrist, of course, disagrees with me.

What about some relationships with others whom you encountered in early years, who may have been proxies for parents or teachers?

The generosity I received—it seems to me that the generosity most people will receive as young men and women—is inestimable. Malcolm Cowley singled the article "Expelled" out of a pile of unsolicited manuscripts and sent me a telegram, which was exciting. And now, at sixty-five, I trust I can do something of that sort for the young.

You encountered some older writers when you went to New York, did you not?

Yes, I think I was perhaps the only man in the northeast who talked with Sherwood Anderson. E.E. Cummings was a dear friend. I met him when I was eighteen, loved him immediately, and very much love his memory. Dos Passos I knew, and thought him rather dull, but pleasant. Edmund Wilson I met again and again, and we both detested one another. Cummings was very exciting and very helpful. I was in the army for four years, in an infantry company, and got a letter from him which included a ten-dollar bill, an autumn leaf, and the line, "I too have slept with someone else's boot in the corner of my smile."

You were living, certainly in no affluence, in New York in the thirties. Some of your acquaintances were very political people, and you had some experience of the Second World War. Yet one doesn't

*feel the wind, in your work, of the kinds of literary influences that
politics brought to bear on much of the writing in the thirties, and that
the war brought on much subsequent writing.*

On the political matter in the thirties, it seemed to me that the
Communist Party attempted to take over, to direct, writing. This was
very serious. People—Newton Arvin, for example, who was a friend
and a very good critic—decided that the only literature was the
literature that would provoke social change. This struck me as being
rubbish. And then, when I was perhaps twenty, I was singled out by
Marxist critics in *New Masses* magazine as the final example of
bourgeois degeneration. This more or less closed any political relationships with the Communist Party. On the war—I have written
about it, but very little. My feeling was, when I found myself in the
particular chaos of the infantry, that there must be deeper, richer
strata to life. There are, of course.

And what about your life with Mary? Your family life?

I claim to have been married for forty years. My wife claims, I
think, thirty-five. It's been an enormously rich, various experience.
We've thought of divorcing once a month, at least, over these forty
years. Perhaps the most exciting thing in life for me has been the
birth of my children. In interviews people always say, "Well, what was
the most exciting thing in your life?" And I say, "The birth of my
children." And they say, "Well then, after that?" The amount of
richness that children bring into the lives of their parents is indescribable. I've never been rich. When I wanted to be a writer my parents
said, "Well, you may be a writer,"—this is again the voice of New
England—"so long as you don't pursue fame or wealth." And I said,
"Well, I have no idea of being famous or wealthy"—an idea I've
often regretted.

*For me, one of the things that makes your work so moving and
powerful is a sense of tension which is very complex and seems to
produce an immense, sometimes oppressive, yearning on the part of
many characters. Some of the tensions that I think of are between the
ideal of voyaging and stasis; enlarging and diminishing; nostalgia and
the sense of the present moment; pleasure and pain; confinement
and freedom; light and dark; love and carnal knowledge; and
obviously life and death. And I'd like to ask you about some of them.*

Nostalgia is the word that strikes me most strongly. I woke—

yesterday morning, I suppose—with the sense of one of those landscapes that we all so richly know, and that we all so richly love. It was a field, some trees, a stone wall, which had not been denied to me, but which I hadn't quite achieved. The sense of nostalgia is very much a part of my life and, when a book is widely accepted, I assume a part of the reader's life. That one is in conflict with oneself—that one's erotic nature and one's social nature will everlastingly be at war with one another—is something I am happy to live with on terms as hearty and fleeting as laughter. These conflicts—between love and death, youth and age, war and peace—are simply that vast vocabulary we use for the divisions in life. And it seems to me that literature is the best way we have to refresh this conflict, to embrace it, to admit it into our lives.

In "Goodbye, My Brother," the husband and wife go to a costume party at a club. She dresses as a bride, he as a football player. They discover, to their amusement at first, that there are a dozen women who come as brides, and enough football players to have a good scrimmage. Do you see nostalgia as a reaching back? As a wish for a past in exchange for a present that's less pleasant?

That would be, I think, much more regressive than nostalgia. Nostalgia is the longing for the world we all know, or seem to have known, the world we all love, and the people in it we love. Nostalgia is also a passion, a longing not only for that which is lost to us, or which has been destroyed or burned, or which we've outgrown; it is also a force of aspiration. It is finding ourselves not in the world we love, but knowing how deeply we love it, enjoying some conviction that we will return, or discover it, or discover the way to it.

In a story about a well-digger named Artemis, you say his drill "struck the planet sixty blows a minute." And that trivial activity of trying to find water for one house begins to have music of stars in it because you've enlarged it by that one strange choice of the word "planet." There are other characters, though, who seem to make things smaller. "The seraphic look she assumed when she was listening to music was the look of someone trying to recall an old phone number."

I think one has a choice, with imagery, either to enlarge or to diminish. At this point I find diminishment despicable. When I was a younger man I thought it brilliant. But as a mature novelist I think one's responsbility is to perhaps get a few more details in and come out with a somewhat larger character. Chekhov, in his journals, urges the writer to know as much as he possibly can about a character—his shoe size, his liver condition, any tendency he might have to lordosis, his lungs, clothes, habits, intestinal tract—and then, from this glossary, to pick one detail. It is a judgment of character by a single attribute.

On pleasure and pain. You once said to me that you had no memory of pain, but you have, at any rate, a clear memory of pleasure. You see your characters, time and again, responding almost ecstatically to things around them, even when the general situation of their lives may be quite terrible.

That has been my experience.

These are memories?

In Bulgaria, where we were recently, someone said, "You are a naive optimist." Of course, it's a very general term—one I would qualify—but I would be quite happy to be classified, in Bulgaria, as a naive optimist.

Finally, there is the tension between light and dark. The sky appears in almost every one of your stories, usually with a vivid sense of welcome. It's terribly important in Falconer, *that little patch of sky that's seen outside the prison windows.*

Light is very important to me, very important to my moods. Blue sky. I always go back to William James, of course. A blue sky is quite mysterious, mysteriously heartening, a source of indescribable joy. Light and dark, very loosely of course, mean good and evil. And one is always seeking to find out how much courage, or how much intelligence, or how much comprehension, one can bring to the choice between good and evil in one's life.

One of the most exciting things to me, in having followed your work over the years, has been the occasional leap you take—as if the force of gravity releases you from time to time. You did it in Bullet Park, *and now in* Falconer. *Is this partly because of external experiences?*

It seems to me that writing is always in the nature of an adventure, and that one never wants to repeat oneself. A novel means a newness. It is a discovery. Every good novel takes the great chance of an explorer. You find out not only how far you can go, but how far your reader can go with you. How far you can go and still give to the experience its universality. One is walking in the dark. And in a sense the reader shares this. No one really knows how its going to come out. If it is successful, it is that shared memory which, up until this point, none of us comprehended.

Could it be that the heart attacks you had some years ago, and your struggle with drinking and triumph over that in your life, were realized in the kind of leap that Falconer *has achieved?*

Obviously there's a connection. I resist admitting it because this puts the novel into an autobiographical context. I had started to write *Falconer* when I was in Boston, when I was drunk and drugged much of the time, putting hats on the statuary on Commonwealth Avenue, and so forth. However, I did not complete the novel until I had some rather grueling experiences in both alcohol and drug withdrawal, and I was delighted to be free. That, obviously, is part of the book. I'm very reluctant to admit it because I would not want the novel to be thought an account of Cheever's escape from a rehabilitation center. I wanted to write as dark and as radiant a book as possible. I didn't know that the hero would get out of prison until I was about halfway through. I came running out of the house and shouted, "He's going to get out. Hey! Hey! He's going to get out." I was probably convinced that he was going to escape before I started, but it was at some more obscure stratum of my intelligence. I wanted to write about confinement.

An Interview with John Cheever

Jacqueline Tavernier-Courbin and R.G. Collins/1978

Reprinted from *Thalia: Studies in Literary Humor*, 1978, pp. 3–9, by permission of Jacqueline Tavernier-Courbin.

Eds: Much of the theorizing about narrative fiction seems to have included acceptance of a *basic* tie one way or another, between fiction and comedy or humor. Do you see such a connection?

JC: I can't offhand think of a piece of fiction in the history of literature, beginning with the classics, that doesn't use comedy and humor at one time or another. With the exception, of course, of the Greek dramatists. No, of course, they use humor, too. No, I can't think of anything in literature that doesn't rely on humor for some force of emphasis.

Eds: Do you think there's a foundation in what might loosely or generally be called our conception of life that involves humor, comedy? Some basic conception of life that manifests itself as humor or comedy, which underlies fiction, as opposed to, say, high drama or philosophy, in a general sense?

JC: Well, first, as to philosophy and the sort of fiction I work in. It seems to be a sameness, but of course vastly different. The kind of fiction I do is an improvization and has, since its beginnings, been an improvization; and philosophy, of course, is a series of systems. I don't have any general or absolute theories on fiction at all, beyond the first canon of aesthetics being *interest*. Fiction is obviously one aspect of life that I associate with newness, with light; and in fiction one tries to have fiction play the same role in a narrative that it plays in one's life, in short. I shall read this evening from a story in which I use very loose reference to *The Divine Comedy*, describing a supermarket in which people are the Damned. In the middle of the paragraph—this is not calculated at all, it's simply instinctive—I describe one of the shoppers as, speaking of himself, a native American wearing buckskin jump boots, pants, chino pants cut tight

161

enough so that his sexual organs are discernible, and a rayon acetate pajama top printed with the Santa Maria and the Nina in full sail. All this is not thrown in as a calculated laugh. It *is* a laugh and it is meant, of course, to suspend briefly the realization of the fact that the description of the supermarket is meant to refer to eternal damnation.

Eds: You speak of improvization there almost as a synonym for the craft of fiction, as though it were a searching after life in all kinds of situations. Is that true?

JC: Yes, that's as I see it, yes.

Eds: Do you, then, consider your earlier writing to be substantially different from the latest works?

JC: Oh yes, yes. As I am now, of course, very unlike the young man I was.

Eds: Well, given that difference in the observations you made about improvization, do you think, then, that fiction is the record of sensibility and time in some kind of fixed sense, let's say, as well as in an inevitably changing sense? That is, is there an underlying similarity of self, despite constant change?

JC: Well,there's certainly a sameness of purpose, yes. I write at sixty-six with precisely the same purpose as I did at 16 which, of course, is to make some sense of my life and perhaps to assist other people in making sense of their lives as fiction had helped me or continues to help me. To make my life useful and coherent. It is, of course, triumphant, the writing of fiction. It seems to me very close to the triumph over chaos.

Eds: So that each story you write or a situation that you develop is a series of assaults upon and triumph over some kind of disorder.

JC: Yes, it is to clarify. Yes.

Eds: In the *Newsweek* article which appeared last week, you justified the short story on what I understand to be different territorial ground from that of the novel. In doing so, you mentioned its versatility or flexiblity in dealing with the new or perhaps even the currently fashionable. Could this also be a problem or perhaps even a weakness of the short form? The fact that, at least as you speak of it in this particular essay, it has different things to do, or has different capacities than the novel?

JC: Well, it seems to me the short story's as determined as the novel and as poetry, as I understand it. Its length or its shape—I think of a piece of fiction as possessing shape—is determined by the impulse to create. I did speak of the short story as being suited to experience that is episodic and characterized by its episodic nature, its intensity and very often its interruptive quality. I do think the short story is very good at that. It can also encompass very often a much broader territory than you find a mediocre novel. I think, for some reason, of De Maupassant's "Boule de Suif" which is thought to be a short story.

Eds: The novel itself is turning very much, or at least some writers of the novel are turning very much, to a borderline fiction by the use of thinly disguised history. What do you think of that sort of thing?

JC: I feel very strongly that fiction is not cryptoautobiography, nor is it ever current history. One of the glories of fiction, it seems to me, is the inestimable force of memory that is brought to bear in the description of a single scene. When people say "Was that your mother?" it strikes me as comical. The character may have had, perhaps, a ring my mother wore, but the character also has a voice that I overheard in a Vienna airport. I will have a woman, perhaps, whose letters I read, that were written a hundred years ago. I seems to me in fiction one completely transcends autobiography and current history. Cocteau, I believe, said that fiction is a force of memory that is imperfectly understood and it is very much profound, an expression of some profound aspect of the subconscious. The glory of it is, of course, that it is shared strata of memory, which is why one's works can be translated into Bulgarian or Latvian and understood.

Eds: You speak of "intensity" there with respect to the short story. As you say that, I find myself struck very much by its appropriateness the short story. Do you think, in that sense, that the short story is a kind of ideal module for fiction? Without, of course, the advantages of looseness of the novel but. . . .

JC: I don't quite know what you mean by "module."

Eds: Well, in the intensity of characters. The intensity of character you spoke of as related to the short story. One would think, from the outside at least, that the artist has the opportunity to do something that the looseness of novel does not encourage in the same sense. There might seem to be here a possibility for pursuing the art at least for short bursts in a way that the novel does not encourage, as I say, because of the demands the longer form has.

JC: Yes, well, the word "bursts" is very well taken. That is precisely what a short story is. It is a burst. And to use, for example, a burst in a novel is to destroy the architecture of the novel, of course. The intensities of the novel, of course, all have to be interrelated, all the way through the novel. If you had a successful, as you say, *burst* in a novel, people would then close the novel and think—why should I read any further.

Eds: Well, with reference to this, the short story, I think some people would say, has seen better days in terms of public acceptance, given the fact that there were formerly far more popular outlets for it. Today, authors seem reduced to only a few, such as *The New Yorker,* and *Esquire,* occasionally. Is there something about its very quality that makes the short story genre vulnerable?

JC: Well, literature, of course, is vulnerable. That, of course, is the sense of it. That is the source of its strength. I've said that the death of the novel is the concern only of bores, that anyone knowledgeable knows that the forms of both the short story and the novel count for their vitality on their iridescence. Their life has always been precarious and, has been, I think, since the earliest of the bards. I don't think there's been any noticeable decline either in the short story or the novel. You mentioned Flannery O'Connor at lunch. I think she's one of the greatest short story writers we've ever had. Italo Calvino, in Italy, from time to time turns out an extraordinarily brilliant short story. Yuri Trifinov, in Russia, is now a very good short story writer. Actually, the field has never had hundreds of people. There was a very happy period in my life when Nabokov, Irwin Shaw and Mary McCarthy, Jean Stafford, J.D. Salinger were all turning out something like seven short stories a year, which was very good. That we seem to have passed out that period I don't think involves a decadence. I'm sure there will be happy, or as happy, or even happier years ahead of us.

Eds: You don't really, then, take personally your own reference to your collected stories as a lemon on the lists of book publishers this year.

JC: Well, no, that was put down, I thought, with conspicuous irony.

Eds: Yes.

JC: It is on all the best-seller lists, of course. Which is also very heartening to me . . . and for the short story. It's the first time that a short story collection has been on the best-seller list. I'm not speaking of the merits of my work, I'm simply speaking of the merits of the form. It's been a major choice of the Book of the Month Club, and I'm absolutely convinced that it will, for example, outstrip some of the bulkier pieces of rubbish that customarily repose as number one on the best-seller list. And I'm very pleased with this, of course, quite selfishly and also unselfishly, because it seems to verify the merit of the form.

Eds: Why are publishers reluctant to invest in short story collections?

JC: Quite simply, they feel they don't sell.

Eds: Why do you suppose they don't? Given the fact that, as you say, and I think quite accurately, the short story has flexibility to a degree that is remarkably satisfactory in its effect.

JC: Well, I think people feel they belong in periodicals and, of course, periodicals in the United States have suffered terribly in the last 15 or 20 years. Some of this is, I think, quite unnecessary. The marvelous thing is that the reading public completely escapes any survey, any computer analysis. Nobody knows who they are, or where they are, or how numerous they are, and publishers are *always* astonished when a serious novel sells something like 400,000 copies in hardcover. It seems to me that they are surprised much more often than they are willing to admit, because to anticipate accurately is an exercise of taste. And since publishers are in merchandising, they don't rely on their tastes; they lack the courage, it seems to me, to take advantage of serious fiction. I do feel that some readers—and here again I say the reader is totally unknown—would sooner read the short story in a periodical. When they invest money in a book, they like to feel they can read uninterruptedly until the ending, whenever it is.

Eds: Going back to the question of intensity, and bursts, or whatever, that you've pointed out with respect to the short story, do you think there's anything there that is particularly suitable to humor, or comedy, as content?

JC: I really can't answer that. I don't think of form as being particularly suitable to humor or comedy. I think of literature entirely as a means of communication. Perhaps the the most intimate and acute means of communication we possess. But it would be very unlike me, not in my wildest dreams, would I break it down into aspects of humor or tragedy.

Eds: You speak, I think, in your *Newsweek* essay also of *story,* as such. . . .

JC: Narrative, I think.

Eds: . . . as surviving in literature, while other arts—painting and so on—dissolve into parallel modes of order, and I think you said that you'll fight to the end to preserve stories?

JC: With my life, yes. I think this is terribly important, because, talking as I sometime do with painters, I say, you know—well, the protrait, the still life, or the landscape—and particularly the nude— are still very deeply a part of our dreams; and you've lost them, and thus you've lost the ability to correspond to our dreams, to appeal to us at that particular level of profundity. And they usually, if they're intelligent or sympathetic, will exclaim: "You miss the nude, think how *we* miss the nude! How alienated we feel without this whole area of communication." Well, in fiction we still have the traditional nature of the language. The language we use to express the pain of love or death is precisely the same language we use, of course, to buy groceries or airplane tickets. It is a practical means of communi- cation. Experiments in language, I think, are, in general, failures. I think invariably failures. So that we have the traditionalism of the language and the element of cause and effect in narrative. It needn't be conspicuous but, as I said, the principal canon, the first canon, of aesthetics is interest. And cause and effect is inevitably involved.

Eds: Do you think that basic plot, then, of a fairly predictable sort is apt to lie underneath most successful fiction? Allowing, of course, for the differences, the flesh on the bone, so to speak, of the individual writer?

JC: You'll have to give me that again.

Eds: Speaking of story. Do you think that basic plot of a fairly predictable sort. . . .?

JC: Well, of course, fiction shouldn't be predictable. If it is predictable, then it is contrived. The imagination of the reader is superior to that of the writer, and then we have a failure.

Eds: So in other words, there is always shock, or reversal, or perhaps delight?

JC: Delight, yes.

Eds: Let's go into language now, from the question of story. Most humor of the intellect seems to be based on a play of words or images or whatever, including what we call wit, of course. That shock of delight that comes from the unexpected but nonetheless startlingly appropriate joining of certain words or ideas. You do this frequently in your own writing. How conscious is it for a writer, for you, say? What I'm talking about, I suppose, is the consciousness of style.

JC: Some humor, of course, depends entirely on style. This . . . I suppose, we're speaking not here of humor but of wit, which seems to be virtually a style . . . I'm very careful. I knew Dorothy Parker, and she seemed to be a very good example, conversationally, of that wit that is basically founded on destruction. Her cut was always acid and always diminished the situation. That was basically her premise. A contemporary of Dorothy Parker's, a quite serious novelist named Dawn Powell, her humor was, I think, quite as sharp as Parker's. But she was actually more creative than Parker. Here, again, it was entirely a question of style and word play. When I was a very young man I went to a party. Archibald MacLeish was there. He was leaving for the Pacific, and in those days the trip was thought to be quite hazardous, and we were all wishing Archie—I believe I was 19 years old—we were all wishing Archie a good journey and a safe journey, and so forth. As he went out the door, Dawn, who was rather a small woman—she described herself as "pretty little Dawn Powell"—said "Archie, Archie," and he said "Yes Dawn?" and she said "Don't take any wooden pillows." It struck me as being a precise use of word play and wit, but it was amiable. In a way that Parker was not.

Eds: Interesting, because Parker, of course, we associate with the Algonquin Wits. And the question of datedness comes to mind immediately when you say that. People such as Robert Benchley. Is there something built into that?

JC: In that particular period?

Eds: Yes.

JC: I think not. No, I think we'll have it again. Parker was a very stylish humorist. She was superb actually, but it was partly delivery. She got lines off splendidly. But as I say it was always knocking out one of the legs of the table. It was always basically this—not malicious, destructive.

Eds: Is there something more social than individual about that? I mean, does it seem to relate more to lashing out at the world, perhaps, rather than actually addressing any individual?

JC: Well, in her case, it would seem to be constitutional. That's what she'd been brought up doing. Almost as if she'd been born doing it.

Eds: Another question or two on the business of humor. Social comedy seems to involve men in fairly normal *patterns* of behavior with others, however eccentric or outrageous a specific individual's character or personality or response might be. But the pattern which is involved is fairly much a question of normalcy. How would you compare this with black humor? Does that have a non-social, or anarchic, basis?

JC: I don't any any clear definition for black humor, actually.

Eds: Well, is there anything distinct you can see about it, as opposed to social comedy?

JC: Well, it seems to me, that social comedy is something we haven't enjoyed thoroughly since the end of the 18th century, really. It does, of course, involve social structure, which can endure attacks. Can you think of an example of social comedy in the last century?

Eds: Well, I suppose, people like Aldous Huxley. Even writers such as J.P. Marquand and . . .

JC: I don't think Marquand particularly estimable, and I think of Huxley never as a comedian.

Eds: Do you think there are any valid generalizations in terms of distinction wiith respect to the fiction of the 50s, 60s, & 70s?

JC: None. Absolutely none. I choose to think of fiction since its beginning as a kind of Bergsonian river with all its turns, profoundities, and depths and so forth. One to which one makes a contribution. It could be very small, or massive. It doesn't seem to make much difference so long as one's made a contribution, perhaps, to keeping up the quality of the stream.

Eds: Certain writers—Barth, Barthelme, Gass, writers who have emerged in the past 15 or 20 years—are being referred to as fabulists. I suppose there are some implications there of alternate worlds that are being created by them. Do you find the word *fabulist* or the underlying conception meaningful in any way?

JC: Not in the case—no, as a matter of fact, the word fabulist is a word that has almost no connotations for me. It is not in my vocabulary. On the work of Barth—with the exception of one story, involving a rather old-fashioned identity crisis in Pennsylvania Station—well, I care very little for his work. If you are interested in a humorous story: I was dining with Barth and Jean Stafford, and Jean said, drawing me aside, but not so far that Barth couldn't hear what she was saying: "John, your reputation in American literature is very, very shaky. God knows what will happen to it, but if you put a knife in his back, you will be immortal." Barthelme, I think, is a very brilliant man, and I think his work basically violates the kind of aesthetics which I consider to be interest. His readers seem quite swiftly bored.

Eds: How about Barthelme, who's even more—ah—unique?

JC: *Barthelme,* I was thinking of.

Eds: How about Barth himself?

JC: As a person?

Eds: No. I was thinking of his work.

JC: As a writer? I find him unsympathetic, as I say, with the exception of one story about a man losing his identity in Pennsylvania Station. I did not enjoy *The Sotweed Factor.* I think Barth, I may be incorrect here, is one of perhaps a dozen writers who've lived their life in an academic environment, who've been forced to teach to make a living and whose work is generally, it seems to me, enjoyed by their academic associates . . . they've got many of them. I was for awhile very enthusiastic about the work of Coover. Coover struck me as one of the few men—perhaps the only one—who could write an abstract line, that is a line that held my attention for as long as a page, during which I could not describe what was going on. But then he wrote a book on the Rosenbergs which I thought dreadful, and my interest in him has diminished. Gass, I think, is still a very useful and good critic, but I think his fiction is actually quite dull.

Eds: Going back to the question of academic entrapment of writers. You speak of Barth in this connection. Barth in *The Sotweed Factor* is writing a pseudo-eighteenth century novel . . .

JC: Yes.

Eds: . . . while Fowles in *The French Lieutenant's Woman* is writing a pseudo-Victorian novel. This technique of projection means kind of assuming a different identity almost before writing the novel. Do you find any part of such an approach to be valid, interesting?

JC: Well, it seems to me you ought to be aware of what has been done and that you're quite free to go back and exploit a method that was very generously invented for you perhaps a century earlier. The trifling example is that Thackeray, as far as I know, invented the invitation list, which was then picked up by Fitzgerald in *Gatsby*. It's perfectly beautiful. You can use an invitation list as a lyrical poem. A sort of evocation. I believe I've used it once or twice. That's simply a light skip-over. This is something that someone invented, and it seems to me it lies in the public domain, and so one helps oneself, from ancient and recent literature.

Eds: Moving around a little bit more: Looking back to a generation that preceded you—I'm thinking now of people such as Faulkner, Hemingway, Fitzgerald—what do you consider to be their mark as a generation, if there is one?

JC: It seems to me unfortunate that we should try classifying. It seems to me to be absurd. I can't imagine where the term "generation" came from. Faulkner, Hemingway and Fitzgerald were all roughly the same age, of course, but Fitzgerald died much sooner than the rest of them. But no generation seems to be . . . it almost seems to be bringing the terms of utensils into something as irregular and rich as the lives of men and women . . . generations, of course, have shared very general things. They were men, and, unfortunately, in all three cases they were suicides.

Eds: Yes, I suppose you're right. I've been doing quite a bit with Faulkner—that is, rereading him a lot, lately—and there does seem to be the reflection of a man looking at the world in all of his stories, or of men looking at the world from a more individual point of view than the writers I asked you about earlier—people such as Barth and Gass and Pynchon—and I suppose that is the origin of my question. But that in itself would, I suppose, be sufficiently explained by different lives, different times and . . .

JC: And different parts of the country in Faulkner's case, of course. Because not only of the Mississippi past, but the Mississippi cadence.

Eds: Do we have, by the way, anything which you can see that essentially represents something like an international novel, the sort that Hemingway wrote, say, or Faulkner in his early days?

JC: You mean international in its reception or international in its scope?

Eds: Well, perhaps both.

JC: Well, American fiction, of course, is greeted today with immense hospitality. John Updike's novels and mine, I suppose, go into 12 or 14 languages. I don't know which other writers this is true of. I know some of the commercial writers are not translated and one of them, Arthur Hailey I think, is his name—wrote a novel called *Airport*. It is not translated in some of the countries in which I've traveled. He travels with two secretaries, mistress, and so forth. In *grand luxe*. And keeps asking why his books aren't translated. It's because, of course, one likes to think those people are basically interested in serious literature. Oh, but I do think that Updike, for example, is translated into Korean, Japanese.

Eds: What do you find, in your traveling, most interests foreign readers of American literature?

JC: That's very hard to define. As a matter of fact, there are a multitude of things that interest them, of course. The crudest interest is of the United States as a very strange nation composed mostly of blacks or Indians or enormously wealthy and self-destructive people. That is, as a very strange creation. This is, I think, the most superficial sort of European reader. Then, beyond that, we have people who look for profound correspondences between American experience and theirs. This, of course, is a much more desirable reader. *The Wapshot Chronicle* and *The Wapshot Scandal* are extremely popular in Germany, for example. It's a sameness, I think, rather than an oddness. My last novel has been recently translated into French, and something like 90% of the French reviews roughly say "What's happened to Huckleberry Finn?" or "Where are the American Indians?" However, of course, there are half a dozen reviews that understand the novel at a serious level, as an experience that we might all share at one time or another.

Eds: Do you think there's a greater interest in American society as a society than there was when the French were reading Faulkner for his Gothic relationships or when Hemingway became as generally popular as he did in Europe, France, in particular?

JC: I've never read Hemingway in French. How does it read?

Eds: It reads well, actually.

JC: Of course, his English is harsh. Which we would lose in French. I was talking to a student yesterday about the Cubists. Of course he was associated with the Cubists, and that was an influence in his work. No one, of course, speaks in that simple way; it is not a speech.

Eds: No, of course. Do you find any difference, by the way, in the success your books seem to have in places like Russia or Bulgaria as opposed to—well, France, you've already distinguished, but let's say the other countries?

JC: I like to think that the interest is roughly the same. This may be self-deception. I always announce quite clearly—*Bullet Park* was very successful—this is not a work of social criticism, nor is any of my work intended to be social criticism. They seem quite sympathetic to the remark; and whether this is hypocrisy or not, I don't know. I do know that in the mail that I receive from Eastern Europe—I always cherish a letter from a small mountain town in Rumania where a woman wrote enthusiastically—I had to have the letter translated— complimenting me on describing one's response, the *power* of one's response to watching autumn leaves being driven through the head- lights of a car. It is that sort of thing, I think, that gives me the feeling that one is really operating at a much deeper level than political criticism. My work or a great deal of my work in this new collection of stories is quite apparently of subterranean *water,* with wells, with streams, with a search for water, and with a sound of rain, and the Russians perhaps because they were largely an agricultural nation until recently always are very sympathetic to the sound of rain. I like to think it's in such humble matters, humble and profound matters as that, that we're sympathetic.

Eds: Two final questions. First, what do you consider to be your best work to date?

JC: I don't assess my work. I can't think of any other writer who does.

Eds: Well, then, the final question. Do you have any sense of where you want to go in your writing, now? Is there a sense of future need, or activity, that you consciously have at this point?

JC: Yes. I would like, of course, one *always* likes, to do better. One of the great difficulties in assessing one's work—I find it very difficult to read my work—is that I think, "God, it isn't nearly as good as it should have been." Simply to do something that would be an improvement over what I've done. I can't really think of anything else.

Behind the Best Sellers: John Cheever

Herbert Mitgang/1979

Reprinted from the *New York Times Book Review,* 28 January
1979, p. 36, by permission of the publisher. Copyright © 1979
by The New York Times Company.

In the last of the 61 stories in *The Stories of John Cheever,* the
narrator says: "My real work these days is to write an edition of The
New York Times that will bring gladness to the hearts of men. How
better could I occupy myself? The Times is a critical if rusty link in my
ties to reality, but in these last years its tidings have been monoto-
nous. The prophets of doom are out of work."

The tidings are that Mr. Cheever's stories, published by Knopf,
have brought gladness to the hearts and minds of readers without
necessarily changing the headlines that drive us all mad. A little of the
world and what a writer can—or cannot—do about it creeped into
our conversation the other morning.

"I don't put politics into my stories. I don't possess an estimable
political sense. Of course I vote carefully. As a writer, I think there is a
difference between politics and literature. It seems to me that literature is a broader concern.

"I was not interested in prison reform when I wrote *Falconer*—all I
wanted to stress was the mysterious quality of one group of people
imprisoning another group. Prison reform, anyway, is too complex
and begins with the judiciary.

"In my stories, I also avoid anything that's primarily historical, such
as wars and depressions. In *The Wapshot Chronicle,* which spanned
40 years, I managed to skip two wars."

Didn't his own involvement in war get into stories?

"I served with a line rifle company, 22d Infantry, Fourth Division,
mostly in the South, then the Pacific, but never in combat. I did write
some Army stories, they appeared in my first collection, *The Way
Some People Live.* But they were embarrassingly immature, and I

have never gone back to wartime themes. None of those stories appears in this book."

The stories in this book, he notes in a preface, "seem at times to be stories of a long-lost world when the city of New York was still filled with a river life, when you heard the Benny Goodman Quartets from a radio in the corner stationery store, and when almost everybody wore a hat."

We talked about the fact that Cheever—like F. Scott Fitzgerald during the turbulent 1930's—has been criticized for not having characters engagé. Fitzgerald's high-hatted lovers did not bounce off the page one headlines; nor do Cheever's.

"I seldom go looking for a story—I don't research them. Journalism and literature are very different. I would rather be thought of · as writing about men and women. The soul of man doesn't need a locale. I'm fond of the degree of free will within an environment."

How do Cheever stories originate?

"I often try to put my experience in the form of a story that seems to illuminate. If people find it familiar, then there is illumination. Light is an image that I am very fond of. I literally try to put some of my characters in a strong light. Another image that I use a great deal is water. I come from a seafaring family. I went fishing yesterday out of New Rochelle, past the Narrows. You can catch a lot of fish out there, but not yesterday."

Both you and John Updike are longtime New Yorker writers. What is the difference between John Cheever and John Updike?

"Well, I'm 20 years older than John. I'll be 67 on May 27. Updike writes far more explicitly about sex, for one thing. Explicit sexual scenes don't particularly interest me. Everybody knows what's going on. I can't think, in the whole history of literature, of an explicit sex scene that was memorable, can you?"

What were the big Cheever themes?

"Love and death," he said, softly.

Conversations with John Cheever

Bruce Benidt/1978

Reprinted from the *Minneapolis Star*, 30 December 1978, pp. 9–12, by permission of the publisher.

The Hudson River broadens as the commuter train shudders its way up the east bank of the river toward the bedroom communities of Westchester County.

Left behind is the towering architecture of New York City, the constipated traffic, the strident cab drivers, the uniformed doormen at the Sutton Place apartments, the feeling of excitement around Broadway, the tawdry glow of Times Square, the sudden pause of Central Park.

The buildings dwindle, the population thins, the last ripples of the Appalachians end in palisade cliffs at the Hudson. The train runs north, past Tarrytown, once home of Washington Irving. It was his stories of New York and the Catskills that started the long flow of American literature.

Above Tarrytown, between the riverside hill towns of Ossining and Croton-on-Hudson, about an hour from Grand Central Station, lives John Cheever.

The train from New York moves through the landscape of Cheever's vision—the giant city, the suburban world from which commuters daily trek to work, and the open spaces where wind, water and light can dance through a person's senses and into his soul.

"It's perfectly all right," John Cheever is saying as I apologize for getting off at the wrong train station, Croton North instead of Croton. His laugh and his smile put me at ease.

This, then, is John Cheever, a renowned author of four novels and 40 years of short stories. A recently published collection of some of the best stories of his career, *The Stories of John Cheever,* has been received like a gift by the reading public.

175

And here he is, a small man in rather worn, comfortable clothing, by himself in a small car (a Volkswagen Rabbit) in a small town. No agents, no photographers, no feeling of celebrity. Just a winter day and a friendly and gracious man.

His voice still carries the gentlemanly tones of Quincy, Mass., where he was born and raised. His words, though, occasionally disintegrate into a grating cough as his throat recoils from nearly constant cigarette smoke.

As he drives through Ossining toward his house, he tells the history of what used to be a small river port but has since expanded with commuters and slums.

Here's where the whorehouses were; there, the hotel where people stayed when they visited famous gangsters in Sing Sing prison; here lived a purveyor of an all-purpose pill who named streets for his children, and there's the best view in town of the bluffs across the river. A guided tour from an author spinning tales.

Cheever talks almost tenderly about the town as it passes. The hills, the houses and the people are like books on a shelf to him. They're there to be studied, learned from, enjoyed, occasionally chuckled over. He says he likes this town because it lacks the pretense of other Westchester County enclaves.

People around his neighborhood don't fuss over him, he says. "I'm simply old Mr. Cheever on his bicycle or old Mr. Cheever with his dogs, which is precisely what one would want. I just don't have a job that keeps me on the trains."

In restaurants and other places around town, he is greeted and treated well, and some people look at him with interest. But, in his brown pullover sweater and rumpled corduroys, he blends in with the rest of the townspeople and goes on his way without interruption.

He is a great writer, but that shouldn't scare people away. His books and stories are not thick, heady, intellectual fare. They're deep, all right, like memories, if you want them to be. But it's as easy to read a John Cheever story as it is to walk across a meadow in July.

What makes Cheever important is that he is so good at making contact with the very human corners of us all. His writing so often touches a place in our own experience, makes us remember, perhaps helps us understand. He illustrates so well, so simply, our frailty and our power.

Cheever drives past a shopping center being built near the train
station, and laughs at the computer that chewed on income and
population figures and spit out a projected success here.

What the computer doesn't know, Cheever says with delight, "is
that the commuter is a totally driven creature. He gets off the train
and runs to his car and drives through rain and snow, through
stoplights and over people, to get home. And he's not going to stop
for a head of lettuce or a suit."

When he smiles, as now, his eyes sometimes have an almost
impish quality. Not self-conscious, just the look of a man who's
enjoying himself.

Although Cheever occasionally drops a sarcastic comment about
someone nearby, and although his writing sometimes shows the base
side of humanity, he is not a cynic or a misanthrope.

He says that even suburbia, which he sometimes draws with dark
shadings, can reflect the hopefulness of man. Even where the houses
are identical to start with, he says, people strive to improve their
places with landscaping and shrubs, by adding or subtracting something of their own. "Vulgarity is overwhelmed by invention," he says,
pleased by the thought.

Cheever's car climbs a hill, ducks under a bridge, rolls down a long
driveway, and we are in front of the house where he and his wife
have lived for 22 years.

The house was built in 1799, and was restored by a banker in the
1920s. Inscribed on the stone gateway leading to the house is
"Afterwhiles," named by a former owner. Cheever says he changed
the name to "Meanwhile."

The house has two fireplaces, two thick stone walls with beautiful
chimneys, a white oak-paneled library and a small oval of brass on
the door that says "Cheever."

Three golden retrievers, a bicycle, crosscountry skis, a couple of
good woodpiles and a red-and-black wool lumberjack cap are mixed
together on the long front porch. Around the house are stone
terraces decorated with wisteria, a brook, acres of hills, snow, trees
and a sky clear of tall buildings.

It's where a writer ought to live. Not a palace, but a place where an
author and his thoughts have a little room to wander. The location
was a compromise between Mary, his wife of 38 years who wanted

to live close to New York City, and John, who wanted more solitude. Although traffic from a nearby road can be heard, it is a good compromise.

The first order of the day's business is a walk with Cheever's dogs, Bathsheba, Maisie and Edgar. They are all rather gray in the muzzle, and they all love attention. Cheever wrestles lightly with them, talks things over with them, runs his hands through their oily coats. All three dogs are spayed females. The Cheevers can't keep male dogs because they would wander too close to the busy road, but Cheever has verbally changed the sex of one dog so he can have a male companion.

"I changed Edgar's name from Tara because I was an old man and I thought I ought to have a dog. And he's been very accommodating to me, urinates on trees and all that."

We walk off through the woods, dogs bounding around us, Edgar bent on carrying a tennis ball wherever he goes. Cheever talks easily about writing, about himself, his history, his excitements.

Cheever is an aging man with youth in his eyes, a man who listens to the past while he closely observes the present. His smile is real and comes from inside, and when he laughs the smile widens and nearly splits his face. His laugh starts slowly and low, and then accelerates in short bursts, bearing a great feeling of mirth.

In a short time, it becomes apparent that Cheever carries both joy and sadness with him, alternating like sunlight and dark under a cloud-scattered sky. He is an emotional man, an affectionate man, a man who could have been called sentimental before that word took on a pejorative tone.

He has known sadness and torment. He has suffered from tuberculosis and a failing heart. He has known the horror and despair of alcoholism, drugs, sexual depravity. "Very squalid," he says thinking back. Asked if that squalor makes the wind and the rain . . . "Much sweeter," he breaks in, and then his expressive eyes slip off into reverie. He mentions literary colleagues who have succumbed to whatever pressures bedeviled them and taken their own lives. He has had those thoughts, too.

"Regret, sadness are very much a part of my life," he says. But so is "the endless pursuit of summer which one carries on with a good deal of vitality."

His work, and his life, include both optimism and pessimism. "It's pretty much a Monday-Wednesday-Friday situation for us all, isn't it?

"I like to think, as my life is, that it's divided between the two. . . . One must weave the dark side of the street in with the sunny side in order to live a life of any stature."

Although his characters confront the raw material of despair, and react sometimes with self-destructiveness, his writing also tries to share the message that "usefulness in love and usefulness in one's work is what one pursues," and that "one can succeed in love and usefulness."

"Of course, the decline of the west is the easiest thing in the world to prove. But once that's shown, then we go on. One is alive, one can love, one is full of high spirits."

And the woods, just now, are full of light and cool clean air.

Cheever is only about 5-foot-6, but he walks with a stride that makes a 6-footer work to keep up. His ankle-high shoes crunch in the snow, and only when he slips do you remember he's 66 years old. He walks for miles, sometimes with his dogs, sometimes on longer walks, alone or with a friend.

While he walks, as while he does everything else, he's working on his writing. "One tries out word combinations or cadences, you know, when you walk."

And while he walks, he's pulling in his surroundings with all his senses. He sniffs at the world, listens to it, sucks it in with his eyes.

The woods that surround his house are research and relaxation to Cheever. He may not be able to address all the flora by Latin titles ("That's a red-berry bush over there.") but he knows intimately the quality of light that flitters through a beech tree or the shape of a pine formed by the north wind.

"I don't go into New York much. I'm not very comfortable there any more. So much of the light is gone. Light is very important."

A little brook flows through his front yard, and on the walk he follows it up through the hills to the pond where it rises. Water, carried by the thundering wind, curling explosively on the sand, confined seductively in a swimming pool, pouring like youth over a dam in the spring, is the fluid of his soul, the cradle of his memories.

(Taking me to a motel in town later, Cheever spies the Sheraton's swimming pool glimmering in a strange puddle of modern architec-

ture. The pool calls to him, the author of "The Swimmer." His eyes
are stuck on it, glowing. "You could swim there," he says with
thoughtful slowness. He has no pool himself, and swims at a
neighbor's pool in the summer, in exchange for a case of champagne.

(We go back to his house to pick up swimsuits. He circles to the
deep end of the pool and dives straight in. The water is warm, like
blood, like urine. "It's womblike," Cheever says, laughing. "I haven't
been in so much warm water since before I was born.")

Cheever is not a nature writer, but the exhilarating power of the
natural world is strong in his stories. He writes about facing a
morning wind laden with summer sounds and fragrances, and a
"grace of light (that) would make it an exertion not to throw out your
arms and swear exultantly. . . ."

Many of Cheever's stories tell of escaping the city for that special
province of summer. His characters flee New York to the shores of
the east, but they could as easily be leaving Minneapolis for the lake
cottage up north.

The tense dynamics of families pressed together in a summer cabin
for the specific purpose of having a good time and relaxing, and their
reactions as they brush against the wind and water of the season are
easily recognizable by any reader who was ever a child or a parent,
near a shore.

"Summer, of course, means paradise; it means youth. It's very
ancient. 'He leadeth me into green pastures.' " Cheever speaks with
soft excitement. "Summer is our sense of serenity, light, warmth.
Summer is when we fall in love. . . . Felicity and serenity are perhaps
the most fascinating ideas ever to cross one's mind." And they cross
Cheever's mind, and his pages, with tremendous grace.

Back at the house, the cleaning lady is gone and the smell of
ammonia, which Cheever calls "the perfume of cleanliness," has
faded. Soon the smell of a fire, lit by copies of a magazine that wants
an interview with Cheever, fills the front room.

He brings out a bottle of Russian vodka and another of Bulgarian
brandy, but these are only for his guest. Rather than drinking himself,
he tells stories of drinking vodka with poet Yevgeny Yevtushenko
during trips to the Soviet Union.

Cheever won't touch alcohol or drugs now, not even aspirin. He
drinks iced coffee now instead of vodka or gin by the bottle. One of

the reasons he stays away from New York City more now is that, when it gets dark in the city, he feels that age-old pull toward the clubs where he used to drink. Caffeine and nicotine are the only drugs he'll trust to his body after the fight to tear himself away from addiction.

For dinner, Cheever's wife brings out a huge pan of pasta made by the woman the Cheevers brought back with them from Italy to be a housekeeper. She doesn't work for them any more; Cheever says they can't afford her. But she lives nearby and still makes phe-nomenal pasta.

Mary is an attractive woman, dark-haired, polite, friendly and intelligent. She talks of authors and books, articles about her hus-band. Christmas preparations, and her sick cat. Cheever says he and his wife have separated periodically after quarrels, and sometimes spend parts of the summer apart.

The Cheevers have two sons and a daughter, two of them writers and one in college.

Later that evening, a neighbor, a bright and cheery-looking woman stops in to ask Cheever to autograph several of his new short-story collections she's giving for Christmas presents. Cheever apologizes that he can't give her any books, saying he gave *Falconer* away but this one is just too big.

"A terrible thing happened last night, John. Our cat died."

"How should I sign this now?"

She tells him which relative and what to say. He has three books in front of him, 2,100 pages, 7½ pounds of finely hewn short stories. He scribbles inside the covers. His neighbor continued to tell how the cat apparently choked on a crow, and Cheever interrupts again to ask how to inscribe the second book.

"I don't talk much with cats," he says with a twinkling look toward his reclining retrievers.

The next day brings a long walk to a huge masonry dam on the Croton River. It was built in 1904 by Italian workers as part of the water system for New York City. It looks like something the ancient Egyptians or Aztecs would have built and Cheever loves to show it to those who'll make the 45-minute hike into the woods.

No dogs along this time. They get confused in the woods, chasing animal tracks, and then Cheever has to spend hours calling for them.

(That's another reason Cheever changed Tara's name to Edgar—he says he feels less foolish calling into the afternoon for Edgar than for some lost land of the romantic south.)

Cheever is more open to interviews and readings now than in the past because he has realized the value of communicating with his audience.

"I used to despise readings. I'd sit there and leer at the people. I'd knock over the water pitcher and glass with the first gesture. I thought that anyone who took a bath and went to an auditorium to hear someone read was a cretin."

Then, he says, he realized his dependence on his readers. "I have come to think of it much more as a field of communication," he says of writing. "Why do I write? Actually, it's to exchange my innermost excitements and intimacies with other men and women."

He draws a careful distinction between communicating with readers and merchandising. He says merchandising serious fiction is an impossibility; it's just too intimate to be marketed. He stays away from autograph parties in bookstores and from the national circuit of talk shows. He did, however, as a neighborly gesture, go into town later than afternoon to autograph some books in the local bookstore.

Talking about his audience as he walks, Cheever starts with a jab at a favorite target—the computer that proclaims misdirected analyses and plans.

"Surveys and polls and computers always come up with a large number of people with limited intelligence," he says through a mischievous smile. "But the reading public is a group of discerning, mature and intelligent men and women.

He says he's not dismayed that his books, like most serious fiction, don't sell as well as the mass-marketed paperback thrillers and sex books. "Considering what you expect from the reader, maturity and discernment, a couple of million people doesn't seem to be that small."

Asked if he ever longs for the kind of sales popular author Sidney Sheldon has with *Bloodlines*, Cheever says quickly, "Oh, Lord, no," as if he's veering sideways to avoid stepping in something. "There are only just so many discerning and well-informed men and women in the world." This doesn't mean he's addressing an elite, he points out, because these readers represent a cross section of society.

"I feel that writing is one of the most intimate and intense media of communication that we possess. Not everyone is open to it."

He says that for a long time he didn't really know what his readers were like. Then indications came in the mail, a great deal of which came after his fourth novel, *Falconer,* was published in 1975 and after his interviews with Dick Cavett on public television this year.

The qualities he now sees in his readers are "intelligence, maturity, and after that I should say loneliness, particularly from the Cavett show. You'd get letters from North Dakota, and from places where public television is the people's only contact with the world of letters."

Wading through his greeting dogs back on the front porch, Cheever moves upstairs to his own world of letters, his library. It's a wide room with a fireplace and a door to a broad front porch, and with bookshelves filled with classics and contemporary literature, mostly American, and the fine leather volumes of his own books, which are a publisher's gift to an author.

A few steps from the library is a small bedroom, used by one of his sons when he's home. There's a bed, some books, a door to the outside, a small desk and a typewriter. "I work wherever nobody else is," he says. Here is taking shape another novel, and an original play for public television.

"I work every day, sometimes with a great deal of enthusiasm, and sometimes with a great sense of insecurity." Cheever says sometimes he is not sure of his ability "to match what you experience with your vocabulary."

That a master like Cheever occasionally feels unequal to the task of catching the world in words is perhaps encouraging to all struggling writers. Who else could write of a man seeing a beautiful young girl for the first time: "he experienced in his consciousness that moment when music breaks glass"?

Cheever works every morning, rising about 6 and sitting down to his typewriter at about 8:30. "Sometimes I spend 10 days on a page and sometimes I write 10 pages a day. If I write 10 pages in a day, I'm usually quite high, and impossible to live with."

When he's writing well, he says, he warns his family to be wary, and he can write a long short story in four days. He gets excited, his metabolism shoots up, and his sexual appetite increases. When he used to drink, he'd have three martinis after he finished writing for the day, although he says he never wrote anything while he was drunk or on drugs.

His writing, especially in the short stories, is crisp and almost poetic, in the sense that into every line is distilled an astonishing amount of meaning. He makes vivid pictures with quick detail strokes of his typewriter keys—"She was almost sixty and she made an intense nurse. From morning until dark, she gripped Carlotta's hand in hers."

Writing in the preface to the new short-story collection, he says some of the stories evoke a lost world "when the city of New York was still filled with a river light, when you heard the Benny Goodman quartets from a radio in the corner stationery store, and when almost everybody wore a hat."

His writing can carry you somewhere and then make you delight at your presence there. He writes of a man looking out a window and seeing "the strong sun lighting the trees on the mountains, pouring its light onto the flat water of the lake, and striking at the outbuildings of the big, old-fashioned place as commandingly as the ringing of iron bells." This same man steps onto the terrace and discovers "the air smelled as if many wonderful girls had just wandered across the lawn."

Writing, for Cheever, is partly self-examination, he says, when he looks at what he has done that is evil and what he has done that is good. He says that writing in different modes, such as short stories and novels, "is rather like a gait; run, walk and canter. . . . The short-story form is determined by the fact that the experience is fragmentary, and a novel is a sustained experience."

He says he has always written, so he doesn't know what it would be like to not be creating. "I wouldn't say I'm addicted to it, but it seems to be my principal usefulness, and I'm really quite pleased by it."

He should be pleased. His descriptions so often hit dead center. Of a man emptily confronting his wife—"After five years of marriage he seemed to have been left with nothing to say. It was like being embarrassed by a shortage of money." Of a loft where volunteer firemen meet in a small town—". . . the sense that the maleness of the place was embattled gave it the snugness of a tree house."

Cheever writes with reverence and longing about women. His words can make you want to put down his books, and fly to the soft, warming shelter of a woman's cloud-white sweater. ". . . and now when I took her in my arms she was a swan, a flight of stairs, a fountain, the unpatrolled, unguarded boundaries to paradise."

Sometimes what Cheever doesn't write about is as intriguing as what he does. In the novel *Bullet Park,* a man stays overnight in a rooming house, "where I was kept awake most of the night by noises that I do not choose to describe." In Cheever's first novel, *The Wapshot Chronicle,* we're told that "Moses' work in Washington was highly secret—so secret that it can't be discussed here."

Cheever's writing is uniquely tuned, but it is right in the mainstream of contemporary American literature, reflecting back and forth to John Barth, John Updike, Saul Bellow, Kurt Vonnegut and John Irving.

Cheever says he isn't concerned with immortality, with his work lasting through the ages. He claims he wouldn't be dismayed if his stories and novels were forgotten tomorrow.

"I think of it as a stream, and one makes a contribution," he says of writing, invoking his beloved water images. "The assumption is if my work is forgotten, it won't be forgotten in the techniques of somebody else." He talks of writers working in a wilderness, and when one person makes a little clearing, the others are appreciative of the light he lets in.

"One would like to be remembered as an honorable man, that's about it."

The sun sinks red-edged behind the western bluffs of the Hudson. The bluffs look like dinosaurs reclining with their snouts downstream, sniffing at the drifting fumes of the city that lies beyond their comprehension at the mouth of the river.

A tanker rests on the textured silver-blue water, and the engineless commuter train moves along the shore under its own power like an insect, carrying hundreds of people from the tributary communities into the city.

Buildings grow beside the river, becoming taller as the train approaches the sea. Outside the window now are monumental, drab high-rises, massive vertical walls of crowded humanity, El Capitan cliffs of apartments. Forlorn Christmas tree lights burn in one window high in the stratosphere. Can there be optimism here, where the individual is lost in the structure?

"Ladies and gentlemen, they've just turned this train into a local, and it will be making all stops between here and Grand Central Station," the conductor intones as he walks through the wobbling train that had been, until a moment before, an express.

A sigh rises from the passengers, who sag back into their seats, giving themselves up to another wait, a waiting that is the story of New York City.

A well-dressed woman pulling a legal pad from a briefcase shakes her head, setting her dark hair in fluid motion, and smiles over at the man across the aisle. Yes, yes, of course there is optimism, here in this woman's smile. Look no farther.

And the train moves comfortably into the subterranean darkness of Grand Central, seeking home.

John Cheever: The Long and the Short and the Tall

J. W. Savage/1979

Reprinted from the *Chicago Tribune Magazine*, 22 April 1979, pp. 30, 31, 33, 35.

"Nobody has been expelled from Thayer Academy at 16 and later received an honorary degree from Harvard," says writer John Cheever while padding barefoot across the lawn in his usual garb of faded jeans and torn polo shirt. "It was worth a new suit, you know."

There are some literary critics who think that John Cheever should be measured for another suit. They are speculating that this is Cheever's year for the Nobel Prize. Of course, this is just speculation, but through his hundreds of short stories that have regularly graced the pages of such magazines as the New Yorker, Atlantic, and New Republic, and his novels such as *The Wapshot Scandal, Bullet Park,* and *Falconer,* Cheever has unleased thousands of characters that have earned him such awards as the O'Henry, the Benjamin Franklin Short Story, and the National Institute of Arts and Letters.

"When the house fills up with Swedish reporters, then I'll know damned well that I'm up for the Nobel," says Cheever in a voice that has a touch of British accent and a tinge of nasal intonations when he drags out the long "o." "This has happened twice already. I don't know whether I'll get it or not. Anyway," the 66-year-old compact gentleman of 138 pounds continues, "I really shouldn't speculate on whether or not I'm going to win a prize." Adding with a shrug of his shoulders and a wink from his intense blue eyes, "Or, at least I don't."

In 1976 there was speculation that John Cheever would get the Nobel Prize. It did not happen. Again, in 1977 for his book *Falconer,* now in fourth printing and being translated in foreign languages, there were many who believed Cheever should receive the coveted award. It did not happen. Perhaps '79 will be Cheever's year.

187

His new book, *The Stories of John Cheever,* won the National Book Critics Circle award in January and is a leading contender in the fiction division for the National Book Awards, to be announced tomorrow. This collection of stories has left critics baffled as to what category to put Cheever in. So far he has been pigeonholed into such slots as "the writer who swallowed small New England towns"; later, "the writer with promise from the East Sixties of New York"; and, most recently, the "Chekhov of the suburbs." Whatever his description, Cheever can be proud of a 49-year writing career. Not bad for a fellow without any formal education and who "drilled myself. No, wait a minute. I was taught writing, of course, by those writers who had gone before me."

As a child, John had an immense reading appetite and was encouraged by his parents; that is, until he developed a strong interest in Shakespeare. "They thought twice about my enthusiasm for Shakespeare. My parents saw it as unseemly, perhaps even dangerous." He chuckles. "After all, I might do something like become an actor." Near the age of 11, John dutifully approached his parents, in the tradition of the early 1900s, to discuss his desire to become a writer. "That was fine with them, provided, 'you don't pursue wealth or fame.' I said, 'I have no interest in wealth or fame.' Although, I've regretted it from time to time when I've been broke.

The Cheever family operated under the fashionable propriety common to a wealthy North Shore of Boston Yankee household. "We were rich. Thus we would not worry about money. My father did have some money until the early '30s. Sometimes it was ridiculous. During the Depression, mother sold almost anything of value we possessed. One time I said to her: 'You can't sell this. It doesn't belong to you.' And she said, 'Well, do you have $100?' A good deal of it was pretense.

"You're talking about Massachusetts at a time when demon-strativeness was completely forbidden. It was a guarded culture." His father, whose lineage dates to the late 1700s, was "50 years old when I was born, and he seemed to make it quite clear to everyone in the family that he could be expected to do very little for me. It was not a requited relationship." Lighting another cigaret, Cheever speaks through the smoke that hangs in the air. "I felt the lack of my father's love. One of the things I did in *The Wapshot Scandal* was to invent a father. In many ways I wanted to requite the relationship. As a great many people did at that time, he kept a journal. On the evidence of his journal, which I used, I thought I wrote a portrait of him that he would have very much enjoyed."

Though John's father was aloof, his mother was eccentric. "Mother used to gather strays. My brother and I used to accuse her of hanging around the New York, New Haven, and Hartford trains trying to pick up someone who looked lonely to come to lunch. It got to be quite a joke. Mother was not demonstrative in any way, either. There were very seldom warm embraces. Her rules of decorum were rigidly observed." Clasping his hands behind his head, Cheever recalls: "Even when I was older, the same attitudes prevailed. My brother and I decided to take an apartment in Boston, and Mother was delighted to hear it. She made arrangements for the furniture of the old house to be taken to the new place Fred and I had rented.

"I always remember this image clearly. We were backing down the driveway, and she was standing on the hill, when suddenly the headlights struck her face. Both Fred and I saw her face gleaming with tears, and neither of us said anything about it." Sitting up straight, John looks down and begins fiddling with an ashtray, saying softly, "It would have been totally incorrect to observe the fact that she was crying. It would have broken the rules of the way we lived." Through a long sigh, he exclaims, "Thank God, the world has changed greatly since I grew up!"

Seeking love, John turned to his only other sibling, his older brother, Fred. "I loved my brother very much. It was perhaps the strongest relationship in my life. He had a mustache, played bridge for high stakes—very debonair. Later we went abroad together and were known as the Cheever brothers. When I was 19, we were going to buy a house together. He was going to be the industrialist, and I was going to be the novelist. It suddenly struck me as being a dreadful situation. We could very easily have passed for the Cheever brothers, always as a pair, for the rest of our lives. And that, I was not going to do. God Almighty!" John says shaking his head quickly as though hit by a sudden chill. "I simply packed up and said, 'Fred, I'm leaving,' and again with the attitude typical of those times, he said, 'Oh, are you?' and we shook hands and parted."

John has tried to reconcile his upbringing throughout his life and now feels he has learned that "one can declare one's love without any suspicion of homosexuality. It has been thought by some psychiatrists, and not by others, that the love of my brother was fundamental, or perhaps aberration is the word. It's apparent to me now that he was instrumental in my growing and so instructive in the nature of love. He played all sorts of roles for me and worried about me until the end of his life. In fact, he married an old girlfriend of mine."

As his writing began appearing in the New Yorker, or New Republic, his parents "never admitted to having read anything I wrote." Even if his mother had read a story, she would never admit to it. Although, John says, "I expect she did. One time she said, 'Oh, I read in the newspaper that you won a prize.' And I said, 'Yes, Mother, I didn't tell you about it because it wasn't terribly important to me.' And she blandly said, 'No, it wasn't to me either.' "

Cheever's early lifestyle in New York was that of the fabled starving writer. "I lived in a furnished room for $2.50 a week. Of course I was hungry—very nearly starved. I used to eat stale bread, buttermilk, and raisins. I almost destroyed my teeth, but I needed the iron. Sometimes we got food from the government, usually free rice and canned fish. I was not really eating well, and I just didn't have enough vitality." Besides writing for the New Yorker, which paid "relatively little, but enough to live on," Cheever freelanced for Metro-Goldwyn-Mayer doing 10-page synopses. "I got around $5, very little money. But I felt quite lucky to have this job because I remember I could do five of them and have $25 to spend on Saturday night."

During those years, he met his wife-to-be, Mary Winternitz, in his agent's office. They were married in 1941. Their marriage has never been mentioned for the couple of the year award. After 38 years of a relationship that has been mostly a roller coaster ride almost breaking loose weekly, John explains: "Mary is a first-rate poet. When you put two creative temperaments together, it can be difficult." Then smiling, "Today is only Tuesday, so we have a few more days left." More seriously John concedes: "I suppose we'll be married for the rest of our lives. The bonds are indescribable." Indeed they should be. The former Mary Winternitz has spent a lifetime married to a writer whose poignant writing has been described as the "all-seeing eye for the

absurdities of the world and the foibles and weakness of humankind"
by fellow novelist L. Woiwode.

As John Cheever began making a name for himself as a writer, he
stuck to the Yankee promise he made his parents. After a sip of iced
tea, Cheever comments: "I'm not a money player. So long as I can
keep the house warm in the winter and feed the family, I'm not
terribly concerned with money. In the past. I've always refused offers
to go to the West Coast for a weekly salary of $2,000 to $3,000. All
I've ever wanted to do was fiction, not film." He also wanted little to
do with reviewers, interviewers, and the general public until a few
years ago. To avoid publicity, John would retreat to Bulgaria or Italy
weeks before publication of one of his books. "If there were any
questions, I'd simply go away until it was forgotten." A skiing accident
that kept him home forced Cheever to take another look at the
public. "Finally it occurred to me as an old man that I was more
dependent upon the reader than the reader was on me." Tossing a
tennis ball across the yard for Edgar, one of three dogs, to chase,
John goes on. "Until *Bullet Park,* I simply escaped and avoided
reviews and interviews. Only in the last four years have I become
quite comfortable with my readers. Now I enjoy meeting them. The
marvelous thing about the reading public is that it escapes any
market survey or computer analysis. Nobody knows who the hell
they are. They just seem to be everyday, interested, independent,
and mature people. It's like being a shoemaker, or any other
craftsman, when people know your work and enjoy it. It is a great
pleasure because it seems to me a friendly thing."

Still Cheever doesn't follow reviews of his books and refuses to
promote his works through cross-country tours or through late-night
talk shows, except for Dick Cavett. "I think I've done three Cavett
shows mainly because I find Cavett friendly, and he seems to have
read the books. There is not an open plug for the book on his show.
He doesn't even show the jacket. Many people will not go on a talk
show unless the book jacket is on camera for a full minute. They can
split the minute into four ways." Rocking forward in his chair with a
loud laugh, he says, "Cavett occasionally does not even mention the
fact that you've written anything."

Four years ago was a major turning point for Cheever. Not only

did he come to accept the public and critics, but he also jumped on
the alcoholic wagon after a heart attack. After lighting another cigaret,
and taking a long drink of his favorite new beverage, iced tea, he says
in a wandering voice: "Yeh, I used to take liquor. Hell, after a quart
of hard liquor and a few pills of valium or some marijuana, I'd almost
be catatonic. Drinking became so bad for me that I sat down with a
jughead in the grass and drank out of a paper bag.

"I thoroughly enjoyed drinking. I thought it was terrific, until it got
out of hand. My drinking was progressive, it simply got worse and
worse. I got more and more dependent on it. I have what is known as
an addictive disposition." This "addictive disposition" becomes more
apparent as he lights up another cigaret and flips the match into an
ashtray almost filled with butts that was empty a few hours earlier.

"I've been to a psychiatrist and to an internist about my drinking.
None of it did any good." After the heart attack, "Mary told me I had
to do something about it so I went into a rehab. It changed
everything. Now I can work again. When I was younger, I used to
work a full day. Now I find if I work a full day I can't sleep at night. I
get too excited, so I keep it to about five hours a day. The only
element I take into consideration is my age, of course, and the
fatigue. When I was young, I think my favorite stories were usually
written in the space of three days. I'd start out on a Monday morning
and finish the story by Thursday."

Walking back to his stone house, built in 1799, John points to the
back lot and comments on one of his diversions from writing. "I
scythe. All these woods and the field beyond the peony patch, I've
scythed. It's difficult to get equipment into these woods, so the
scything is very important, otherwise the scrub takes hold. I was
brought up to do these things."

He offers guests their choice of drinks while he refreshes his iced
tea. In the spacious downstairs dining room, Cheever sits in a
straight-backed chair at a long polished table. There is a quiet
moment that sunlight splashes upon his face from a nearby window.
There is a portrait of John Cheever at peace with himself.

He offers nothing but encouragement for struggling writers. "I've
never seen a good story or a good novel go neglected. I've never
known any truly talented or industrious person frustrated." On
occasion he will critique material sent to him. "If it's strikingly good,

you can usually tell in the first paragraph. Malcolm Cowley (New Republic) pulled that piece 'Expelled' (Cheever's first published short story) from a pile of unsolicited manuscripts. I would very much like to do that for somebody else. Literature is our only continuous history of man. I don't think of myself, for example, as being read when I'm long dead. It doesn't matter if your books are forgotten. It doesn't matter at all."

As he watches the ice cubes swirl in his glass, John speaks as a reformed alcoholic. "I miss it. I'll miss it for the rest of my life. But, now I don't miss it so much that I don't remember the loss of dignity, the loss of self possession, and the fact that it had become a contemptible addiction. I'm sure it made my family miserable. They've been very nice about it."

John Cheever now still tries to atone for any embarrassment he caused his family and is extremely proud of them. His book *Falconer* is dedicated to his youngest son, Federico, who is a student at Stanford. The eldest daughter, Susan, is working on a book in Paris, and his first son, Ben, is an editor at Readers Digest.

Relating drinking to writing, Cheever argues that there is no relationship between the two. "I never went near the typewriter when I was drinking. Obviously, I did incline to melancholy because I had terrible hangovers. I don't think the collected stories *(Stories of John Cheever)* show any discernible difference between Cheever sober or Cheever drunk. I think very few writers go near the desk if they've had anything at all to drink. One realizes that the intelligence," pointing to his temple with his index finger, "loses its discipline. Collins, of course, wrote *The Moonstone,* which I think is a mar- velous book, under the influence of opium. But I don't think any writer works when he's either drugged or drunk."

"John Cheever Is at Home"
Melissa Baumann/1979

<hr />

Reprinted from *The Boston Monthly,* November 1979, pp. 13–15.

He is much like the others, prim in their knickers, pullovers and bow ties and not quite resigned to being photographed. The year is 1930; the setting, the steps of Thayer Academy in South Braintree, Massachusetts. John Cheever, a junior that spring, would not return to Thayer in the fall. Instead, he would commemorate his departure from that institution with "Expelled," an essay published in *The New Republic* that inaugurated his literary career. His class proceeded without him. "John Cheever is at home," read the pronouncement on the erstwhile scholar in the yearbook of 1931. An inauspicious beginning, certainly, for one who has written four novels, been a regular contributor to *The New Yorker* and won the Howells Medal, the MacDowell Award and, for his collected short stories, the Pulitzer Prize.

Cheever, as he repeatedly reminds his audience, is now 67. There are few persons left who remember him from his schooldays; Louise Pennock, his art teacher, does not recall him with any particular distinction and Harriet Gemmel, the "very nice" but rigid English teacher characterized in Cheever's first essay, has been dead these past few years. Frances Aldrich, two years his senior at the academy, remembers him as "a pudgy boy, just another kid at Thayer, really" and Louise Saul, his freshman English teacher, describes him as being "sloppy" in punctuation and grammar, one who "didn't take well to discipline." The man himself, although apparently hale, hedges on resurrecting his youth. He has not returned to Thayer since he left, although administrators there hope to lure him back this spring when his niece graduates. The closest he has come to his native Quincy recently is a visit to Boston in April, when his son ran the marathon.

Cheever bristles at the suggestion that St. Botolphs, the town featured in his first two novels, *The Wapshot Chronicle* (1957) and *The Wapshot Scandal* (1964), *is* Quincy, and quickly obscures other parallels drawn between his childhood and his fictionalized experience. "Fiction is not crypto-autobiography," he insists, as he did not long ago at his eighteenth century Dutch farmhouse in Ossining, N.Y. His stories, as he states in the preface of his latest collection, are inspired by "a love of light and a determination to trace some moral chain of being." They are tales of vanity, self-delusion and disillusionment—yet hope, as well—enacted by suburbanites, expatriates, children, a prisoner and New Yorkers of another generation. They are *not,* we are told, transliterations of the author's life.

Cheever, perhaps, is more willful than forgetful. On the terrace of his home in Ossining, the small, sandy-haired man, notorious for his sardonic chuckle, was uncomfortable in his reminiscences. Between sips of iced tea and reprimands to Edgar, his rambunctious golden retriever, in a patrician Yankee accent he made it clear: certain subjects were best just skimmed. He looked relaxed enough, slumped in a canvas chair in his jeans, loafers and beige sports shirt, but his mind was preoccupied with selection, meticulously isolating the memories he chose to disclose. Fifty years, he was saying, reflecting back on his youth, did not permit succinct recollection. Yet certain experiences, evidently, were all too clear; certain people, namely the former headmaster of Thayer Academy, were unforgettable. "To the Thayer Library," Cheever wrote in 1977 when inscribing a copy of *Falconer,* his bestselling novel, for his alma mater at a Boston book fair. "From someone who remembers Stacey Southworth vividly."

Other recollections are less keen, numbed by time and the author's selectivity. Yet it is the prerogative of writing, and writers, to discriminate, and to dramatize. Cheever has, after all, given us what he terms his "most intimate and acute form of communication" in his fiction. If we are bent on uncovering connections between his life and his work, he will not do it for us; we are left to infer what we will.

"I was born and brought up in Quincy. And that's certainly true. But, as I say, I'm not an autobiographical writer. I mean, I . . . those are the only beginnings I know, so presumably I've written about them. In the Quincy in which I grew up, to want to be a writer, or to want to be involved in the arts, because of the vicinity of Boston and the importance, really, of the Boston Symphony Orchestra, wasn't thought, actually, to be freakish or a waste of time. A very close friend of my mother's, Margaret Deland, was a successful novelist. Mother always took me to visit Mrs. Deland. My aunt was a painter, I had a cousin who was a concert pianist, all of which I have written about in a peripheral and in a fictional sense. So that to be a writer wasn't terribly unusual.

"I went to a school that was founded partly through my mother's exertions. I went to school in South Braintree [after attending Wollaston Grammar School]. I went to Thayerlands, founded when I was a kid, the grade school for Thayer. And then I went on to Thayer. My memories of Quincy are actually quite pleasant. There was also a writer who lived in Quincy named Henry Beston, an outstanding writer who had a book called *The Outermost House*. It was about a year he spent on Cape Cod, which was very successful. Henry's dead. He's a good deal older than I. He was a great friend. Then, my memories of Quincy are actually all quite pleasant. The five and ten cent store used to look like Shakespeare's birthplace. It was a reproduction of Shakespeare's birthplace.

"I grew up on Wollaston Hill, in a large, comfortable Victorian house. I have no idea of the street number. It was torn down years ago. Now, I'm 67 years old, right? I was last in Quincy for my mother's funeral. I really have no idea what year it was." (He adds later that it was about 15 years ago.)

"Fiction is not crypto-autobiography and this has got to be made clear. I had a brother. I also had parents. There are perhaps 100, or 200 parents in the work, but you just cannot confuse fiction with, . . . you can't say 'my brother appeared.' The experience with my brother was a very profound experience and the theme of a brother, or the relationship between two brothers, is very strong in the fiction. But this is not autobiographical. He was older than I was (seven years), a businessman, in advertising. He has been dead about three years. He died in Hingham. He and my parents are buried in Norwell.

"I loved both of my parents dearly. My father was 50 years old when I was born. The age difference made it difficult for us to know one another. Also, in that particular period, intimacy between fathers and sons was fairly uncommon. You were simply expected to do what was thought correct, and that was about it. I was being photographed a few days ago and I was asked to touch my face as I would customarily touch my face, and I said I was brought up not to touch my face. They said, 'What would they do if you did touch your face?' and I said, 'They would cut my hands off.' You ate your peas off a fork, you were polite, you got to your feet when old people came into a room. You were taught what was acceptable decorum at that time in history.

"My father had a small shoe factory in Lynn called Whittredge and Cheever, which he sold at the end of the twenties and invested heavily in Kreuger and Toll International Match. He lost all his money. My mother then opened a gift shop in Quincy Square, which she ran for a great many years supporting herself and her husband. I don't know if it's still there. The granite church, the Unitarian church, is still there. My father and brother were Unitarians. I was raised as an Epicopalian. My mother was an Episcopalian. My mother was English. My father wasn't particularly pious and didn't go to church, really. We went to the church of my mother's choice. What else is still there? Since I haven't been back in 20, no 15 years, I really haven't any idea."

Although Cheever has roosted in Ossining, a sleepy town on the Hudson best known as the home of Sing-Sing prison, geography hasn't any claim on him. His Yankee heritage, however, is detectable immediately.

"I think of myself neither as a New Yorker nor a Bostonian. I think of myself not as a regional writer. I don't think of writers as being regional—excepting, perhaps, the Southern writers. If you were born in Quincy, of course, you were not a Bostonian. It was quite simple. You get that through your head clearly. You don't go to Milton and I didn't go to Harvard. But I did get an honorary degree from Harvard last year.

"I think of myself as a Yankee, yes. I was brought up by seafaring people in a maritime tradition. I was taught to keep a journal or a ship's log, I was taught to be punctual. I still keep a journal. I was taught to check the direction of the wind the first thing in the morning. I don't quite know what you mean by 'Yankee tradition.' Puritanical I am not.

"I think it's largely genetic. The first Cheever, Ezekiel Cheever, came to the United States. No one seems to know what ship he came on. He also founded the Boston Latin school and wrote a Latin grammar which was used up until about 100 years ago. He, I think, settled in Boston in 1637. My father was very much a Yankee. Mother was a vigorous, eccentric woman. My father came from the North Shore, Newburyport. My father and my grandmother and my uncle—I had an uncle named Hamlet, that was his first name. Hamlet Cheever, yes. My grandfather was very enthusiastic about Shakespeare. They came from Newburyport in a ship called the *Harold Currier,* which was the last sailing ship to leave Newburyport. They came from Newburyport to Boston. I don't know how old my father was then. I really don't know. It was all so long ago."

Cheever's more immediate past took shape when, as he describes it, his "memory became active, shall we say, in about 1914, 1916.

"I was born in 1912 and left, I suppose, in 1931 or 1932. I had moved to Boston with my brother in the meantime. I remember Quincy as rather pleasant, relaxed, one of the early suburbs of Boston. The Baileys lived slightly above us and had a tennis court. All of them played tennis. It was very much the last century, I should say. We all had one car. And we used to go swimming in Wollaston Beach. There was a man named Delcevare King, who was president of the bank, who had his *own* beach. He was president of the Granite Trust Company and he was the son of a man named Theophilus King. Very much turn of the century. The air was clear because of the nearness of the water. There was relatively little smog there. All the women had gardens. And there was something in Quincy called 'The Neighborhood Club,' where we all went for New Year's Eve. It was for everybody. Smoking was rather unusual. I think there were various rooms, as I suppose there are now, where you weren't allowed to smoke. And the dances were black tie, as I recall. Very middle class.

"We used to swim a lot, we used to play hide-and-go-seek, hoist the green sail, croquet. An awful lot of bridge was played. It was quite rural, there were woods—we used to go into the woods and make cigarettes out of cedar bark and toilet paper and smoke them. There were streams. We used to swim in the streams. There was a place called 'The Meadow,' quite near the center of town, which when I was a kid used to have cows.

"I read a great deal. Before I was old enough to read, I was read to. I used to bicycle in the Blue Hills, we used to hike. Occasionally we went to the Cape to go fishing. In the summer we used to go to N.H. until I was about ten, and then we went to the Cape, and then I went to scout camp for a couple of years, a camp on a pond named Gallows Pond. I believe a pirate was supposed to have been hung there. This was in Plymouth, south of Plymouth. And in going to scout camp I got to know everybody who didn't go to Thayerlands. Thayerlands was a relatively small school and confined my friend-ships. However, when I was 12 I went to camp and got to know everybody in Quincy. I was very happy about it."

Thayerlands and Thayer, nevertheless, are central to Cheever's boyhood memories; he preserved Thayer for posterity in "Expelled," in which he wrote:

> It is strange to be so very young and to have no place to report to at nine o'clock. That is what education has always been. It has been laced curtseys and perfumed punctualities.
> But now I am nothing. It is symmetric with my life. I am lost in it.

His sentiments haven't much changed.

"Thayer Academy was a day school. One of the principal teach-ers—although she died when I was young—was a cousin of my father's, Anna Boynton Thompson, who taught classics. It was an old-fashioned, New England academy at which Greek was taught until, I think, two years before I entered. Classics were important. It was a preparatory school for Harvard. I was expelled, I was expelled principally for smoking. I don't recall it with any particular vividness. I had wanted to be a writer for a good many years and it struck me that—my quarrel of course was—that the school was not education; it was simply college preparatory. Questions weren't answered or subjects raised unless they would be featured in one's freshman year at college or college board examinations. Which seems to me perfectly legitimate but it is not, of course, a way of educating, or learning. I remember the school, I remember the smell of the school, quite clearly. And it had—Anna Boynton Thompson had brought back—an exhaustive collection of plaster of Paris bas-reliefs, classical plaster of Paris bas-reliefs and statuary which dominated the interior of the school, which I remember pleasantly. The people I knew at Thayer—my closest friend, a man named Faxon Ogden—seems to

be dead. Well, he had called me. I was on the cover of *Time*
magazine some years ago and he was interviewed by *Time*. And then
he called me. We met in New York for lunch. I saw him once.
Someone called from Thayer last winter and I asked them to check
back on Fax, and it was 'address unknown.' "

Cheever is uncertain of the degree of his academic success; any of
his stories, however, suggests his erudition, which he bears modestly.

"It seems to me that I have no more curiosity than most people but
I've had plenty of time. And I've learned languages, and it seems to
me that most people, most writers anyhow, given a writer's schedule,
read a good deal, pick up languages. I've been fortunate enough to
travel. I lived in Italy about 20 years ago, for a year. We return every
eight years. Why Italy? I suppose you might say because I can speak
Italian. Because I loved Italy. I loved the people. I loved swimming in
the Mediterranean. I was very happy there.

"I went to Europe when I was 17 with my brother. We spent the
summer in Europe. Coming back, I lived in Boston. I don't know if I
lived in Boston for a month . . . presently, I went to New York, in any
case. And I made a living doing synopses of novels for Metro-
Goldwyn-Mayer. Made a very poor living at it. But I stayed alive. I
did that for a couple of years, I guess. It was not at all gratifying. I
guess I was lucky to have a job. I started to publish, as you know,
when I was 17 and published pretty much continuously until now,
when I'm 67. And I continue to publish." He grabbed his dog by the
scruff of the neck. "Right, Edgar, right? Right?"

Cheever is prolific in print; he is less free, however, in offering oral
commentary on his work.

"I don't comment on it. I don't reread it. I write about men,
women, children and dogs. I sometimes write about cats, and I've
been thought to be very cruel about cats."

Asked to explain his religious stance in his stories, and the possible
forgiveness he affords his characters, he is candid, and unwavering.

"It is extremely difficult for one to talk about one's religious feelings
in any case, but to talk about them in one's work is virtually
impossible. There is an interview with John Hersey in the *New York
Times* in which the subject was brought up. I think that's about all I
can say and I can't remember what I said then. It was very

ambiguous. It had something to do with light. It's not a question of unwillingness. I can't. I don't think anybody's religious experience can be simplified.

"Am I forgiving toward my characters? I wouldn't say I was forgiving. I do try to comprehend them, as I try to comprehend the men and women I know, and as I try to comprehend myself. I'm not always successful. I'm not in a position to be forgiving. That's presumably as though I were passing judgment on people. Fiction is not a series of judgments. Fiction is . . . fiction is, oh, you know, The Bright Book of Life. It should never be concerned with judgment. An author is not a judge. An author is a traveler.

"I don't think any writer is in a position to make a critical assessment of his own work. I've been interviewed maybe 1,000 times. I've never, nor has any other writer I know, made an assessment of his own work. That doesn't happen to be our task. Our task is to *work*. I think we probably know less about what we do or how we do it than almost any other craft or art. Literature is, as far as I'm concerned, an acute and an intimate means of communication. It is the only continuous history of man's struggle to be illustrious.

"I write as a means of communication. No, I don't think of anything as 'quintessential Cheever.' I write because it seems to me that I have something to say that strikes *me* as being urgent. It might not strike anybody else that way. And sometimes it's successful, and sometimes it isn't. Any self-consciousness about my work is very uncommon. I don't say, 'Oh, how rich, how colorful my themes have gotten.' My preoccupations have been, roughly, with the mystery of love and death."

Critics have compared Cheever's work to that of F. Scott Fitzgerald, but Cheever himself shrugs off the comparison, as well as comparisons to other writers. He acknowledges, however, that his debt to other writers is interminable.

"I wouldn't say there is any marked influence, but I'm keenly aware of the greatness of Melville, of course, Hawthorne, Thoreau. I've read some Emerson. The list of writers who have influenced me is so long, beginning with *The Egyptian Book of the Dead,* that to give it to you would be the equivalent of giving you the Manhattan telephone directory. I've been compared to Scott Fitzgerald; it is not I who makes these comparisons. I don't compare myself. Writing is not a competitive sport. Long before I had any success at all it was quite plainly not a competitive sport.

"What one wants to do, of course, is to make some sort of contribution to literature. It could be a very small contribution—a short story—or it could be twelve novels. I have no idea of the importance or unimportance of my work. It's a matter of absolute indifference to me. It's terribly important—the first canon of aesthetics is interest, which of course involves having a reader. The collected stories has been a huge success. The mail I've received from people who have enjoyed the book is very gratifying because these people are all mature and well-informed. I trust I will finish a novel and publish that. I have done an original for television (WNET-TV in New York) and three stories of mine are being dramatized on television (also on WNET) the last two weeks of October and the first two in November. But I've never spoken about work-in-progress. It's generally thought to be unlucky, among other things.

Cheever's literary contributions over several decades appeared in *The New Yorker,* in which he published approximately 150 stories. He recalls his connection with the magazine, which ended a few years ago, as "an extraordinarily happy and profitable relationship.

"I sold my first story to *The New Yorker* when I was in my early twenties. *The New Yorker* was interested in serious fiction and paid for serious fiction as highly as other commercial magazines paid for trash. Sort of like $400 a story. The fiction editors and I were very close friends. One still is. Bill Maxwell. And Gus Lobrano, my fiction editor for many years, was also a fishing companion. I've never had heavy editing anywhere. What I had from *The New Yorker* was encouragement."

Which is not quite what he received from his parents when he first broached his desire to write; they did not, however, obstruct him.

"I told my parents at age 11 that I wanted to be a writer, and they said they would think it over. In those days one went to one's parents for approval, hypocritically or otherwise. At the end of a couple of days, they said, 'well, we've thought it over and we think it is perfectly all right if you want to be a writer, providing you do not pursue fame or wealth.' And I said I had no intention of becoming either rich or famous. And they said, in that case, I could be a writer."

There seemed little chance, judging from his early days at Thayer, that Cheever would ever be anything else. This abiding addiction to writing, a profession long-associated with troubled souls, might prove divisive in many writers' families, but not, evidently, in Cheever's own. The home in Ossining, from Cheever's description, is a refuge for him and his wife, Mary, and a crossroads for their children Ben, Susan and Fred. It is, Cheever says, an environment "quite different from growing up in Quincy"; secluded among willows and ever-greens, covered with ivy and sheltering bicycles on its porch, it is an image of comfort and well-being.

Cheever is at home there.

"I cannot think of my being a writer as problematic. I don't see any of the problems as being insurmountable or serious. As I see it, it's a loving family. We're all very happy to see one another. I was a very bad alcoholic. I no longer drink. I no longer smoke, either. I bicycle ten miles a day, I swim, I was chopping wood when you came. I certainly wouldn't describe myself as a health fanatic. I wouldn't describe myself, really . . ."

His wife called from an upstairs window that the telephone was for him. He dismissed himself politely, and returned minutes later. He was restless, and called an abrupt end to his reminiscences.

"I must take the cleaning lady home. She's waiting in the car. Life goes on. That's fiction."

Cheever's Story

Christina Robb/1980

Reprinted from the *Boston Globe Magazine*, 6 July 1980, pp. 11–13, 27–31, 35, by permission of the publisher.

John Cheever sits down to breakfast talking about Yankee brown eggs. Brown eggs are hard to find in Ossining, New York. Cheever gets his from a farmer who also sells blue eggs, packed with protein and laid by hens with feather-covered faces. This sort of barnyard eccentricity is as Yankee as brown eggs, he feels, and it delights him.

Cheever is eating lox and dill bread in Howard and Nancy da Silva's open first-floor kitchen-dining-living room while he chuckles about old-fashioned New England brown eggs and the latest blue ones. The da Silvas are neighbors, and Howard, the actor, worked with Cheever on the adaptations of stories and the original screenplay, *The Shady Hill Kidnapping,* that Cheever wrote for public television this winter. Their wide, shallow, three-story farmhouse is built on the same plan as Cheever's and went up at about the same time, 1780 or so.

But the da Silva's house is all studio, full of open white space, books, and music that clearly belong to working artists. Cheever's house would probably look like home to the colonial farmer who built it, if the farmer was prosperous. The upstairs parlor and downstairs sitting room are furnished with antiques and heirlooms out of Cheever's Yankee past—his grandmother's ivory and paper fan framed so its brilliant Chinese blues and greens won't fade; a lowboy from Newburyport, where the Cheevers settled generations ago; an oil portrait of Cheever as a boy with rosy lips and a palette in his hand, a sort of portrait of the young man as an artist that his aunt painted after Cheever declared at an early age that he wished to become a writer.

Cheever's brother, Fred, named for his father and seven years older than John, has a matching portrait of himself as a businessman.

204

The portraits are important to Cheever, and so is his memory of the aunt who painted them. Ten years ago, he says, a doctor told him he was going to die shortly. His response was to write "Percy," the only story of his career that he'll admit is autobiographical, about his painting aunt. In the story, shortly after her father dies and her family is left destitute, Percy declares that she wants to be an artist. And she does become an artist. But she compromises with taste and commerce and gives up Renaissance-sized canvases and Paris garrets for magazine covers and marriage to a philandering physician.

Cheever has been on the covers of *Time* and *Newsweek*. He won the National Book Award for his first novel, *The Wapshot Chronicle,* and a Pulitzer Prize last year for the collected stories he started writing in the 1930s. He has not compromised with taste or quality. All of his compromises have been with the tough New England tradition he found in his family, and they have been more like lover's quarrels and battles for his freedom than compromises.

"Mixed with the love we hold for our native country is the fact that it is the place where we were raised, and, should anything have gone a little wrong in this process, we will be reminded of this fault, by the scene of the crime, until the day we die," he wrote in a story called "The Bella Lingua," about an American expatriate in Italy. For Cheever, Boston and its South Shore were the scene of the crime. He can't forget the place. He loves it; but he was shaken to the core over and over again in the years he spent there, and he's never outgrown a need to rebel against the way his family seemed to expect him to take that kind of upset. He left Boston in 1930 for Europe and New York, and when he came back in the mid-seventies at 62, to teach a semester or two at Boston University, he was almost continually drunk, and so disorderly that he was, he says, almost arrested. "I think I picked up where I left off. I did everything that would have infuriated my parents," he said when he was interviewed in Boston in 1977, on the wagon.

Before the middle of this decade, Cheever's life made two complete cycles of gaining and losing all security. When he's in Boston, he's reminded of the catastrophes that befell him and his family here before he was 17, and of the rigid way he felt required to deal with them. He lost his home and his school and a sense of order and balance about the relationships in his family. He moved to New York

to start again, and wrote about city life in the nineteen thirties and
forties. He starved and worked to establish himself, married and
settled in Westchester County, using its commuter life as the basis of
most of his short fiction in the fifties. And when that life began to be
established and honored, he all but lost it to liquor. Loss and the pain
of loss have rolled up and down his life and work like the rock of
Sisyphus. Now, in a good time, when he's at home in Ossining,
Boston reminds him of the good, stable, simple things of the New
England tradition—the family skating, the confident unpreten-
tiousness, the brown eggs that he found a way to keep when he
moved to New York.

"I have a friend here—the one Yankee in Westchester. We spend a
great deal of time together eating brown eggs" and talking about New
England traits and foibles, Cheever says as we drive into Mount Kisco
to pick up his bicycle. Fifty years ago, when Cheever first left the
South Shore of Massachusetts for New York, he and E. E. Cummings
used to eat brown eggs together, when they could afford them, or
talk about New England and about how Cheever felt the weight of a
heavy Massachusetts farming and maritime family tradition damning
him for going to New York. Cheever's parents had told him "that if
you had any character, you would be content with Boston," Cheever
says. As far as they were concerned, "New York was bad"—a den of
showy nomads. "And I took all this quite seriously."

The poet, with Cambridge and Harvard behind him, made the
break more easily than Cheever (known to his friends as Joey in
those days) and encouraged him. "Cummings said, 'Get out of
Boston, Joey! It's a city without springboards for people who can't
dive.' "

John Cheever was born in Quincy on May 27, 1912. His father,
Frederick L. Cheever, was descended from Newburyport sea cap-
tains. He and a partner ran a shoe factory in Lynn, but the older
Cheever chose to live on the South Shore. Though he was a good
New England Unitarian himself, he married an Episcopalian, Mary
Deveraux Liley (rhymes with Riley), a tiny Englishwoman whose
father had come over from Old Windsor. Like his own father,
Frederick Cheever sired his children late—Fred when he was 42 and
John when he was 49. And throughout his career as a father, till he

died at 82, his life was full of whiskey and women and his talk was
spare and seaworthy.

"He spent most of his life on a catboat that he would call 'a wide-
waisted sloop that sailed like real estate.' He had a very good New
England style," Cheever says, "precise, laconic New England," and it
grounded Cheever in "that careful speech which is basically nautical,
I suppose," and which makes as little as possible of any event.

"End of September business at Mansion House slow as molasses,"
Leander Wapshot, the New England patriarch, writes in a telegraphic
journal in *The Wapshot Scandal,* Cheever's second novel about his
New England. "Some northerly winds. Also fine weather. Bright sun.
Warm air. Breeze up and down the mast. Wouldn't blow a butterfly
off your mainsail. Walked often on beach with Thespian before
commencing tour of duty. Delightful company. Lingered in various
coves, nooks, also aboard catboat. Property of hotel. Tern. Fifteen
foot. Marconi rig. Wide waisted. Sailed like a butter-tub. Small cabin
with no amenities. So the days passed."

All his life, Cheever's father liked to drink, and he set an example
of New England laconism for his sons by which it was all right to
drink to excess as long as you didn't talk or act immoderately. Misled
by this example, both of his sons became alcoholics. Cheever
remembers introducing his father to martinis as an adult: "He'd never
had one and he asked me to make him one. I made him a martini
cocktail and he said, 'Strong enough to *drawr* a boat.' "

John Cheever grew up in a big Victorian house on Winthrop
Avenue in Wollaston Heights. The family tastes were simple and
cultured. They read Dickens aloud and sailed and skated together.
The first ten thousand cars in Massachusetts had license plates
numbered 1 to 10,000, and the Cheevers' car had license plate
3088. It was all right to drive with 3088 on your license, but when
Cheever's brother forgot to renew the license, Cheever's father
stopped driving, John remembers. It was a world where "the first
thing a male did in the morning was draw a foot of cold water," and
"it was only sensible to wake yourself up by pouring water down
your spine because everything else was going to be worse."

Manners were simple. When in doubt, you said no thank you. "No
thank you was on the family escutcheon. You always say no thank

you" to honors, awards, or anything special so that no one will notice you or check up on your finances, Cheever laughs. When Cheever was 10 or 11, he decided he wanted to be a writer and announced his decision to his family. He loved to read, and he knew that writing fiction was something acceptable people did. Margaret Deland, whose husband coached the Harvard football team, was a novelist (she wrote *Iron Woman*), and his family knew her. They took John's announcement under advisement and reported back to him in a day or so. "It's all right with us if you want to be a writer, so long as you are not seeking fame or wealth," they told him.

"Coming from Quincy, dreams of fame and wealth were totally unsuitable," he explains. He was expected to live a hard-working, inconspicuous life, "because that is roughly the way everyone lived in Massachusetts." He was made to feel "it's like eating white eggs": If you're from Massachusetts, you don't do it. The fortunes of Cheever's family altered radically during his life, but their views about decorum in Massachusetts never changed. In 1954, when Cheever was 42 and his mother was nearly 80, he won the Ben Franklin Award for short fiction, and the *Quincy Patriot Ledger* reported it. Soon afterward, he talked to his mother on the telephone. "Mother said, 'I read it in the newspaper that you got a prize.' And I said, 'Oh yes, but I didn't mention it to you because I thought it wouldn't interest you.' And she said, 'Oh, you are so right. It doesn't interest me at all.' Now that is Massachusetts," he says. "I don't know what my father made of my literary career" because he never mentioned it.

Cheever has been able to weave from these stoic strictures and eccentricities a sense of tradition he values. He has inherited a rocklike sense of stability and practiced a profession in which it's all too easy to wander right off the deep end. His sense of pleasure is rooted in the physical sports and work that his family enjoyed. He's skated all winter, he says, on nearby Teatown Pond. He skated every day for six weeks, and when a conference in New York looked as if it were going to keep him till after dark, he got anxious and wanted to leave early so he wouldn't miss a skate. "Skating wouldn't have been as much of a pleasure to me had I not been brought up skating on Braintree Dam, and had I not skated with my mother and father," he says. "I'm very fond of living with a reasonable amount of phys-icalness," and he finds a lot of it in skating, skiing, swimming, biking eight to fifteen miles a day, riding, a touch of touch football, and in work like cutting wood, vegetable gardening, and scything. The physical ground under his feet supports his mind and spirit, in his life and in his writing. "The physical world is extremely important to me. It's the world by which I live. It contributes a great deal to my bearings, which is why I bicycle and skate," he says. His writing always moves from sensuality to morality, and his characters' moral and psychological insights are always rooted in physical perceptions.

"How to write a summer's day in an old garden?" he asks in the fifth chapter of *The Wapshot Chronicle*, his first novel about Massachusetts and about Leander and Sarah Wapshot and their sons, Moses and Coverly. "Smell the grass, we say. Smell the trees! A flag is draped from the attic windows over the front of the house, leaving the hall in darkness. It is dusk and the family has gathered. Sarah has told them about her journey with Mr. Pincher. Leander has brought the *Topaze* in to port. Moses has raced his sailboat at the Pocamasset club and is spreading his mainsail out on the grass to dry. Coverly has watched the table-silver-company ball game from the barn cupola. Leander is drinking bourbon and the parrot hangs in a cage by the kitchen door. A cloud passes over the low sun, darkening the valley, and they feel a deep and momentary uneasiness as if they apprehended how darkness can fall over the continents of the mind. The wind freshens and then they are all cheered as if this reminded them of their recuperative powers."

The positive part of the tradition was the sense of order and discipline it lent life. The negative part was its cloistering taciturnity. You simply did not notice if anything untoward was happening. By the time he was out of grade school, Cheever had decided to buck this "no thank you" attitude to life by becoming a writer. And that was in good time, because from about then on, Cheever's life in traditional Massachusetts was one calamity after another.

First he lost his home in a puzzling way that was never explained, because things are not explained in Massachusetts. All he knows is that he overheard his father quarreling one night with a man called Mr. Pinkham, who owned the local Granite Trust, while they were playing bridge. His father told Mr. Pinkham that he, Frederick Cheever, was a humane employer of forty-two people whose birthdays and names he remembered, and coldhearted Mr. Pinkham simply dealt with money. The next *day*, the Cheevers moved out of their house in Wollaston Heights into a house they owned in Hanover, and the Quincy house was razed to the ground. John was 15.

In 1928, when Cheever was 16, his father sold out of his shoe company for a nice profit and invested most of his share in "safe stocks like International Match." In the spring of 1928, Cheever was expelled from Thayer Academy, in Braintree, for smoking. "I was a fairly tractable student, but I was a chain smoker," he says.

The next year, Cheever's father lost everything in the stock market crash, and his mother opened a gift shop and began to support the family. His father was crushed and his mother was delighted. But they were both shocked. This sort of reversal of roles was not supposed to happen in Massachusetts. "They were so bewildered by the turn of events that it was hard for them to make sense of their lives," Cheever says. But Cheever hung on to his ambition—writing— because he wanted "not fame or wealth but a way of making sense of my life." He wrote an essay about what had happened to him at Thayer Academy and sent it to Malcolm Cowley at the *New Republic*, which printed "Expelled" when Cheever was 17. "If I had left because I had to go to work or because I was sick, it would not have been so bad. Leaving because you are angry and frustrated is different. It is not a good thing to do. It is bad for everyone," he wrote.

Cheever's moral sense is sharper and subtler than any American writer's since Hawthorne, and even at 17 he was not afraid to use words like "good" and "bad," or to see how they fit the world around him, which was falling down. In two years he had lost his home, his parents had lost their place in the world and their respect for each other, and he'd been kicked out of school. He lived with his brother in Boston for a while, writing stories and seeing a few of them printed in *Story* magazine or in *Hound and Horn*, which Lincoln Kirstein edited in Cambridge. But he was still reeling from the fall his life had taken.

Even now, his recollections of that time can come back and shake him. "The commercial violence of those years . . . is still so powerful. I sometimes find in streets in Boston my self-possession shaken," he says. He loves Symphony Hall for its sound and for his memory of his mother in her tricornered hat telling the usher she was Mrs. Cheever and the number of her seat every Friday rather than using something so outlandish as a ticket. But he doesn't like to go to Symphony Hall, he says. In 1931, he and his brother went to Germany for the summer, and he saw Nazism and its myth of Aryan conquest for the moral poison they were. "The idea struck me as being absolutely sinful the first time I knew of it—which was when I was what, 17?" Cheever does not believe that his moral acuity is exceptional or was precocious. He says he finds nothing remarkable about the fact that he realized after this trip that he couldn't go on living with his brother because he loved him too much, and it would be narrow and wrong to spend his life on that one passion. And that's what happened. Cheever moved to a $3-a-week room on Hudson Street in New York. his brother sent him $10 a week till John got a job writing synopses of novels for Metro-Goldwyn-Mayer with Paul Goodman and James Farrell.

"My brother and I had been extremely close, and it seemed to me to be a relationship that should be ended," Cheever says. "I felt that I should leave my brother and spent the rest of my life trying."

This turn, away from a homosexual attraction to his brother and toward a family and posterity of his own, was the turning point of John Cheever's life; he has turned it over and over and over in his mind and in his work ever since. This decision was all the harder to make because Cheever and his brother did not discuss it or anything else about their relationship. After all, they were from Massachusetts, and "the laconism of that part of the world was also observed by the family. If the house were on fire, you did not if possible mention it." Cheever only began talking publicly about this decision after his novel *Falconer* was published in 1977. Recently, he and his brother have mentioned it casually. "I think the last time I saw my brother, I said, 'Oh, Fred, I killed you in the last book.' He said, 'Oh, good, good. You've been trying for years."

Something extraordinary happens when Cheever first brings up this subject of leaving his brother. I ask him to clarify and expand on what he means and on what happened, and he simply jumps away from the topic. To know how striking this break in the conversation seems, you have to understand that Cheever is very polite and very warm and easy about his politeness. He grins and brightens boyishly at some point in about every third sentence he speaks, continually footnoting good cheer. He is also a master of the mysterious and dynamic Yankee silence that directs conversation away from unacceptable topics before they are brought up, so that no one ever needs to change the subject because all unacceptable subjects are somehow silently spotted and banned before they are ever mentioned. In this case he brings the topic up himself, but when I ask for more, first he describes his family's way of not talking about important emotional realities, and then, without pausing, he talks about the party he's going to in Boston for people who have been on the cover of *Time*. Then he talks about "seven or eight generations" of Cheevers, lots of Aarons and Ezekiels, that his father searched out of the Newburyport records. (He doesn't remember exactly how many generations there were. His memory stops at Benjamin Hale Cheever in the War of 1812, he says later, and "for some reason I threw all the papers away.")

This is Massachusetts asserting itself with a vengeance, almost independent of his will. It tells me that even though Cheever introduced the subject of his relationship with his brother, I'm going to have to approach it very slowly and carefully, the way Cheever approached it himself in his own literary career.

Cheever's women are often cramped into suburban New York dollhouse roles or distended by New England eccentricities that make them foils for men; his men are usually beautifully if agonizingly alive. The beauty of men and of male relationships, and the motif of leaving a man, saying good-bye to a man, haunt his work from the beginning. The very first story in Cheever's collected stories is the small masterpiece "Goodbye, My Brother," set on an island like Martha's Vineyard off the coast of Massachusetts, and his last novel, *Falconer,* is about a fratricide.

When Cheever left Boston, he deliberately left the scene of all the crimes against him and the place that he felt was too "hospitable to eccentricity" and would have let him and his brother collapse into an effete symbiosis all too easily. (The plan was that his brother would go into textiles, still the businessman like the boy in "Percy's" painting, and Cheever would write Jamesian novels in a house they would share in Boxford.) And he left off writing about Massachusetts, too.

For two decades, while he was meeting and living with and

marrying Mary Winternitz, fathering children, and finding a market in the *New Yorker,* he wrote stories about New York commuters that largely left New England out. He found his own voice on his own, non-Yankee subject matter, and only much later, in his first novels and in *Falconer,* did he return to New England and the shape of his early life. And that is how our conversation in Ossining goes. We discuss the work and the life that intervened between his decision to leave his brother and his decision to talk about what that meant to him. Then we come back, and he can talk without balking about his decision to leave his brother.

"It would have been by my lights a perverted love," he says. "It would have confined my knowledge critically—my knowledge and my emotional life." The choice was a moral one, and he saw it in black and white. "There are the loves of darkness and the loves of light, and it certainly hasn't changed. As I crowd 70, I still have them." He sees light and darkness in all relationships, and chooses them for light. "Light is characterized for me by boundlessness, by openness. Darkness seems to me second best," he says. He thinks everyone sees this way. "It seems to me that every person knows from time to time what is craven, what is sinful, and what is joyous, what is courageous," he says. "Courage is an aspect of enthusiasm. . . . Courage is part of the air we breathe."

But some things have changed in his lifetime, he feels, and one of them is that homosexuality is no longer wrong because "relations between men and women that are not procreative are no longer moral choices." In his own Massachusetts tradition, they were. Ship captains couldn't have homosexuality aboard on two-year voyages or there would be havoc; small farmers in underpopulated New England had to produce offspring to survive, he says. When Cheever turned away from homosexuality, it was because he felt it to be empty and wrong. "Fruitless, or sterile, is what I mean—unnatural, less than courageous."

Courage is a word Cheever uses easily, and he has found plenty of use for it in his life. It took courage for him to leave his brother and turn toward an unknown development and assimilation into civilization. It took courage for him to move to New York to write stories and starve for four years till he found the *New Yorker,* at 22. "I was cold. I was hungry. It was very rough," is all he says.

It took courage for him to knock on Malcolm Cowley's door after his schoolboy essay appeared in the *New Republic* and Cowley invited him to his first New York cocktail party. Cheever wore his gray flannel suit and drank five Pernods "to make it apparent to everyone that I was very sophisticated," and then he walked out into the hall and threw up. After this introduction, Cowley became "very much a surrogate parent" to Cheever when he moved to New York.

Cowley advised him to set aside some of the very long stories he was writing and write a few very short ones. "I have always been rather prolific, and I wrote about five. He submitted them to the *New Yorker*. Katherine White took one. The *New Republic* took another—about a burlesque girl" Cheever had seen in Boston. ("I used to hang around the Old Howard.") While he was finding his feet as a writer, Cheever managed to get out of the cold during a few visits to Yaddo, the writer's retreat near Saratoga Springs, where he's now a vice-president, succeeding Cowley.

It took less courage for Cheever to ask out Mary Winternitz, his agent Maxim Lieber's assistant, after he saw her in the elevator at 545 Fifth Avenue and thought she'd make a good date. The woman he was to marry had a more extreme form of his own Yankee and foreign parentage. Her father, the dean of the Yale Medical School, had grown up in Baltimore, the son of Viennese Jews; her mother was a Salem and Weymouth Yankee whose father, Thomas A. Watson, was on the other end of the line when Alexander Graham Bell made the first phone call in 1876. Watson founded the Fore River Engine Company, in East Braintree, in 1884. Cheever and Winternitz lived together for a couple of years and married in 1941. His daughter, Susan, a novelist herself, was born three years later, and his son, Ben, an editor at *Reader's Digest* and a father (of Joshua, 7), was born five years after that.

Cheever represented his Massachusetts tradition in the Second World War by entering the army, where he spent four years as an infantry gunner, never mentioning that he was the young writer whose short stories had begun appearing in the *New Yorker*. "Here again, this is Massachusetts: 'I want only to be taken as a soldier.' " His platoon's intended landing in Africa was delayed, which was a lucky thing, he notes, since everyone who made the landing was killed. He "marched around Georgia for two years, and then suddenly someone discovered who I was and I was pulled out. This

colonel said, 'What are you doing in the infantry?' and I said, 'I want
to be in the infantry.' " But Cheever was transferred to the signal
corps and ended up in the Philippines. "I tried to get back into the
infantry but I couldn't, fortunately, or I would have been killed," he
says drily.

Massachusetts. Even after the *New Yorker* started accepting his
stories and Cheever realized he could—just—support his family by
writing for them, he kept fame and wealth at arm's length. Like many
writers, he got calls from Hollywood to adapt novels into screenplays,
and he turned them all down so he could go on writing stories for the
literate, intelligent audience and inspired editors he felt the *New
Yorker* provided him. He wrote more stories for the magazine than
anyone but John O'Hara—120 or 130 by now, he says ("I never
counted"). Finally, in 1950, the four Cheevers made their suburban
break. They moved to a rented house on an estate in Scarborough,
just south of Ossining. They loved upstate living and the outdoor life
and decided to buy. Cheever found a house way up in Saratoga,
nearer good skiing than Westchester, but Mary didn't want to leave
her downstate friends. In 1956, MGM purchased the movie rights to
Cheever's story "The Housebreaker of Shady Hill" for $40,000. The
movie was never made, but the Cheevers bought their house in
Ossining and traveled to Italy on the proceeds.

When Cheever was 45, his mother died. His father had died a
dozen years before, in 1945. Cheever had been writing stories for
nearly thirty years, and he'd been married for fifteen—two long
relationships, with a craft and with a woman. In his youth, when "all I
knew were interruptive experiences" and "meetings that were involuntarily terminated," short stories were all he could appropriately
write, he felt. But after fifteen years with a wife and two children, "it
seemed to me it was an obligation, really, to celebrate" sustained
experience in a novel. The novel he wrote was modeled on the
eighteenth-century picaresque novels of Fielding and Sterne, and the
sustained experience he celebrated was growing up in a mythical
South Shore Massachusetts town, St. Botolph's, in a mythical family,
the Wapshots. And their myths were his.

The Wapshot Chronicle won the National Book Award in 1958,
the year that Federico, the son of his late 40s, was born in Italy, his
antidote to Massachusetts.

Cheever spent part of every year for the next ten in Italy, and then he went to Russia, where he's returned twice, though now he prefers Bulgaria. "I find Eastern Europe quite mysterious and quite powerful," he says. "I've always been quite a lonely man, and perhaps it is because in Eastern Europe I'm a *very lonely* man." His fears about going to Russia the first time were totally unjustified. "My life has never been so highly valued, so esteemed" as he felt it there, he says. In spite of language barriers, his Eastern European admirers have managed to convey what they value him for—if only by throwing their arms around him and shouting, *"La grande poesie de la vie!"* he says.

Americans typically talk about possessions. "When I was young I used to think it was ridiculous." But now he accepts this American habit as a kind of poetry. "We use possessions as metaphors," he says. But in Eastern Europe, "possessions never play a part in a conversation," and "loneliness and melancholy are quite acceptable topics of conversation." And that never would have been allowed in Massachusetts when Cheever was growing up.

The Wapshot Scandal, whose opening brings heaven and hell to earth in St. Botolph's more subtly and gladly than Hawthorne in "My Kinsman, Major Molineux," appeared in 1963. In 1964, Cheever was on the cover of *Time.* In 1965, the American Academy of Arts and Letters awarded him the William Dean Howells medal.

Bullet Park, Cheever's chilling and loving novel of suburban New York, followed in 1967. It was badly reviewed on the front of the *New York Times Book Review* and sold badly. Cheever declined in more than reputation. Slowly—like the priest in *The Wapshot Scandal,* after years of daily and very wet conviviality—Cheever became a drunk.

He had always drunk liquor joyously and with gusto, like his father before him. "I used to feel that the classical libation was very much a part of life. I drank very happily until I found that I was an alcoholic." What proved to him that he needed to stop drinking wasn't that his work suffered and almost stopped. "I never wrote when I had been drinking," he says. "But then there were fewer and fewer days that I could write." And it wasn't his near arrest for drinking in Boston when he came back to teach at BU in the early seventies, after he'd taught creative writing at Sing Sing, the prison near Ossining where he did his research for *Falconer*. It was death.

He quit drinking five years ago, he says: "I'd had two heart attacks, which is why I stopped. If I'd gone on drinking, I would have been dead." He faced a choice between light and darkness, life or death. "And so I went to the hospital and got detoxified," joined AA, and four years later, choosing life again, quit smoking. Though he still holds a glass of tea in his hand almost incessantly, for the familiar feel of the glass, he says smoking was a more threatening loss than drinking, because he feared his work would suffer. He never drank while he wrote, but he used to smoke all the time when he worked at his Olivetti portable in the basement of his New York apartment or in his daughter's room or, lately, in Ben's room. And he was used to arriving at his desk at eight a.m. and "pulling on a cigarette for the clarification of my thinking."

Cigarettes and drink appear on almost every page of his novels and stories, he says. They are still very important to him. They are metaphors for all our pleasures and the choice we have about whether our pleasures will become addictions. But it's only lately that Cheever has been able to write about addictions explicitly. In fact, for a long time he rejected addiction, homosexuality, and sexual explicitness as fit subjects for fiction—they are high on his disapproved list in his odd fictional essay "A Miscellany of Characters That Will Not Appear," for instance.

"I started *Falconer* when I quit drinking," he says. The novel is about a heroin addict who finds a male lover, methadone, and epiphany in prison, where he has been sent for killing his brother. "Farragut (fratricide, zip-to-ten, #734-508-32)" is Everyman: "Farragut was a drug addict and felt that the consciousness of the opium eater was much broader, more vast and representative of the human condition than the consciousness of someone who had never experienced addiction. The drug he needed was a distillate of earth, air, water and fire. He was mortal and his addiction was a beautiful illustration of the bounds of his mortality. . . . Only the opium eater truly understands the pain of death. When one morning the orderly who gave Farragut his methadone sneezed, this was for Farragut an ominous and a dreadful sound. The orderly might come down with a cold, and considering the nature of the prison bureaucracy, there might not be anyone else who had permission to issue the drug. The sound of a sneeze meant death."

In *Falconer,* Cheever focuses on the characters he had said would never appear, and their struggle for freedom, kindness, and pleasure sheds as much light as his stories about the similar struggles of suburban families. He wrote the novel in the first months of his victory over the addiction that had been killing him. And Farragut, who is a professor and has a Yankee tradition behind him, moves so confidently and bravely toward freedom, from a position of such extreme, addicted vulnerability, that the whole novel has the ring of an anthem of praise. Much of this tone comes from Farragut's religion, which he preaches to his bishop (and no one else) in a letter: "I truly believe in God the Father Almighty but I know that to say so loudly, and at any distance from the chancel—any distance at all— would dangerously jeopardize my ability to ingratiate those men and women with whom I wish to live. I am trying to say—and I'm sure you will agree with me—that while we are available to transcendent experience, we can state this only at the suitable and ordained place."

One of the major differences between Cheever and the New England Calvinists who created the tradition that nags and guides him is that he's Episcopalian, like his mother. Cheever's father used to go to the Unitarian church and sit by the bankers, though Cheever stresses that "he was a pleasure-loving man." But his mother made sure that John was christened in the Episcopal church in Quincy. "Then Mother veered wildly into Christian Science, and I didn't follow at all. And then I was highly skeptical, I think, until I fell in love at about 20. It was love that seemed to open up the whole area of imponderables," he says, and when he was 22 he started going to church, though he wasn't a member till his late 30s, when "out of a sense of enormous gratefulness" he was confirmed. Now he goes to communion at eight-thirty every Sunday. He read the second chapter of *Bullet Park,* which is about churchgoing in a suburb not unlike Ossining, at a recent evensong service. He loves the old Book of Common Prayer and hears "all the tread of Latin" in the General Confession, but he doesn't care who else marches along. His children have been baptized and confirmed on their own (except for Susan, in Rome, because "the Romans were after her").

"My sense is not in any way evangelical," he says. But he needs to use religious conventions in order to write about the transcendent events of every life. *Bullet Park,* for instance, ends with an attempt at human sacrifice that might be mistaken for an impulsive murder attempt if it didn't take place in church. A warm and ritual-filled religiousness that avoids the austerity and arrogance of Yankee Calvinism is important in his work because "it's an acceptance of imponderables and the mysteriousness of life and an agreed use of a set of symbols for this."

John Cheever loves life—loves his dogs Edgar and Maisie, loves "the whole phenomenon of winter," loves movement, loves foible and the brown eggs of existence, loves his family. But he's had to struggle with darkness, as he calls it—with obsessive passion and addiction—and with the aftermath of losing his home, losing his sense of support, expulsion, the penury of a four-year literary apprenticeship, four more years of war, and "Massachusetts." His stories and novels are steeped in a sense of loss—and often of loss overcome. But the losses are never of wars or elections; like the New England theocrats who came before him, Cheever sees our power struggles as moral, never political, struggles. And the greatest losses he records are of the meanings, the moral and spiritual meanings, that lost things have.

The husband of a woman who craves a house in the country closes the door on a house that she wants and he doesn't in the early story "The Common Day." He closes the door on her dream of safety, and she responds to the loss of a dream, not a house: "She looked behind her as if he had closed the door on her salvation, and then she took his arm and walked beside him to the car." Although they're full of realistic detail that he treats with irony and love, Cheever's stories seem timeless because they are never built on politics or trends but on the moral meanings that underlie politics and keeping house.

He insists on this moral dimension; the passions and conflicts of his characters are never merely or even mainly psychological. When Moses Wapshot's wife, Melissa, becomes obsessed by an infatuation with the grocery boy in *The Wapshot Scandal,* she refuses to treat her infatuation as nothing more than a fashionable neurosis. She knows that "the world, the village would forgive her her sins if she would go to Dr. Herzog, whom she had last seen dancing with a fat woman in a red dress, and unburden herself three times a week for a year or two of her memories and confusions. But wasn't it her detestation of bigotry and anesthesia that had gotten her into trouble, her loathing of mental, sexual and spiritual hygiene? She could not believe that her sorrows might be whitewashed as madness. This was her body, this was her soul, these were her needs."

Cheever loves writing and literature with the same energy he has for all his other loves, because he's used his work as a tool for living. All his life the literature that he's read and the literature that he's written have nourished him with pleasure and direction. He believes that literature is the first mark of a civilization and that civilization requires us "to make sense of our lives and to discover what is useful and beautiful." He feels that is what he's spent his working life doing.

As a boy, "I very much loved as I do today the feeling of bringing unrelated—totally unrelated—areas of life together as one can in fiction," he says. "That, it seems to me, is one of the great pleasures of my life," and one of the great aids. Fifty years after he first realized it, "my ambition to be a writer does seem to me the best way of making sense of my life." Life needs making sense of because "this is the world one finds oneself in and of but at the same time one finds oneself a stranger," and literature makes that strangeness familiar. Cheever enjoys the whole stream of literature, which "begins with the Egyptian Book of the Dead and goes through the classics in translation—Homer and Virgil—and Dante, all the novelists," including Flaubert, whose *Madame Bovary* Cheever has read twenty-five times in French and English.

"These are the only lights one has to go by," he says. "You have to know what's been accomplished by other writers before you can know where you can proceed on your own." Without benefit of a college education or even a complete high school education, Cheever found out what other writers had accomplished, and he developed a classic style that college and high school students study now.

He hasn't learned from every writer in the canon. "What one learns is what one needs for one's particular journey," he says. But his house has been full of literature all his life. As a child he heard his father reading Shakespeare and his mother reading Dickens and Stevenson (Poe was forbidden). As a father, he and his wife and children would recite poems they'd memorized on Sunday afternoons, and his were most often poems of Donne or Yeats. Mary's first book of poems is to be published this fall.

Cheever enjoys his contemporaries—like Bellow, Malamud, and John le Carre—though he's not part of any literary group. "In the United States we don't actually have a literary congregational community," but "most of the writers I esteem I love. I love Saul Bellow, but we meet once a year," he says. "Our friendship is obviously not in this world."

He learns from other languages, too—enough Latin, French, and Italian to give him perspective on English and to intensify and vary his "sense of how profoundly different we are at times from one another."

His audience—the "large, you might say electorate out there of mature, well-informed people" who've been reading him in the *New Yorker* and elsewhere for forty-five years—is very important to him. Writing is communication. "It is rather like a kiss. It's something you can't do alone, as I see it." And he is careful to maintain the tone of a conversation, or of a story that is told *to* someone, when he moves from the physical to the mental and moral in his writing. "In using a word like beauty, you want to make sure the reader is with you," he says. "The vocabulary of choice is hammer, nails, fire and water, earth, air, a more elemental vocabulary. . . . As soon as you cease addressing other mortals on practical matters such as how to get in and out of the house, you lose them, and you lose yourself, too."

But at a moment when the pace of a story allows a variation, Cheever is a master of the brief digressive essay. "The discursive thing I love. I still use it. When you have the reader's attention, then you can completely do something else," he says. "It's almost like making a change of key in some kind of musical development, which rather has the quality—if you bring it off—of laughter."

He's working on a novel and won't talk about it. He's working on a story that may end up in his novel. He may write another screenplay if the one he wrote for public television this winter finds a sponsor. "I go back and forth all the time" between short and long forms, he says. He never talks about his work while it's in progress because "if I use something in conversation I seem to deplete the drive to put it down on paper. I never when I was younger would tell anyone about what I was working on because I thought I would diminish the drive," but now once in a while he'll talk to Mary or to one of his children.

"It's never been an intensely literary marriage," and in the past, Cheever often implied that his wasn't an intensely married marriage and it might come apart any time. He and Mary discussed divorce weekly, he would insist. And when he went to Boston to teach at BU in the early seventies, the separation was serious. His return to Ossining was a return to marriage, he says, and now he talks about his gratitude for the support Mary has given him "by being my wife, the mother of my children, by living with me for forty years. Nobody else has." His children "are remarkable in that they presented very few causes for anxiety." And his life has given him a lesson to teach them that astonishes and comforts him: "You can succeed in love and usefulness and pursue life for those rewards." He says he tells his children to "improvise, because everything is unprecedented. I mean to be expelled from Thayer Academy for smoking and to get an honorary degree from Harvard is unprecedented, and all we can do is improvise—and everybody seems to be successful in usefulness and love."

In 1977 he was on the cover of *Newsweek,* for *Falconer.* In 1978 he got his honorary degree from Harvard. Last year he won a Pulitzer for his collected stories. He's 68. Malcolm Cowley is 81. "I went to Chicago this fall and put a wreath on his head at the Newberry Library." After a spring lecture trip to Venezuela, he came to Boston in April for the *Time* cover party, then to Syracuse, back to Chicago in May, and then to Warsaw. "But if you asked me if I traveled I would say no." He doesn't feel like a traveler. He feels like a writer, and his "only certainty," he says, is that he's going to finish the novel he's working on. He's a homebody who feels he loves his vegetable garden and the field he scythes beside his house too much to leave for long after all these years. He reads free to public libraries within twenty-five miles of his house. He likes giving readings now that he's always sober when he does it.

"Growing old is certainly not as interesting as maturing, but it is some part of 'the great migration that is the life of man,' Edgar," he aphorizes mock-heroically to one of his two golden retrievers, calling him out to walk, through the field that he scythes to the hill above it for a look at the wide Hudson.

He strides along in his boots, corduroys, tweed jacket, suede vest, and button-down shirt, as preppy-looking as the day he left Thayer Academy. Tolstoy liked to scythe, too, he says. The skill and rhythm of the stroke are restful. "You get to look at the sky and you get to think a lot."

He's old enough to know what his story is but not old enough to have finished telling, or living, it. "The brothers story I've told fifty times, I guess. Sometimes I think I'm not telling it, but I am. It's one's destiny, of course. I don't believe in absolute free will," he says. "As a young man, of course, I hated it, which was natural of course. When you are young, you detest the ordinations of the old. But now . . ." Age has brought him a new perspective. And life has brought him "usefulness and love."

He tried dutifully to avoid fame and wealth; but fame found him. At 68, he feels safe from its ravages: "It really doesn't amount to much if you don't much care about it." What amounts to something is the feeling that he's lived a life he has made sense—and use—of. He has not evaded any of the human drama of his life, and so far it's a deep and complex comedy. It isn't over, though.

"It's a continuing performance and I don't know—of course it could be tragic. I still find it quite thrilling and mysterious," he says quietly, never afraid to use the big words, for the imponderables, when they fit.

John Cheever's Affirmation of Faith

Joshua Gilder/1982

Reprinted from *Saturday Review,* March 1982, pp. 16–19, by permission of the publisher.

The winter day I arrived in Ossining, New York, to interview John Cheever, the wind whipped off a Hudson River choked with ice. It was the second meeting we had scheduled; our first, almost a month earlier, had been canceled when the extent of Cheever's cancer had been diagnosed. Since then he'd been undergoing radiation treatments that have helped, but left him gaunt and exhausted. Still, he was determined if at all possible to go on with business as usual. *Oh What a Paradise It Seems,* his new novel, was coming out soon, and he wanted to talk even if he had to give the interview in bed.

As it turned out, he wasn't feeling well enough to leave his bed, so we talked in his room on the second floor of his Dutch-style wooden house. He looked physically tired, but alert. Reclining against his pillows, Cheever was, as always, polite and cordial, maintaining decorum even in the sick room. "I was realizing this morning," he said, looking out a window at the snow-covered woods that surround his yard, "this is the first snowfall I can remember when I haven't been out skiing. There's almost no inch of snow that I don't remember fondly. There's something marvelous about it, swaying down a well-covered slope.

"So," he said, getting right down to it, "you see before you a very sick man." Cheever had originally been unwilling, when we were making plans for the interview, to have the details of his cancer publicized; but he said now that he felt it important to discuss it. "It's not me," he said, resigned to being the reluctant "host" to this invading disease.

Cheever had an operation in July for the removal of a cancerous kidney; it seemed successful, but a short while later he developed a limp. "I thought it might be a pulled muscle; and then there were

224

pains in my chest. It occurred to no one that it might be cancer. But then, all of a sudden, it was." The cancer had developed in the bones of his legs and a spot in his rib cage. "The radiation treatment is really extraordinary. I wasn't able to walk without it. I now limp, but I can walk. Also I had a burning spot in my rib cage, which was continuously painful and for which I had to take painkillers all the time—and that's gone, absolutely gone. So that much of it appears terrific.

"Having cancer is a whole new world, of course. Memorial Hospital, where I go for treatment, is a cancer hospital, and suddenly to find yourself with thousands and thousands seeking some cure for this deathly thing is an extraordinary experience. It's not depressing, really, or exhilarating. It's quite plainly a critical part of living, or the aspiration to live."

Cheever didn't always share in that aspiration. For several years in the 1970s, he was in the depths of a severe, self-destructive alcoholism that came close to claiming his life. At its worst, he was washing down several Valiums at a time with a quart of hard liquor, drugging himself into an almost comatose state. His family and friends were convinced he was going to die, and his only feeling about it was "so what."

A more basic instinct for survival, however, got him through the worst and into Smithers, a rehabilitation clinic. From there he emerged, about six years ago, with a determined will to live, and a renewed sense of the importance to him of writing. His daughter, Susan (now a novelist in her own right), has said that when her father came out of Smithers, he seemed to be on a kind of high: He sat down and wrote *Falconer*—considered by most critics to be one of the great achievements of his career—in a little under a year.

And he didn't, as he usually had in the past when his novels were published, run off to some foreign country to avoid the press. He welcomed interviews, and said he had discovered a new respect for his audience, being genuinely gratified by the intelligent and feeling letters he received from readers. "Literature," he will tell you now, "is the highest form of communication between intelligent adults." And on a more personal level he will speak of literature as the only vehicle for expressing certain modes of feeling and of love. "Though I'm very close to my son, there are still things I can say to him only in fiction."

Even before his cancer was diagnosed, Cheever was talking of the setbacks of aging, and that "as one grows old there's always the possibility that one won't be able to write." During a recent Dick Cavett show, on which he appeared with John Updike, Cheever compared himself to his friend and younger colleague. Updike, he said, is "at the peak of his powers, while I'm an old man reaching the end of his journey."

Cheever is now 69, but except for the possible disruptions of illness, there is no evidence that his literary powers have declined with age. The evidence points much the other way. *Falconer*, published in 1977, was in many ways a creative breakthrough; it was his longest sustained narrative, formally his most successful novel; the Wapshot books read more like collections of short stories and *Bullet Park* is unconvincing structurally. Still, Cheever is not a literary long-distance runner; he tends toward brevity. *Falconer* was a short novel. His new book, *Paradise,* at about 100 pages, is even shorter, going by length it might be more accurate to call *Paradise* a novelette or even a long short story. But it reads like a novel. The story's continuity and the skill with which two narrative lines are woven together are evidence that *Falconer* wasn't one of a kind, that our best short-story writer has consummately mastered the somewhat different craft of writing novels.

Paradise—"really the first ecological romance," said Cheever—opens with a lyrical passage like the beginning of a fairy tale:

> This is a story to be read in bed in an old house on a rainy night. The dogs are asleep and the saddle horses—Dombey and Trey—can be heard in their stalls across the dirt road beyond the orchard. The rain is gentle and needed but not needed with any desperation. The water tables are equitable, the nearby river is plentiful, the gardens and orchards—it is at the turning of the season—are irrigated ideally.

Into this peaceful, melodic vision (surely one reads Cheever as much as anything for the harmonious cadences of his prose) comes a disturbing note. The town council of Janice, apparently in collusion with the Mafia, is profiting from the dumping of toxic wastes into Beasley's Pond, a once-beautiful, deep body of water surrounded by forest at the north end of town.

Some weeks before the dumping begins on a winter day in January, Lemuel Sears—"an old man but not yet infirm"—is up

skating on the pond, an experience of almost divine pleasure:
"Swinging down a long stretch of black ice gave Sears a sense of
homecoming. At long last, at the end of a cold, long journey, he was
returning to a place where his name was known and loved and lamps
burned in the rooms and fires in the hearth." The pollution of
Beasley's Pond seems a desecration. Sears has some money and he
hires a lawyer to investigate.

In the meantime, waiting on line in a bank, he meets Renée
Herndon, a divorcée, in whose features he sees "very definitely a
declaration of paradise." When he asks her what the music is playing
over the loudspeakers (it's a ragtime version of a Brandenburg
concerto), she laughs sweetly and says, "You don't understand the
first thing about women." It's the beginning of what becomes an
intensely erotic relationship, but all Renée ever seems to say to Sears
is, "You don't understand the first thing about women." She even
interrupts sex to look up at him and say it. Though their relationship
is intense, it's short-lived. Renée finally deserts Sears, and about two-
thirds of the way through the book, she vanishes completely from the
narrative.

Renée is not exactly a replay of the virtuoso-bitch performance of
Farragut's wife in *Falconer*—a portrait that prompted Susan Cheever
in a *Newsweek* interview with her father to wonder just how, exactly,
did he feel about women. But Renée is mysterious—she regularly
attends meetings about which she refuses to tell Sears—and she is in
the end perfectly cold to his entreaties before she leaves. "I never
thought of Renée as being particularly cold," said Cheever. "She's
capricious; and she stands him up—twice. But she's terribly nice to
him a good deal of the time." Still, when she stands him up, isn't he
devastated? "Oh, yes," replied Cheever, "the 'Balkans of the spirit.'

"I don't know how successfully that's conveyed. What I meant was
some absolute wilderness—yes just that, a wilderness. But then Sears
is left with the memory of what a paradise it seems." Are romantic/
erotic relationships always doomed? Could they survive only as
pleasant memories? "No, on the contrary, I think they can be
consummated and endure to an extraordinary length of time, longer
than I believe I have ever heard anyone declare."

The purification of Beasley's Pond becomes more than a metaphor;
it's almost the means of Sears's spiritual purification. "I think that if he

wishes to discover any purity in himself, "Cheever said, "he's not
going to find it in himself; he's going to have to find it in some larger
sphere of which he is, of course, a part. Sears means to succeed in
loving usefulness, and actually he is quite useful. He purifies a large
body of water. There really is little one can do that's comparably
useful today."

John Cheever occupies a special place in the pantheon of great
American writers. Cheever and Updike are often compared for the
elegance of their prose and because they both write out of their
experience as WASP suburbanites. But while Updike seems to wax
poetical at the slightest provocation, Cheever's lyricism is all the more
powerful for its restraint. And traditional WASP values survive more
intact in Cheever's fiction, though not without conflict. In the introduction to his collection of short stories, Cheever describes his work
as determined to "trace some moral chain of being." He writes that
although Calvin played no part in his religious education, "his
presence seemed to abide in the barns of my childhood and to have
left me with some undue bitterness."

Cheever looked a bit bewildered at the suggestion that in some
ways one might think of him as an ethnic writer; he smiled and found
amusing the proposition that one could draw a parallel between
himself and Philip Roth. "No! Philip is a good friend, and I admire his
work immensely—in fact I don't think of Roth as an ethnic writer,
either. I think that's a limitation." As an attempt to pigeonhole
Cheever's writings it no doubt would be, but it's not typecasting either
author to acknowledge that each comes out of a definite heritage,
and for each it is a source of tremendous ambivalence.

At his broadest, Cheever can produce an ethnic slapstick to rival
Roth's: the Wapshot family of Yankee eccentrics, for example, with
Moses Wapshot scampering naked over the roof to Melissa's room in
The Wapshot Chronicle. The crumbling mansion itself, its windows
broken and electricity out and all its priceless paintings forgeries, is a
comic symbol of fading aristocracy. Then there is the husband in
Cheever's short story, "The Fourth Alarm," whose wife joins an
avant-garde theater group: "Adultery and cruelty were well-marked
courses of action [for divorce] but what can a man do when his wife
wants to appear naked on stage?" In *Falconer*, there is also the
darker burlesque of the two brothers' mutually fratricidal impulses,

and the scene in which the father brings an abortionist home to dinner to introduce to his wife when she's pregnant with Farragut. As Farragut says later, in prison for fratricide and hooked on methadone, how could one help being a drug addict with a history like that?

While Roth's characters scream their emotions at the top of their lungs, Cheever's human comedy is characterized by what is left unsaid. His prose masterfully works its way around emotion. The feeling is there—it often looms much larger and more ominously for being unexpressed—it's simply that there are certain things that one just does not talk about.

A seminal work of Cheever's early career is "The Enormous Radio." In it, a young couple living on Sutton Place buy a large radio that supernaturally picks up the revealing private conversations of their neighbors. Cheever wrote it at a time, he said, when he could still be shocked that behind their upright exteriors people carried all sorts of shames and vices; and there is a touch of adolescent righteousness to the story. But though the moral thrust of the piece may be simple, the unraveling of the young couple's lives in remorse and accusation is Cheever at his most devastating.

Because Cheever's fictional characters have followed him from his starving-artist beginnings on Hudson Street to Sutton Place and from there to the Westchester suburbs, people assume his writing is autobiographical. It's a misconception that Cheever has probably despaired of ever setting right.

Just as Balzac could find a Lear in a Parisian vermicelli manufacturer ("My bourgeois novels" he said "are more tragical than your tragic dramas"), Cheever discovered the themes of great literature dwelling among suburbanites. At first, his work found favor with intellectuals because his dark vision, often shading off into the depressive, seemed to confirm the then-fashionable disdain for American values as exemplified in the suburban middle class. Even the Soviets adopted Cheever as one of theirs, believing that his writings showed up the moral bankruptcy and decadence of capitalist society. This was a misreading of Cheever. His view of humanity would be the same no matter where he chose to situate himself or his fiction. If his characters lead less-than-perfect lives, if in fact they sometimes appear to be teetering on the edge of a spiritual abyss, this, to Cheever, is the universal human condition.

The author shares an identity with his characters, not in an autobiographical sense, but in a Christian one. Cheever is empathically inside his fictional creations—even Charles Pastern in "The Brigadier and the Golf Widow," marching around the locker room shouting "Bomb Cuba! Bomb Berlin! Let's throw a little nuclear hardware at them and show them who's boss." In the end, his wife realizes that he's urging on the atomic holocaust because only the end of the world can end his own spiritual death. But his vision of apocalyptic imminence is too close to Cheever's for ironic detachment: Cheever has stood with Pastern on the edge of the abyss.

One can only admire a compassionate understanding that can embrace Charlie Pastern in the "Brigadier," and in *Paradise,* Betsy Logan's simple pleasure shopping at the local Buy Brite:

> She liked—she loved—to push a cart with nice rubber-tired wheels through a paradise of groceries, vegetables, meats, fishes, breads. . . . It is because our fortresses were meant to be impregnable that the fortresses of the ancient world have outlasted the marketplaces of the past, leaving the impression that fear and bellicosity were the keystones of our earliest communities, when in fact those crossroads where men met to barter fish for baskets, greens for meat, and gold for brides were the places where we first grew to know and communicate with one another. Some part of Betsy's excitement at Buy Brite may have been due to the fact that she was participating in one of the earliest rites of our civilization.

The music coming over the Buy Brite Muzak system that morning is a Brandenburg concerto, chosen

> by a nephew of one of the majority stockholders, who seemed to think that there would be some enjoyable irony between eighteenth-century music and the tumult of a contemporary shopping center. He was, spiritually speaking, a frail young man who would amount to nothing, and the irony he so enjoyed would be discontinued and forgotten in a month or so. There is no irony, of course.

Cheever is not one of those writers who explain the world to us. He is not a psychological writer, and there is no sense in his writing that life has a meaning to be discovered. There is ugliness to cause despair, and there is beauty to celebrate—but there is nothing to explain. This is partly seen in Cheever's attitude toward psychoanalysis. He has tried therapy at several different times in his life, but has never found it helpful. In his stories, analysts are always underemployed. "Yes," said Cheever, "I am inclined to deal with them lightly in my fiction." They don't, he feels, have much to offer: "Psychoanalysis runs counter to fiction with the idea that everything is symptomatic. Fiction is not about what's symptomatic, it's about what's astonishing in life. Fiction is meant to illuminate."

Illuminate, not enlighten; it is a religious illumination not a humanistic enlightenment. He is in many ways our most religious writer today: The light in his fiction is the light cast by a halo; there is no source but in faith. And the dark side of his vision? "My sense of darkness is the sense of evil. I think there is evil in the world. I've always associated evil with darkness, and I've always associated goodness quite openly with light."

When asked what part religion plays in his life, he described himself as "a churchgoer." When pressed further he said he goes to church "because prayer seems to contain certain levels of gratitude and aspiration that I know no other way of expressing." He stops and considers before he makes this statement, and when he talks it's as if he is reciting the phrases. It is almost word for word what he has said about religion in other interviews, and beyond this he will not go. It's obviously important for him to get it just right: like his prose, perfectly poised between allusion and affirmation.

A short way into our interview, Cheever apologized for his failing strength and said he could talk only a little while longer. I mentioned that "The Death of Justina" is one of my favorite stories. "I'm so glad you like it," he said. "I love it. I used to love giving readings of it. It's short, it would only take about 12 minutes, and if I were going to read a long story, something like 'The Swimmer,' I'd read 'The Death of Justina' to find out what the audience was like, what the depth of their response was. And it used to appeal to almost everyone on one level or another."

In "Justina," Cheever writes, "How can a people who do not mean to understand death hope to understand love. . . . ?" "Yes," Cheever said, quoting from the same passage, "love is a violet-flavored kiss," a line referring to our culture's denial of death, represented in the story by the undertaker and his helpers hiding behind their limousines at Justina's funeral. The end of the passage—"who will sound the alarm?"—had always intrigued me, but if I hoped for an explanation, it wasn't forthcoming. Cheever looked as if, yes, that's exactly what

he meant to say, and to say more would only muddy up the idea with
inadequate words.

"Justina" ends with a personal and strongly felt rendition of the
23rd Psalm; it is at least a partial answer to his thoughts at the
opening of the story on life, death, and the purpose of fiction:

> Fiction is art and art is the triumph over chaos (no less) and we can
> accomplish this only by the most vigilant exercise of choice, but in a
> world that changes more swiftly than we can perceive there is always the
> danger that our powers of selection will be mistaken and that the vision
> we serve will come to nothing. We admire decency and we despise death
> but even the mountains seem to shift in the space of a night, and perhaps
> the exhibitionist at the corner of Chestnut and Elm streets is more
> significant than the lovely woman with a bar of sunlight in her hair,
> putting a fresh piece of cuttlebone in the nightingale's cage. Just let me
> give you one example of chaos and if you disbelieve me look honestly
> into your own past and see if you can't find a comparable
> experience. . . .

Throughout his life, Cheever has tried in his fiction to bring order
to chaos and to exalt the decent and beautiful, though he often
doubted that good would prevail over evil. The despair in his fiction is
palpable. But so too is the abiding faith that answers it.

Interview with John Cheever

John Callaway/1985

Reprinted from *StoryQuarterly*, Issue #19, 1985, pp. 13–36, by permission of the publishers.

John Cheever—long regarded by critics as an American Chekhov—earned many distinguished awards and prizes during his lifetime. He was the author of six story collections, four novels, and one novella. The *Stories of John Cheever* won the Pulitzer Prize, the National Book Critics Circle Award, and an American Book Award. He received the Howells Medal of the American Academy of Arts and Letters for his novel *The Wapshot Scandal,* an O'Henry Award for his story "The Country Husband," and the National Book Award for his novel *The Wapshot Chronicle.* He also was presented the National Medal for Literature for his "distinguished and continuing contribution to American letters." His other novels and novella include *Bullet Park, Falconer,* and *Oh What a Paradise It Seems.* He died in 1982.

The following interview was aired nationally October 15, 1981 and was presented by the Public Broadcasting Service, and was a production of WTTW/Chicago.

Interviewer: (on location in Quincy) John Cheever probably is not a household word in America. In an age of television, few writers are. But some of his critics regard him, because of his short stories and books like *The Wapshot Scandal* and *Bullet Park* and *Falconer,* as one of our greatest, if not our greatest, living writer, continuing the American literary tradition of James Fenimore Cooper, Herman Melville, Edgar Allan Poe. And so it may well be that when the images on the tube have faded to black, his work will live on and on.

John Cheever grew up on this block in Quincy in a big old Victorian structure that stood where this house now stands. He was born to a traditional New England family. They prized the virtues of practicality, reticence, privacy. It was almost a storybook childhood. But there's a darker side to John Cheever's memories. When he was thirteen years old, his father, who was a self-made businessman, lost all of his money. One night John heard his father engaged in a loud and violent argument with the local banker. And the next day, the Cheevers had to move. The house was torn down. And young John Cheever was never told why.

Cheever: After, shall we say, after thirteen, a great deal—a great many violent blows were dealt me or were dealt my family.

Interviewer: Your father went into bankruptcy?

Cheever: My father went into bankruptcy. My parents separated. My mother went into business. A great deal went wrong.

Interviewer: You came from a seafaring family—if you go back a couple of generations.

Cheever: I came from a family of seafaring men, yes. My grandfather sailed to China and Ceylon from Newburyport. And my great-grandfather, Benjamin Hale Cheever, was a well-known ship's master. My father simply sailed cat boats.

Interviewer: And what kind of business was he in?

Cheever: My father had a shoe factory in Lynn. Once a year I was taken and held up in the air, and there was a cord you pulled. And that was the twelve o'clock whistle. Everybody then took their sandwiches out of their paper bags. And that was my participation in the shoe industry.

Interviewer: Was the breakup of their marriage because of the economic circumstances that they faced? That was what—1928, 1929, around in there?

Cheever: That I think contributed a great deal to it. Of course, well, it robbed him of his power. She opened a gift shop to support the family. And it made her immensely happy to find out that she could make money of her own. That she could purchase an automobile, for example, without consulting anyone, was for her an intoxicating experience. My sympathies all lay with him. And I worried terribly about what would happen to him. I was afraid that he would commit suicide. And presently the situation seemed to be insoluble. And I simply left.

Interviewer: Had your grandfather committed suicide?

Cheever: It is rumored that my grandfather had committed suicide. Well, I was drinking with my father one stormy—it was a northeaster. We were in one of the old houses in which we lived. And we had both drunk at least a pint of whiskey. And I thought, Well, under the circumstances I can ask about my grandfather. And I said, "Dad, would you tell me something about your father?" And he said, "No."

Interviewer: It's interesting. You've been quoted as saying that one of the aspects of your writing is that you can say things in your writing you cannot say to your sons.

Cheever: Yes, that's quite true. Well, I think of literature as an extremely intimate means of communication, involving sentiments, passions, regrets, and memories that simply don't belong in the spectrum of conversation.

Interviewer: It was later, wasn't it, that you came to understand your mother's pride in running her own gift shop and buying her own materials?

Cheever: It wasn't until I was in my late sixties that I finally understood this. My wife's poetry is being published this fall. And the joy that she has in having her own name on a book, rather than to find her husband's name on a book, has thrown a great deal of light on the pleasure my mother took in being able to buy a car of her own.

Interviewer: I don't mean to be simplistic about it, this is partially what we talk about when we talk about liberation, is it not?

Cheever: It seems to me the only thing we talk about.

Interviewer: And so you were in your sixties when that caught up emotionally.

Cheever: When I finally understood my mother, yes. Well, she did damage my father. And my father's well-being was very much my concern.

Interviewer: When did he die?

Cheever: He died during the Second World War, sometime in the forties.

Interviewer: Do you remember when you started to read the masters? The good stuff?

Cheever: Oh, I expect I was in my early adolescence. I remember the excitement of reading nineteenth century Russian novels when I was still in secondary school, which would have been when I was fifteen. The Garnett translations of Dostoevski were just coming out and that was very exciting.

Interviewer: But you wanted to write, didn't you, before you started that?

Cheever: I wanted to write. I think I decided to be a writer when I was about eleven. And these were in the days of absolute parental authority. I went to my parents and said, "I would like to be a writer." And they said, "Well, we will think that matter over." And they went into conference. And several days later they said, "We have decided that you may become a writer if that's what you intend. So long as you are not concerned either with fame or wealth." And I said, "I'm not concerned in any way with fame or wealth." And they said, "Very well, then. You may plan on becoming a writer."

Interviewer: And you even said many years later that you weren't a money player.

Cheever: I know very few writers who are, as a matter of fact, money players.

Interviewer: Doesn't go together, does it?

Cheever: It does from time to time, but very infrequently. Most of us have been offered, for example, opportunities in film and various other means of communication, that would be infinitely more profitable and secure than writing what we want to pursue. And almost all of the men I know would say, "No, thank you. It's nice of you to inform me, but no, thanks."

Interviewer: It's not the money per se that's the problem, is it? It's that it would distract you from what it is you need to do.

Cheever: It would rob us of that independence, which of course is imperative to literature. You must make your own decisions.

Interviewer: What is it in your life, that made you want to be a writer and to know that at the age of eleven?

Cheever: I think—I can't be counted on for the truth this late in my life, I think it was—I like to think it was—the fact that I found life immensely exciting. And the only way I had of comprehending it was in the form of storytelling.

Interviewer: What time do you write?

Cheever: I work in the mornings, which is by far the best time for me. And it seems to me that most of the serious writers I knew work in the morning. The legend of the writer who began work at midnight, usually quite drunk, very often debauched, I think is an exploded legend. One works when one is most in command of one's intelligence and one's strength.

Interviewer: You did not get through Thayer Academy. What happened when you were sixteen?

Cheever: I was expelled. I was expelled presumably for smoking.

Interviewer: What do you mean, "presumably"?

Cheever: I believe I was expelled because I was an intractable student. I questioned teachers. Thayer Academy was a preparatory school. I was being prepared for Harvard. There wasn't any point in my remaining a student if I had no intention of going on to Harvard. I had no intention of going on to Harvard. The headmaster, Stacy Southworth, was an extremely understanding and a vastly intelligent man, and felt that he was simply wasting his time arguing with me. I chain-smoked out behind the tennis court, and so he expelled me. However, I did receive an honorary degree from Harvard. So it all worked out.

Interviewer: Have you ever gone back to Thayer?

Cheever: No. No, I've never been back to Thayer. I've been asked to go back for baccalaureates, but that's it.

Interviewer: Then did you go to New York or did you join your brother in Boston?

Cheever: I joined my brother in Boston, and we both then went abroad, and spent some time in Germany. We returned. And then I left my brother in Boston and went on to New York.

Interviewer: And you lived on Hudson Street.

Cheever: I lived on lower Hudson Street, yes.

Interviewer: Did you by any chance live at 323 Hudson Street?

Cheever: It sounds very familiar.

Interviewer: The reason I ask is there is a guard in *Falconer* who says—late in the novel, "Well, I'm going home to 323 Hudson Street."

Cheever: Really?

Interviewer: Yes. He says, "I'm going home to 323 Hudson Street and drink some Southern Comfort." He's gonna drink a bottle of Southern Comfort, and if that isn't enough, he's gonna drink another bottle of Southern Comfort, and if that isn't enough, he's gonna drink another bottle of it.

Cheever: Well. That is a curious trick of memory. I expect it was 323 Hudson. I didn't know that.

Interviewer: What was life like there?

Cheever: On Hudson Street? It wasn't nearly as bad as one would have anticipated. This was during the Depression. There was a longshoremen's strike. I lived on the fourth floor which was the cheapest floor. Rooms were two dollars on the fourth floor. You went down to the third floor, the rooms were three dollars or two dollars and fifty cents, something like that. And it was full mostly of unemployed longshoremen. And with my accent, my gray flannel suit, and my blue buttondown shirts, I was something of a curiosity. And they couldn't have been more helpful.

Interviewer: In what way?

Cheever: They wanted me to take some sort of an extension course. They wanted me to get into the government. They thought I could take an exam for post office work. They couldn't have been nicer. The thought of being locked up in the attic of a Hudson Street rooming house with a bunch of unemployed longshoremen does not in any way anticipate or describe their kindness, their wit, or their pleasantness.

Interviewer: And so here you started to write short stories?

Cheever: Yes. Yes.

Interviewer: Was it hard? Did it come easily? How was that experience?

Cheever: It's always been a great pleasure. And any pleasure, of course, is a matter of mixed ease and difficulty. It's always been an enormous pleasure.

Interviewer: When did you meet the woman you were to marry?

Cheever: I wasn't to meet her until, oh I believe, the year before the war.

Interviewer: 1940. How did you meet her?

Cheever: I met her on a rainy afternoon in an elevator. I can't remember the address—one of the buildings on Fifth Avenue. I'd spent a very pleasant summer working as a boatman and water skiing, which had just come in. And I saw a woman in the elevator.

And I thought, "That's more or less what I would like." And went up and then she got off the elevator at the same floor. And she went into my literary agent's office. And I asked who she was. And I was told she was Mary Winternitz. And I asked her for a date. And presently married her.

Interviewer: You said about your marriage to Mary, "In forty years there's scarcely been as week in which we haven't planned to get a divorce." Why is that?

Cheever: I suppose it's becuase we're both uncommonly contrary people. However, considering the vast discussions of divorce that have gone on within the containment of our marriage, I'm enormously indebted to my wife for having shown me the melancholy as well as the pleasures of a marriage. Had it not been for her, I would never have known about certain degrees of loneliness and rejection. And also had it not been for her, I would never have known about many aspects of happiness—of sustained happiness. It has been, of course, the longest relationship I will ever have.

Interviewer: What is it you learned about loneliness that you learned through marriage? The other—melancholy, joy, all the rest of it. What about loneliness?

Cheever: Through feeling that one had failed as a husband, I expect, is probably one of the loneliest sensations I know.

Interviewer: Did you ever feel you weren't worthy of the—

Cheever: "Worthy" is not the word I would settle on. No, it's simply a question of not having made any money. That, in itself, is quite enough to go on.

Interviewer: You never had a lot—I mean, I don't know what your condition now is, but you know what it is to be broke, don't you?

Cheever: Yes. I do, yes. I've been broke quite recently.

Interviewer: A lot of people think—well, John Cheever, *The New Yorker*—all those stories. All these books, the best seller list here and there. You were broke. I read something where you were broke as late as 1977.

Cheever: I think that was true, yes. I was broke when I was writing *Falconer.* I didn't have enough money to finish the book. And there was a question of a film option. They were going to pay twenty thousand on a film option. And I said, "Fine but you can't. . . ." I had published one chapter in *Playboy*, that was it. And somebody wanted to option it for film for twenty (thousand). As soon as they found out I was stone-broke, they cut the option to ten. Ten would not have solved my problems. Ten would not have paid my debts. And I told them what they could do with ten and hung up, leaving myself with nothing. However, another studio, having heard that studio A was willing to put out twenty—they hadn't heard about the split yet, and they hadn't heard that I was broke—offered forty. So it all ended very happily, and I was able to finish the book, pay the debts, and, I don't know, buy another dog.

Interviewer: Okay. We're talking about ten, twenty, forty thousand dollars. And in the past three years we've read of advances of eight hundred thousand, a million-five; two and a third million.

Cheever: Well, there are paperback sales. But these paperback sales have nothing to do with the work I do, nor have they ever. This is to assume that the cloak and suit business, for example, is one simple business. To assume that publishing is one simple operation is a great mistake. One doesn't mind at all, for example, that a book like *Scruples* sells millions of copies. It satisfies a group of perfectly responsible citizens. And if one is number one or number two or number three on the best-seller list, you're usually cheek-by-jowl with a book that is basically banal and vulgar. It doesn't make any difference. The company you keep makes no difference. It's a question of being recognized by those people you enjoy.

Interviewer: (on location at Sing Sing) John Cheever came here to teach at Sing Sing prison—notorious Sing Sing on the Hudson River, in Ossining, New York, not far from where he lives. Cheever taught English composition to the prisoners for two years. He stopped when he had a heart attack, his second. But the experience here provided the context for his most celebrated novel, *Falconer*, published in 1977.

Falconer is about a college professor who's doing time for a crime of passion—the murder of his brother, but it's as much about the incarceration of the soul as the imprisonment of the body.

Interviewer: I felt that *Falconer* was a—not a departure from what you'd done in the past, but that it went beyond. That it was a—

Cheever: I'm glad you felt that way. A growth or extension, yes.

Interviewer: But even more than a growth. Growth isn't quite the

right word. It was almost a leap of experience. John Leonard said—
and I don't know quite what he meant. I have to get him on here
some day and ask him—he said, the book, it seemed to him, was
almost willed more than imagined. I felt that it was a huge leap from
where you'd been, but totally tied to where you'd come from.

Cheever: Oh, I'm so pleased you felt that way. Of course, all the
work has dealt with the mystery of confinement. And *Falconer*
brought confinement up to confinement in a jail. I was very pleased
with the book. Leonard, I think, gave it one of the few bad reviews it
received. But what sort of reception the book would have, the
publisher didn't know, and the printing was quite small. Saul Bellow
came out for the book very early, which made a tremendous
difference. And then almost all the reviews at an international level—
you know, Germany, Japan—were highly enthusiastic. The only
country where the book has not been published, so far as I know, is
Soviet Russia.

Interviewer: May be wise of them.

Cheever: Oh, it did very well in the underground I've been told.

Interviewer: I don't mean to tie the two directly, because I know
there was more to it than your experience at Sing Sing. But how did
you come to teach at Sing Sing?

Cheever: I had received something like five offers of good visiting
professorships in the space of a month. And had thought quite
seriously and quite mistakenly of myself as a teacher—perhaps I
should show up at Yale or Princeton or Harvard. And then at a party
someone said, "If you're thinking of teaching, Sing Sing has two
thousand inmates and six instructors operating on a straight academic
year." So I went down to the warden and said, "Well, look, you're
short of teachers. I'd like to teach composition." And he said, "I don't
think you do. Why don't you get out of here?" And I said, "Well, you
damn well will take me as a teacher or I'll make a stink about this."
So he took me on as a teacher.

Interviewer: You had to insist. I love it. So what happened?

Cheever: I taught there for two years.

Interviewer: How do you teach in a prison? What kind of a
setting was it? Did they bring people into a hall?

Cheever: Everything in Sing Sing is relatively squalid. The first
class—I think there were close to forty men came in to see what it

was. And I told them it would be a course in writing—a course that would involve writing letters, for example. A course in telling stories. A course, if possible, in making sense of one's life by putting down one's experiences on a piece of paper. And there were enough people who were interested, who stayed with me, to make the course extremely interesting for me and, I think, for them. None of them published. However, a good many of them on parole would write me saying—that very often on parole, they are susceptible to every sort of temptation; that is, every criminal will try to get a man on parole, you know, for drugs or for any number of offenses. And by putting down what they did, who they met, and what they said in the course of a day, they were able to hold onto themselves in a degree that they hadn't enjoyed before.

Interviewer: I can't think of a group of people who might more need and want to make sense of their lives than somebody who's in confinement.

Cheever: Well, this seems, in many instances, to have worked with them. Keeping a journal, which is something I would insist on in any student, is something that several of them did. And by simply waking up in the morning and putting down, if necessary, the weather, the address of the house where they happen to be, and then carry on through the day, they were able to avoid immediately going into drug pushing or anything else of that sort.

Interviewer: How long have you kept journals?

Cheever: I have journals from the age of, I believe, twenty-two.

Interviewer: How do you use them?

Cheever: I use them infrequently these days, but there are aspects of—there is a freshness of experience that one loses. And I can find it if I go back into the journals. It's the excitement of a smell or a sound or of meeting someone who strikes one as being accomplished and exciting.

Interviewer: When you were teaching at Sing Sing, did you feel in any way that a prisoner was teaching prisoners? Did you feel any sense of confinement in your life?

Cheever: I felt a sameness there. But this, I believe, is simply my fondness for anything that strikes me as being heretical; that is, if the cons and I were lined up against a guard, well, I was all with the cons.

It was very simply that. I don't take the stuffier aspects of organized society ceremoniously.

Interviewer: Yet you take the ceremony seriously enough to go to church?

Cheever: If I think it of first importance, of course. Well, then I do take ceremony seriously. But there is, I think in all of us, a glee, a good deal of pleasure in seeing a stuffed shirt exposed.

Interviewer: But when I talk about you as a prisoner communicating to prisoners, weren't you coming, by that time in your life, to terms with your own addictions or your own confinements?

Cheever: I shouldn't say so. No.

Interviewer: You weren't? Did you do that later?

Cheever: No. It wasn't until I'd left that teaching. I had a heart attack when I was teaching at Sing Sing. Which is why I stopped teaching. And it was as a result of the heart attack that I stopped drinking—which had been a great problem.

Interviewer: But then you started again, didn't you?

Cheever: Yes. I drank for another year. And then I had another heart attack and stopped for good.

Interviewer: How did you stop?

Cheever: Oh, I went to a rehabilitation clinic and I joined Alcoholics Anonymous.

Interviewer: Why did you stop?

Cheever: I would have killed myself otherwise. Also the brain damage was—the damage to my—because of the basic loss of dignity. I believe very strongly in the dignity of men and women. And this was a totally ignoble position.

Interviewer: Did it make a difference in your life? It seems to me it's made a difference in your writing.

Cheever: Well, yes. It made what I consider to be a splendid difference. There are people who consider me, now that I'm sober, to be much more of a boor than I ever was falling down. But they seem to be few.

Interviewer: In *Falconer*, one of the characters says, "I'm kind of excited about what's on the other side." He's ready to die, and he says, "I'm ready to die. And I'm looking forward to what's on the other side." Did you have any sense of that when you were dealing with this? People I know who've been alcoholic, and gone all the way to the bottom, have really faced their Maker, in effect, and said, "I don't want to quit yet. I gotta keep going." Did you have anything like that at all?

Cheever: No, I think not. I was certainly at the bottom. I was at totally self-destructive bottom. But with no commitment to see my Maker. What we are concerned with, of course, is living as intelligently as we can in the world in which we find ourselves.

Interviewer: Do you believe in a Hereafter?

Cheever: I've never asked myself that question. It seems to me quite incidental. I am concerned with making as much as I possibly can of the world in which I find myself. And I use the word "find." It's not a world into which I've strayed or a world in which I've entered. It's a world in which I was placed. And to make sense of it, to appreciate it, it seems to me, is a totally absorbing task.

Interviewer: The themes that you have written about—and I may be misusing the word "theme"—but I see in your writing a lot of light and sky and a lot of wonderful rain. Am I mistaken in that these are major strains somehow that come through your work?

Cheever: No. Light is of the greatest importance to me. And it seems to increase in its importance as I grow older. I dislike spending any time in dark cities these days. And the light of the sky, I seem to associate with virtue or with hopefulness. Rain—I love the sound of rain. I come, as I say, from a seafaring family. I don't think my father ever planted a vegetable. I think he regarded people who planted things with absolute scorn. I do have a vegetable garden. And I seem to respond to the rain with the enthusiasm of an agricultural citizen. But I love light. And I do love the sound of the rain.

Interviewer: Isn't that beautiful country where you live?

Cheever: Yes, it is.

Interviewer: I'll never forget the first time I discovered that. I think that's where I want to go sometime.

Cheever: The Hudson Valley is one of the most beautiful places in the world.

Interviewer: I remember I came across from Long Island. I was going to Garrison, New York, and I discovered, not forty-five miles from New York City, the lushest densest forest. It was in the middle of July. And it had rained. And it was just lush and thick and primitive.

Cheever: As a matter of fact, much of it is Precambrian, very early. Laurel and rhododendron are Precambrian, and it's very very strong in the Hudson Valley.

Interviewer: I miss that very much.

Cheever: Well, it's there waiting for you to come back.

Interviewer: Somebody said, "Well, you're gonna talk with John Cheever. He must be reading these articles in *The New York Times Magazine* about how the suburbs ain't what they used to be. And ask him how he feels about that." And I said, "Well, I don't know if that really has anything to do, frankly, with what his work is." You're looked at as a suburban writer. But I don't see you as a suburban writer. I look at you as a writer—as far as I'm concerned—who could have been coming out of Tallahassee, Florida.

Cheever: Oh, I'm very pleased you feel that way. But I do understand being categorized. People categorize everything. It's simply a way of getting a handle on it or comprehending it. Well, I've been criticized—I've been confined by my knowledge of—You know, it doesn't matter.

Interviewer: But as a citizen—forget about your role as a writer— as a citizen, do you get that sense of profound change in the suburbs?

Cheever: The suburbs, as I understand them, have always been an improvisation. It was a way of life that started about fifty years ago when rentals in the city, when raising children in the city, became an impossibility—when schooling children in the city became an impossibility. It still is an improvisational way of life. It still is an invention. It doesn't cling to tradition.

Interviewer: One of the things I like about what you've done, and I talk about it a lot, is that young reporters will complain to me that, "Oh, my God, I got stuck with the zoning thing in the suburbs." I say to them, and I know I sound pious as hell, "You'll find the whole story, the whole human condition, can come out of that zoning hearing—greed, ambition, love, death, it's all there." And everybody says, "Get me back to city hall and Mayor Byrne! Don't stick me out in the suburbs." But isn't it all there?

Cheever: I think it is, yes. It seems to me there's more vitality, more change, in the suburbs than you find in urban life.

Interviewer: Talk to us, if you would, share with us—I think an English teacher I had called it the process of transmutation. You have this rich experience. It's used creatively in fiction. And yet it is not to be confused with crypto-autobiography. How does it work? What is and what isn't? Three-twenty-three Hudson Street? That's a fact. That relates to a factual part of your lie.

Cheever: That was a memory. The process of writing is an employment of an area of memory that is marvelous and that is not yet understood. When one tells a story, one tells it to no particular reader. The marvelous thing about writing and storytelling is that the book-buying public is one public and that completely escapes any computer analysis. No one knows who the intelligent, who the mature reader is. And yet they are there, and they are there by millions. And they would much sooner read a good book than sit through a bad television show or a bad movie or get stoned in a bad disco.

So it's operating in an area of memory that I know really very little about, that is disciplined to tell a story to someone whom I don't know. And yet if it is successful, whoever it is—it could be someone in Israel, or someone in Japan—will write me a letter and say, "Oh, but that story was just what I wanted to read on that particular rainy afternoon." And this, of course, is the enormous pleasure of writing. And I, as a reader, of course, recognize the same thing. Certainly to read a book that strikes me as a clarification—a book that makes me feel that life is full of promise—that not only the present, not only the moment, but also the past is bewilderingly beautiful—is a terrific experience. And of course, when you realize that most American fiction is translated into eight or ten languages, you realize that the audience is international.

Interviewer: Do you agree with John Gardner that the writer has to be connected up to a moral vision?

Cheever: Well, that's an interesting question. But literature is basically an account of aspiration or hopefulness. I have described it as our only coherent and consistent, continuous, history of man's struggle to be illustrious. We have a literature of the decadents. But it is pretty much confined to the end of Rome and to nineteenth century France. Very little of our great literature is self-consciously decadent. Most of it is a question involving, in one way or another, human greatness or the possibility of human greatness and dignity. Most of it involves the mystery, of course, of love and death.

Interviewer: At the end of *Falconer,* Farragut gets out. And he gets out through death. He could be picked up two minutes later, but he's really free in a new sense, isn't he? Isn't he self-possessed, almost?

Cheever: Yes. He's quite free as far as I'm concerned. Of course, you don't know what happens to him after that. But I felt that was none of my damn business. I knew that he was out. And it closes on the word "rejoice"—Rejoice, which I very much enjoy reading in the various translations. Except in the Japanese, which I can't pronounce.

Interviewer: When you came to terms then with your addictions, because you were also—weren't you popping pills with the drinking?

Cheever: I was, yes. Certainly.

Interviewer: When you came to terms with that, and after this book, if I said to you, "Let's get on a plane this afternoon and let's go back to Boston and let's go back to Symphony Hall," would you be comfortable with that?

Cheever: I think not. I think Symphony Hall is a part of the world that I can avoid for the rest of my natural life without any great loss. I was in Boston last week. I walked from the public gardens to the museum and back again. My son, Ben, ran in the Marathon last week.

Interviewer: Ben—who's an editor at *Reader's Digest?*

Cheever: Right. Did the Boston Marathon in two hours and forty-six minutes. Which is very good time. And I don't see any reason to worry about Boston. It is a part of the world in which I came of age in a very troubled way. And there are still memories there that disconcert me. Also, the sense of the past in Boston is very strong. There are a great many Cheevers buried on Cob Hill. My father took me up and showed me the Cheever graveyards. What I do remember about the family, and about Boston, is that Ezekiel Cheever established the first school in Massachusetts, the first school in the New World. And that on his death it was said, "Here lies Ezekiel Cheever. The welfare of the Commonwealth was always upon his conscience, and he abominated periwigs."

Interviewer: How do you feel about what you're doing—what you've been doing with public television?

Cheever: It was not I who did the adaptations. They were done without me. I did an original which is yet to be produced. Public television came to me and said. "Would you do three stories?" And I said, "No."

Interviewer: What do you think about what was done with them?

Cheever: I don't enjoy adaptations of any sort. Prose is meant to go where a camera cannot penetrate. One is writing in an altogether different voice than camera work. A prime example of something that cannot be photographed is *The Great Gatsby,* which I think has been made into at least three or four films. You simply cannot photograph a good novel because the novelist intended that you shouldn't be able to photograph it. If he had wanted to write a screenplay, he would have.

Interviewer: You can do a nice job with a limited piece of writing. You take *The Day of the Jackal,* which is a kind of nice story. It's not literature, but it's a nice action thing. And it's kind of flat. It doesn't have much depth. And it really works nicely. And it's—movies are kind of surfacey.

Cheever: Yes. There was a dreadful novel called *Poldark,* or something like that, which made a marvelous television series. If it's really very very bad, then you can do anything with it. You have your principal characters. You have changes of scenery and so forth. Then you can just run with the ball. But if you really get a good book like *Gatsby*—or it seems to me that most of the work of any of my colleagues—John Updike's works simply will not photograph, nor will Saul Bellow's. You can't do anything with Saul's work.

Interviewer: What do you read?

Cheever: I read most contemporary serious novels. I very much enjoyed this year Tom Wolfe's book, *The Right Stuff.* I very much enjoyed Barbara Tuchman's *A Distant Mirror*—was it—the fourteenth century? Oh, there was a new history of the American Revolution by Page Smith which I very much enjoyed, and I've read most of the novels that claim to be serious.

Interviewer: Do you read mysteries or anything like that, ever?

Cheever: I'm extremely fond of mysteries, yes. And I think Le Carré is first-rate. Although I do feel that he's never done anything quite as good as *The Spy Who Came In From the Cold.* I've read all of Le Carré.

Interviewer: Do you have demands made on you by aspiring writers—"Please read my manuscript?"

Cheever: Yes. My mailbox is full of manuscripts. And I spend a great deal of time taking them to the post office and mailing them back. I cannot read, of course, unsolicited manuscripts. I've been on various grants committees. One is, of course, at my age, asked to judge manuscripts for prizes. And the obligatory reading one does can be overwhelming. It isn't that one lacks the time. It is that one lacks the discernment. There is an hour—two-fifteen, sometimes three-thirty—when one is no longer discerning about the value of a manuscript. And it's absurd to go on reading.

Interviewer: What would you say to the person who considers him or herself a short story writer, but who looks around and says, "My God, Updike, or Cheever, or the great writers have got *The New Yorker* sewed up for the next ten or fifteen years! I'll never be able to break in there! And there's not much left, except the *Atlantic,* and it just seems hopeless." Would you say, "Keep writing," or what?

Cheever: I would say, number one, that was a display of damn foolishness. Anyone who reached that conclusion, I don't think, would have the intelligence to be a writer. Updike and I, of course, have no corner on any market. To the contrary, we're both extremely hospitable, and we'd do everything we possibly could if we thought a good writer was coming along.

Interviewer: But the markets aren't there, are they?

Cheever: The markets are not there. But the success of my collection, I think, does imply that there is a market for a short story, for a good short story.

Interviewer: When did you first write for *The New Yorker?*

Cheever: I think my first story in *The New Yorker* came out when I was twenty-one or twenty-three.

Interviewer: So that would have been in the 1933–1934 area?

Cheever: Yes.

Interviewer: Harold Ross had had the magazine what six, seven years?

Cheever: Yes. It was very much his magazine.

Interviewer: Did you have much of an association with him or did you just send it in through the mail?

Cheever: The first story of mine was sent to *The New Yorker* by Malcolm Cowley. It was sent to Katharine White, who was Ross's associate and partner. I did see Ross. I didn't know Ross intimately. But I lunched with him, you know, a few times a year. Ross was an eccentric. He used to clean his ears a lot. He used to tuck his shirt tails inside of his underwear so that a broad band of underwear, showing something like green dice, could be seen. He used to use strong language at lunch—I think principally because he knew it would make me jump, as it did. And he was, as far as I could see, a genius. He used to say, "Goddamnit, why do you write those gloomy stories?" And he would buy a story, and hold it for three years, four years, and then he would run it. And it would be an enormous success. This used to bewilder him. But he continued to do it.

Interviewer: Now do they still do that? Will they take a story—?

Cheever: I think not, no. No writer would put up with that anymore. We were quite patient. Also we were economically absolutely dependent on Ross. Ross held a story of mine called "Pot of Gold" for four years. And then when it ran, it was an enormous success. It was much more successful than a series of funny jokes, which he thought readers wanted. And he would say, "Goddamnit, why the hell are them gloomy stories successful?"

Interviewer: I love that magazine, and yet there's a side of me that says—well, they, with their standards about how they handle language which seems rough, they could have never published *Falconer.*

Cheever: It doesn't seem to me to make much difference one way or another. My editor there did read *Falconer.* And wrote a very, very understanding note saying, "You do understand of course that we can't publish this, but you also understand how enthusiastic I am about the book."

Interviewer: Is that okay that *The New Yorker's* prudish that way? Should we hope that one day somebody else will come in and say, "We want Norman Mailer's toughest stuff, and we want *Falconer*"?

Cheever: I think not, no. Magazines, very like people, are confined within their own characteristics. And you cannot be a universal magazine, any more than you can be a universal man. You have ways of walking and talking and tastes in clothes and food and sex and so forth. Universality, it seems to me, escapes all of us.

Interviewer: Are awards important to you?

Cheever: Awards, as far as I'm concerned, mean the esteem and very often the affection of strangers. And the esteem and the affection of strangers is something I very much enjoy.

Interviewer: How much mail do you get?

Cheever: It depends entirely on the amount of publicity. For example, if you've been on a television show, and it is understood that you answer your own mail, I will sometimes get one hundred letters a week. I very much enjoy my fan mail.

Interviewer: What do people say to you?

Cheever: They are usually extremely discreet. They realize that they cannot involve you in a lengthy conversation. They very often say that they've enjoyed a story, or they have enjoyed a paragraph in a story. They've enjoyed a novel. I have received very few unfriendly letters. I did receive a letter from a woman who had bought *Falconer* and thought it was disgusting and tried to burn it. She went into some length about how she had tried to burn the complete book, and it would not ignite. And then she had tried to burn the book by taking off the jacket. And it was only by tearing the book in little pieces was she able to ignite it. And then she bought the collection two years later and wrote a letter saying, "I am terribly sorry. I am the woman who burned *Falconer*—and please accept my apologies."

Interviewer: That's wonderful. Do you read your critics?

Cheever: It was very nice. Yes, with pleasure.

Interviewer: Even when they—

Cheever: Well, the assumption, of course, is that one is far from perfect. Their intent is to express their vision of what literature should be. And if this happens to be sympathetic, I'm very anxious to see where they think I've failed.

Interviewer: Have you ever learned from a critic?

Cheever: Yes, I should say I have. If I've disappointed a man whose judgment I esteem, I certainly will go back over my work and see how I could possibly have improved.

Interviewer: How do you feel about this controversy over the National Book Awards, and that they've gone commercial?

Cheever: I haven't informed myself on the matter at all because it seemed to me that if you mix commercialism with publishing, of course you're totally lost. The wonderful thing about writing, and the wonderful thing about reading and publishing, is that it is not angled

for the maximum profit. It has absolutely nothing to do with merchandising, or very little. People write books because they feel they
have something to say. People buy books because they feel that
something may be within the book that they want to hear, or that will
help them live more happily or more usefully, or more beautifully.
And publishers work as an intermediary between the reader and the
writer. And commercialism has no place in this—or very little.

Interviewer: Talking about commercialism, how did you get
involved with the Rolex ads? I saw your—it's a wonderful ad. It's a
lovely ad—in *The New Yorker,* in April.

Cheever: They asked me if I wanted a gold watch. And I said I
certainly did. And then I said, "Well, what do I have to do?" And they
said, "All you have to do is to go in town and be sketched." So I said,
"Great." So I went into town, to an advertising agency in New York,
and somebody drew a picture of me, and I got a gold watch.

Interviewer: How do you feel about your daughter, Susan,
turning novelist?

Cheever: Oh, I'm very happy about Susie's career. I'm very
happy about her success. I'm happy about it in that she's not felt that
being the daughter of a writer is something she ought to be ashamed
of. I'm very happy that she hasn't taken up a career, for example, as
an opera singer. I'm very glad that she's not taking a couple of years
off waiting on tables at Aspen to find herself. She knows damn well
who she is. She knows damn well what she wants to do. I'm very
gratified and pleased with the whole thing. And the book has been
very successful.

Interviewer: *Looking for Work.*

Cheever: *Looking for Work.* Yes.

Interviewer: What did you think of it?

Cheever: I thought it was—well, I was delighted, of course, to find
out that it was not, as far as I was concerned, a crypto-autobiography.
Her father is described as a man who rides with a Myopia Hunt, a
North Shore Hunt, and parts his white hair in the middle. This is, I
think, not a photographic description of what her father is like.

Interviewer: What do you think of your wife's poetry?

Cheever: I think my wife's poetry is first-rate and I'm delighted
that her book is being published.

Interviewer: What does she write about? What can we anticipate?

Cheever: Oh, she writes about men, women, children, dogs, landscapes. She writes about her children. There are poems to all three children. Oh, she writes about the Hudson Valley, which she very much enjoys. She writes not at all, as far as I can figure out, about her husband.

Interviewer: Do you read her material as an editor, or do you just read it as her—?

Cheever: I read it as a colleague. I read it as a man who knows her. I don't read it as a husband.

Interviewer: Is there still as much give and take in that marriage as there was earlier? Is there a different sense of it now?

Cheever: No. No, the elasticity is in no way diminished.

Interviewer: Do you have any advice for anybody about marriage—love?

Cheever: My sons from time to time come to me for advice. And what I convey to them, I think, is that I am perhaps more bewildered than they. But it is not a sorrowful bewilderment. It's rather an exciting sense of confusion.

Interviewer: I haven't asked you about politics, and I won't. But a lot of us feel a sense of political gloom, and a lot of problems that don't seem to be easy to resolve. Could you sum up—how you feel about this civilization, where we are?

Cheever: I think civilization where we are is not in any way a melancholy situation. And as far as the political gloom goes, the president of Bulgaria is an acquaintance of mine. And when I returned to Bulgaria last summer, I said how pleasant it was to be back in his great country. And he said, "Isn't it a great country? I've been president for twenty-three years." And whenever anybody objects to the confusion of the American presidential election, I always think of my Bulgarian friend and his simplified twenty-three-year presidency.

Interviewer: Thank you.

Index